W9-CDE-050

SCHOLASTIC

6+1 Traits of Writing

THE COMPLETE GUIDE FOR THE PRIMARY GRADES

By Ruth Culham

NEW YORK • TORONTO • LONDON • AUCKLAND • SYDNEY
MEXICO CITY • NEW DELHI • HONG KONG • BUENOS AIRES

Teaching Resources

6+1 TRAITS is a trademark of Northwest Regional Educational Laboratory,
101 SW Main Street, Portland, Oregon, 97204.

Scholastic Inc. grants teachers permission to photocopy the reproducible pages from this book for classroom use. No other part of this publication may be reproduced in whole or in part, or stored in a retrieval system, or transmitted in any form or by any means, electronic, mechanical, photocopying, recording, or otherwise, without written permission of the publisher. For information regarding permission, write to Scholastic Inc., 557 Broadway, New York, NY 10012.

Cover design by Lillian Kohli
Interior design by Holly Grundon
Interior illustrations by David Clegg

ISBN 0-439-57412-9
Copyright © 2005 by Ruth Culham
All rights reserved. Published by Scholastic Inc.
Printed in the U.S.A.
6 7 8 9 10 23 12 11 10 09 08 07

For Sam Culham

(1976–2004)

The greatest gift of my life was to be your mother. You taught me everything. The frustration you experienced as a kid who just wanted to learn is what guided this book. When you were a little boy, I watched you question why school had to be so hard—why hour after hour was spent doing things that could have been more interesting, thoughtful, and important. I know you would hate that I put this story here, right at the beginning, but readers need to know you, through your words, and hear your voice. It's the voice of all children who expect more from us, their teachers. The good times shouldn't end because of school—they should start. You knew that. I miss you, sweet boy.

Sam's Funny Life

When I was born my mom and dad named me Sam Allen. I was a funny baby. When I was two I poured flour all over my head. My mom was in the bathtob. It was not hard to find me. She could follow the little white footprints on the rug. Then I poured grapejuice on the wall. By then it was supper time. My mom gave me liver. I ate my bowl of liver. Then my cat wanted some so I felt sorry for her. So I gave her some. My mom thought I ate it. So she gave me more and more. And I Kept feeding the cat. My mom saw it and she . . . was well I really . . . hummm. I don't Know. Then after Lots of days my Dad moved away to Alaska. I was sad. Then I turned three. I had a big caKe. And everybody sang and danced it was a fun day. Then we went on a trip. I got a train. When I turned five Life started to get harder. I had to go to school. and I had to do work. And thats about all. I go to school every day and work. And I come home. Buy. One thing my name now is Sam Culham.

Contents

Acknowledgments

Thank you to primary students, parents, teachers, and administrators for allowing me to visit your classrooms, conduct interviews, gather samples of writing, and collect permission to publish the stories, pictures, and pieces for this book: Scotty Mosquera; Ashley Ryan and Lu Ann Hermreck; A. J. Monterossi; Sarah, Ann Marie, and Brian Wheeler; Leah A.; Marsha Zandi; Sharon Peiffer Pennington; Carrie Collins; Chris Poulsen; Melissa Garner; Karen Davidson; Jessica Tracy; Elise Wright Mull and Courtney Mull; Berta Lopez; Gaye and Dave Lantz; Cindy Tjoelker; Diane Drake; Shelly Treely; Kelly Chumrau; Ursula, Clay, Tanner, and Jeff White; Tony Boyland, and Sergei S.

The principal, teachers, and students at Palmer Way Elementary School, National City, California: Rick Hanks, Janet Malek, Rex Payumo, Rocio Huh, Diane Whitaker, Herb Eckardt, Samuel Garza, Alvin Garcia, Calvin Cabading, Santino Avila, and Lenny Madrigal.

The teachers at Council Rock Primary School, Brighton Central School District, Rochester, New York: Libby Jachles, Betsy Waugh, Sue Martin, Carol Flanigan, Lori Baglione, Pat Ringelstetter, and Lisa Jordan. And a special thank you to Ben McLauchlin.

The teachers and principal at Pleasant Hill Elementary School, Topeka, Kansas: Debbie Stewart, Laura Sadler, and Craig Carter.

And to all who are not mentioned by name, my deepest appreciation for your words, ideas, and inspiration.

Thank you to the visionary people of Scholastic Teaching Resources: Terry Cooper, Judy deTuncq, Eileen Hillebrand, Joanna Davis-Swing, Susan Kolwicz, and Margery Rosnick. Every conversation we have centers on teachers and kids. You make a difference every day. To Holly Grundon, for designing each of my books elegantly. And to Margery Mayer and Dick Robinson for believing my books are good enough to stand on the shelf with the Scholastic name. It's an honor to work with all of you.

Thank you to Laura Robb, Ralph Fletcher, Katie Wood Ray, and Linda Rief for the gift of friendship as I try to find my way.

Thank you to Bridey Monterossi, Beth Sullivan, Rhett and Jean Boudreau, Janet and Larry Slocum, Ann Rader, Bonnie and Rick Snowden, Wendy Doss, and Janice Wright. You came running. There could not be better friends.

Thank you to Mary Sue Fordham. Every day I am inspired by your courage, grace, intelligence, and passion for life. Sam always knew you were amazing; I couldn't agree more.

And finally, thank you to Ray Coutu, my editor and friend.

Foreword

BY CAROL AVERY

More than 20 years ago, John Meehan, a visionary leader from the Pennsylvania Department of Education who was working to expand the teaching of writing in elementary schools statewide, asked me: "We recognize a good piece of writing when we read it, but do we really know what makes it well written or how to teach children to write well?" With that question, he made me realize how difficult it is for teachers to look at student writing, know what young writers need, and then teach them.

John is now retired, but I suspect he will cheer when he reads this new book by Ruth Culham, as I did. I delight in the fact that Culham's long-overdue ideas are now available to teachers. If I had her book 25 years ago, the task of learning how to help children improve their writing would have been much easier. At that time, the groundbreaking research of Donald Graves had reached our state. I was introducing daily writing workshops and, as a result, my first graders were going far beyond any of my former classes. Writing was exploding in elementary classrooms with energy we hadn't seen before. Children were choosing topics and drafting every day. They were rereading their pieces and revising so their words made sense.

But, for many of these young writers, making a piece better simply meant making it longer. Knowing how to help my students find a focus and then develop that focus was challenging for me and countless other teachers I knew. We had lots of writing going on, but we realized that we needed to do more to help young children improve the *quality* of their writing.

Ruth Culham tackles this issue head-on in *6+1 Traits of Writing: The Complete Guide for the Primary Grades*, a thoughtful book that is intensely practical but never prescriptive. She gives teachers and children a language for applying seven specific attributes of good writing to their work: ideas, organization, voice, word choice, sentence fluency, conventions, and presentation. Even more important, while we learn about those attributes, she helps us maintain a developmental perspective and teach responsively based on our observations of individual writers, which is the heart of Graves's research findings.

Culham uses carefully chosen examples of children's writing to lead us through the process of assessing for each trait. The purpose of this assessment is not to slap a grade on the writing or rank it, but rather to recognize the writer's development to inform and guide instruction. Good instruction evolves from good assessment, and the purpose of assessment ought to be first and foremost to inform instruction.

By reading this book and observing Culham's process of assessing children's writing in each trait, the classroom teacher will be able to apply this approach in the classroom. As that teacher internalizes the procedures Culham advocates, she will likely come away with a clearer understanding of how children emerge as writers. I have to admit, I've always been highly resistant to scoring student writing in the traditional sense, but Culham presents a way to assess and *teach* writing while maintaining a developmental perspective that honors the individual writer.

After demonstrating how to assess examples of children's writing, Culham shows us how to address specific traits in our instruction. She does not offer tailored lessons, nor a neat sequence of lesson plans. Rather, she provides ideas that are specific enough for us to implement easily, yet general enough for us to modify or transform completely. A suggestion that one teacher might find just right for her children might prompt another teacher to create something different or more appropriate for her children. I like the range and variety of ideas and, most of all, the fact that they are responsive to the writers in the classroom. That is, they are designed to help us respond to what we notice writers doing (or not doing) as they write.

With regard to conferences, Culham also offers suggestions—not formulas—for responding to writers. Her goal is to show us ways to respond to child writers that encourage the development of specific traits. She provides useful tips for creating momentum in conferences and keeping it going.

In addition, Culham recognizes the important connection between learning to write and hearing children's literature read aloud. She suggests numerous quality picture books to consider reading aloud, organized around each trait. In her annotations for these books, however, you will find no prescriptive lessons. Instead, she encourages us to just read, noticing what authors do and talking about it with the children. Those rich conversations help children grow as writers. How simple. How basic. What fine teaching!

We've come a long way in the teaching of writing since the early '80s. The basics remain: respond to writers, honor their thinking, and learn as much as we can from them so that we can teach them well. Ruth Culham does all of this while taking us further on our professional journeys. She has written a book that respects children's learning and our decision-making processes in the classroom.

You'll enjoy *6+1 Traits of Writing: The Complete Guide for the Primary Grades* and turn to it as you make daily decisions in your classroom. May it stimulate your professional growth and, ultimately, the growth of your students as writers.

CHAPTER 1

Building a Foundation for Writing

Devon sits at his desk, scrunched over his paper, working hard on a piece of writing. In the background, the familiar high-pitched *beep beep beep* of the lunch truck as it backs into the cafeteria loading zone is barely audible over the steady hum of his first-grade classroom. Cocking his head to listen, Devon catches the eye of his teacher. "You know, Miss Peiffer, that bird comes the same time every day." And with that astute observation, he goes right back to his work.

A day in a primary classroom will be filled with delightful moments like this. Students see things we overlook, hear things we screen out, and use their observations to make sense of their world with insight that is honest, simple, and logical. And they bring their developing ways of looking at the world to their conversations, drawings, and early text. They capture snapshots of their thinking that amaze us and, in Devon's case, make us smile.

> *"Writing is a craft before it is an art; writing may appear magic, but it is our responsibility to take our students backstage to watch the pigeons being tucked up in the magician's sleeve."*
>
> —Donald Murray

Learning about the traits of writing—ideas, organization, voice, word choice, sentence fluency, conventions, and presentation—can't begin too soon because they give students a way to think and talk about writing. With a foundation for writing built on these traits, young writers are better able to communicate with readers.

What We Know About Primary Writers

Primary writers are hungry to communicate. They want to write and often find creative and imaginative ways to do so long before they are able to create conventional text. Although their pages may appear to be filled with nothing but scribbles, we must remember that they are writing. Therefore, we must learn how to read even rudimentary text with keen perspective. This book will help.

Berta Lopez, a teacher and parent in National City, California, shares this story:

"I came home from school to find my 18-month-old had taken a black, permanent marker to the door and left a whole series of indelible marks. The babysitter apologetically explained that my young son had slipped away from her and, in an instant, created the damage. I took him to the door and asked, 'Hijito, what is this? What have you done?' And to my surprise he grinned from ear to ear, pointed to the top of the line of marks and said, 'Mama.' And then he pointed to a line of marks toward the bottom and said, 'Papa.' You should have seen his face; it was glowing. My son had written his first letter—a welcome-home note to his mom and dad. Instead of scolding him, I gave him a huge hug and thanked him. I then locked up all the permanent markers and replaced them with the washable kind."

There's an important lesson to be learned from this sweet story: If we reward children generously for their early attempts to communicate in writing, they learn quickly that writing is a worthwhile skill to approach with energy and enthusiasm.

> *"Anne Haas Dyson's studies of early literacy development have shown how children use 'print to represent their ideas and to interact with other people' when they scribble; draw and label pictures; and create, act out, or retell stories. Children can express ideas in writing even 'before they have mastered all the mechanics of standard orthography, sentence and paragraph structure.'"*
>
> *—National Writing Project and Carl Nagin*

Carol Avery (2002) has three assumptions about primary writers: they can write, they want to write, and they possess the knowledge, interests, and experiences to write. Like all complex endeavors, becoming a good writer is slow-going and challenging. However, the younger the travelers, the more willing they will be to climb writing's rocky slopes and traverse its tricky trails.

Prominent educators support that notion. George Hillocks, Jr. (Jensen, 1999), notes that "the research has shown that [very young] children transfer much about what they have learned about language to writing . . . Children can begin using what they do know far earlier than we thought" (p. 27). Peter Elbow (Jensen, 1999) explains that very young children "can write anything they say, whereas they can read only a fraction of the words they can say." He concludes that "writing is easier, quicker, and, in a sense, more 'natural' than reading—certainly more naturally learned" (pp. 22–27).

Noted author and speaker Robert Fulghum (1991) refers to children's early years as the "Yes, I can" stage of life. When asked if they can draw, paint, write, dance, read, sing, or any other task you can put in front of them, primary students respond with "Yes, I can." And their confidence takes them a long way toward reaching important literacy goals. When they approach learning how to write with a positive attitude, they move from the outside of the literacy circle to the inside. Kelly, a kindergartner, for example, proved she made this move when she said, "I can see now that most of my letters are in the alphabet." This is a moment worthy of the grandest celebration. What was once unknown territory—the world of letters and words and meaning—is now home to Kelly. She is literate. When our students observe themselves as writers, we must recognize it and create opportunities for them to become established, experienced writers. We must urge them to write stories, poems, explanations, how

> *"What happens to the child who is not allowed to write? The latest research about the development of intelligence leads us to believe this is dangerous ground. Windows of opportunity that only open once might be missed, and potential for learning lost forever."*
>
> *—Bea Johnson*

to's, descriptions, and any other forms of writing they wish to explore. We must give them writer's notebooks and encourage them to record their thoughts as they learn more about writing. By doing so, we empower them to be writers.

Young writers accept writing tasks with excitement and energy. Ralph Fletcher (1993), author of books for teachers and students on writing, sums it up well: "The writer goes out into the world (or descends into the inner world) and returns with both fists clutching a mass of words, ideas, characters, places, stories, insights, possibly poisonous, hopefully not, and waves them, still squirming, still alive, before the startled reader" (p. 161). As they venture into the world, their "Yes, I can" attitude helps them bring originality to their work, making it a joy to read.

One Student's Story: A Case for Accurate, Reliable Assessment

Primary writers must be nurtured and their work celebrated in order for them to take the next steps toward more complex writing. We're their teacher-coach, whispering encouraging words into their ears at the beginning of each heat: "You can do this. You have the tools. You've trained hard. Now go, do your best." Look no further for one child's best than this example from Leah, a first-grade writer.

1.
When I Walk to School
With My Brother
We dont Talk. I
always Listen To
The husel Busel going
on in people's houses.

First grader Leah shows strong writing skills in her piece, "Walk to School."

2.
I also like to feel
The Breeze hit My
Skin. Most of all
I Like The Way The
Wind RuShes Me.

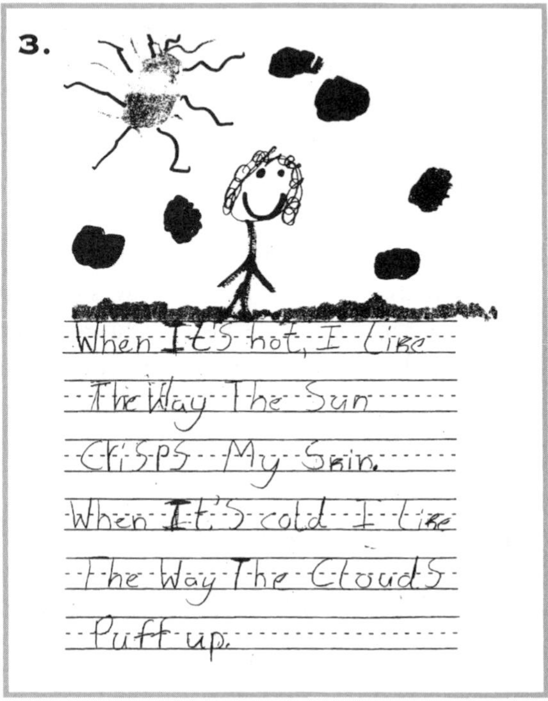
3.
When It'S hot, I Like
The Way The Sun
CriSPS My Skin.
When It'S cold I Like
The Way The ClouDS
Puff up.

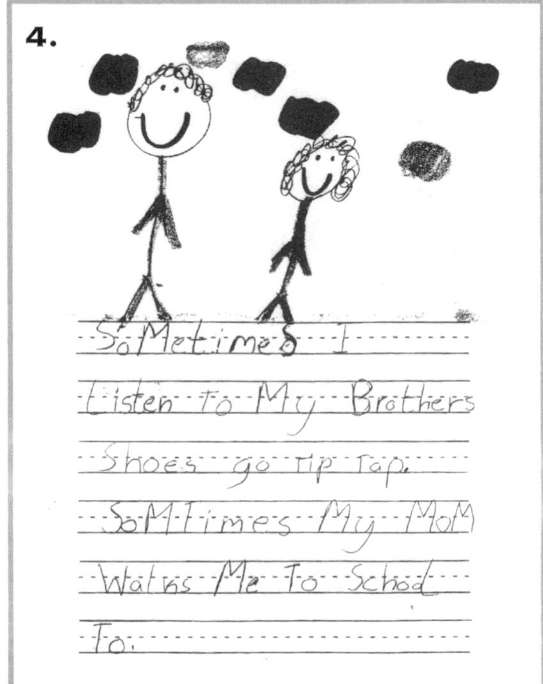
4.
SoMetimeS I
Listen To My Brothers
Shoes go Tip Tap.
SoMTimes My MoM
Walks Me To School
To.

5.
Sch
When Were half Way
There I run so im not
Late. The funis
Thing about Walking
by My Self is
That I Can Tell

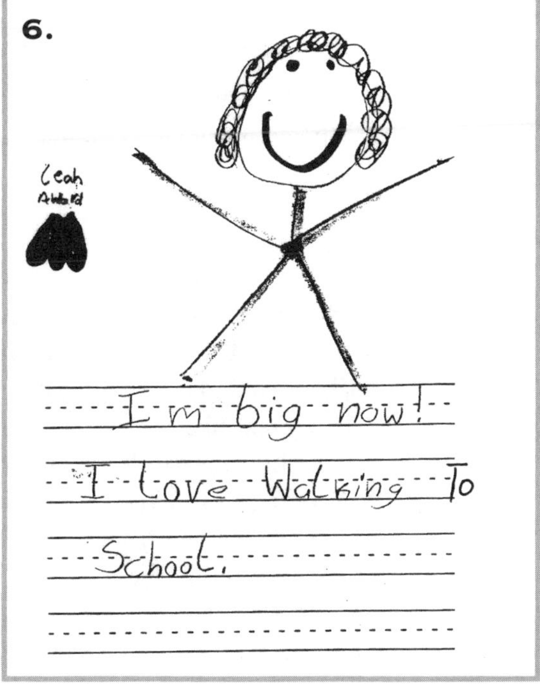

Lucy Calkins (1994) tells us, "I write to hold what I find in my life in my hands and to declare it as treasure" (p. 7). Leah's piece is certainly a treasure. As a reader, I'm right there with this author, experiencing the way the clouds puff up and hearing the *tip tap* of shoes. I feel Leah's sense of pride as she gains independence, able to walk to school on her own. Our students' stories, explanations of how things work, and unique perspectives on life are, indeed, riches to be cherished. As we encourage them to draw, write, and talk about things that interest them, that matter to them, that create questions for them, we create writers who understand the power of words and pictures to connect with readers and create images that last a lifetime. That's powerful teaching.

Now compare my reaction to Leah's work to that of officials from her state. "Walk to School" received the lowest score possible in the state assessment. How can that be? With the intention of responding to the developmental needs of the youngest writers, those officials surveyed the primary teachers and asked which writing skills should be assessed in first grade. The results led them to ignore the traits, fearing they would be too hard for primary writers to apply. So the officials only scored first-grade writing for capitalization. As a result, Leah's paper received the lowest score. The message to Leah was clear: "You just don't write very well." The exceptional qualities of the work were completely devalued by focusing on one small blemish, and Leah was forever branded a "poor writer" at first grade. State officials reduced the comprehensive writing task to a small skill set, easily measured and scored.

This is an assessment horror story. When we tell primary writers they aren't very good, they believe us. So we must be careful to make our assessments comprehensive and constructive, focusing on what is working well, right along with areas of need. If Leah had received such an assessment, she would have been able to hold her head high, smiling, while she worked to correct her capitalization. After all, there is a writing life beyond the writing test.

If we want to see our students' writing improve, we must embrace that life.

> "*Every study of young writers I've done for the last twenty years has underestimated what they can do. In fact, we know very little about the human potential for writing.*"
>
> —*Donald Graves*

Although many youngsters may "write" with pictures and wobbly letters, this is how they tell stories, share information, and capture thoughts. It's real writing, make no mistake about it. These early pieces pave the way for more traditional-looking text like Leah's, but the writer's purpose remains the same regardless of where she is on the developmental spectrum—to communicate clear ideas in interesting ways. High-quality assessment tells writers how close they are to reaching their goals, and tells us what we can do to help them get there.

The spark that these young writers bring to the classroom door is all too easily extinguished when they're handed a single-minded, worksheet-driven approach to teaching and learning. Remember Devon's observation about the *beep beep beep* of the lunch truck? That kind of thinking takes place only in classrooms where it is valued. That kind of thinking is the stuff of good writing.

Consider the insight of this second grader reflecting on his early school experience: "My kindergarten room was full of toys and arguments." What a powerful image. It says to me that the classroom should be a place where play, imagination, and the requisite skills to become effective writers collide. It's a balancing act all the way.

How to Help Primary Writers

Primary writing is about much more than forming words and using conventions correctly. It is about pictures. It is about early representations of letters and words. It is about creative, serious expressions of ideas on paper. So, for the purposes of this book, I define primary writing as work that is everything from random scribbles to simple, multiple-sentence paragraphs on a single topic. Typically this work is produced in grades K to 2. In Chapters 3 to 9, I observe the stages writers go through on their way to becoming confident and fluent, examining the role the writing traits play in this process. You'll find detailed scoring guides for assessing beginning writing, with models to illustrate what work typically looks like at each stage. You'll also find a wealth of practical, ready-to-use focus lessons and activities that develop skills in each of the seven writing traits.

Although I focus on students in grades K to 2, the assessment model and instructional strategies that I provide can be used in the upper-elementary grades as well. It's important to match the assessment and subsequent instruction to the appropriate developmental level of the student. If the student is ten years old, for example, yet working hard to create just one sentence, it's helpful to respond with the assessment scoring guide in this book. Once that student is able to create longer, more conventional looking text, he will be best served by the assessment scoring guide found in *6+1 Traits of Writing: The Complete Guide, Grades 3 and Up* (Culham, 2003).

Regardless of their age, students need specific, constructive feedback to know what is working well and what needs improvement. We must give students feedback that builds on what they know and points them to the next step, especially students who have gotten off to a rocky start in writing. It is not helpful to tell a struggling writer, "You aren't doing very well." They already know that. What they need to hear is what they can do to improve. Beginning writers benefit from trait-driven instruction because the traits are specific, are easily taught and reinforced, and make sense. So, whether the students are six, twelve, or somewhere in between, the ideas in this book will help them understand what goes into crafting a piece of writing and provide the vocabulary to talk about it.

Three Critical Concerns for Today's Writing Classrooms

Bookstores are rife with texts that are not much more than collections of black-line masters designed to "teach" students how to write by giving them story starters, grammatically incorrect sentences to fix, and formulas for organizing their work. Unfortunately, by reducing the writing task to the least common denominator, young writers are led to believe that good writing is achieved by following a series of prescriptive steps.

> *"Children can travel the world as if they are writers, using whatever they do know to approximate writing, while you [the teacher] provide them with constant opportunities to learn."*
>
> *—Lucy Calkins*

Of course, no single path has been discovered that will work for all children, all the time, and in all circumstances. And you won't find one between the covers of this book, either. All the scoring guides, student samples, focus lessons, and activities in the world will not make a difference unless you embrace a philosophy about creating confident, capable young writers. My personal philosophy revolves around three beliefs:

We Must Speak a Common Language Based on the Traits

Look at primary writing according to individual traits and as a whole, using the same working vocabulary from day to day and year to year to develop a foundation for writing assessment and instruction.

We Must Nurture Process Learning

Discover or rediscover the importance of valuing process over product, in a classroom where writing is encouraged and celebrated every day.

We Must Use Criteria to Set the Standard

Use criteria to describe for students what we believe is important for them to learn and to measure how well they're doing.

Speaking a Common Language Based on the Traits

It's just flat-out confusing to students at any age when we use new terminology to describe something they have already learned. Imagine if we taught our primary students how to "add" and "subtract" one year, and then taught them how to "plus" and "minus" the following year. Wouldn't most students think they were learning something completely new? Using new terminology from year to year doesn't help students move toward deep understanding.

Using consistent terminology also gives teachers something we desperately crave: time. We save a great deal of time when we don't have to reteach the same concepts over and over. Instead of starting at square one every year, we can review and quickly move to new work that is challenging and interesting to students.

Analytic Assessment

Through analytic assessment we

- develop a shared understanding of what "good" writing looks like.
- align assessment with instruction.
- evaluate writing with consistency and accuracy.

We can then

- provide meaningful feedback to students.
- enhance our teaching of writing.

Establishing a common vocabulary that captures the key characteristics of writing and using it as a foundation for writing instruction is at the core of trait-based writing assessment and instruction. In the mid-1980s, a group of teachers from Beaverton, Oregon; Missoula, Montana; and other areas worked to create a reliable and accurate tool to measure student writing performance. Using the work of Paul Diederich (1974) as a starting point, they read and sorted stacks of student writing into "good," "fair," and "poor" categories and then analyzed that writing closely, identifying the characteristics that were common to all the pieces. Their efforts led to an analytic assessment model that identified seven key characteristics, or traits, of writing.

- Ideas: the meaning and development of the message
- Organization: the internal structure of the piece
- Voice: the tone of the piece—the personal stamp that the writer brings to it
- Word Choice: the specific vocabulary the writer uses to convey meaning
- Sentence Fluency: the way the words and phrases flow throughout the text
- Conventions: the mechanical correctness of the piece
- Presentation: the overall appearance of the work

Analytic Assessment of "The nit qast"

Analytic assessment—or breaking the writing down into traits—allows us to delve deeply into the core of the text. It enables us to communicate to primary writers what is working well in their writing and what needs work. It's far more useful than any holistic tool that provides only a single score. Beginning writers get rich feedback on their writing. Consider, for example, how much first grader Scotty Mosquera gained from my trait-by-trait analysis of his story "The nit qast."

First grader Scotty shares a complete, original story entitled "The nit qast" ("The Knight's Quest"), which I assess, beginning on page 22.

2.

The cing cald his nit.
The cing told his nit wut to do.
A men flyr brethIg Dragin
has stolln my pOT uv gold.
I wont youTo slay that
Dragin. yes sed The nit.

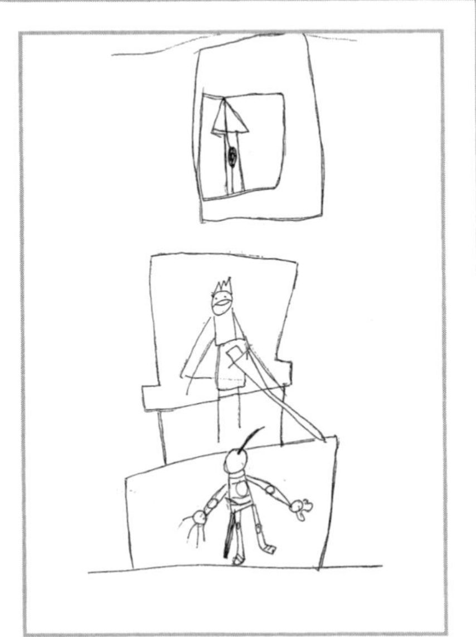

3.

He set owT on his Qast
aumdele.

4.

Then he met the dragIn.

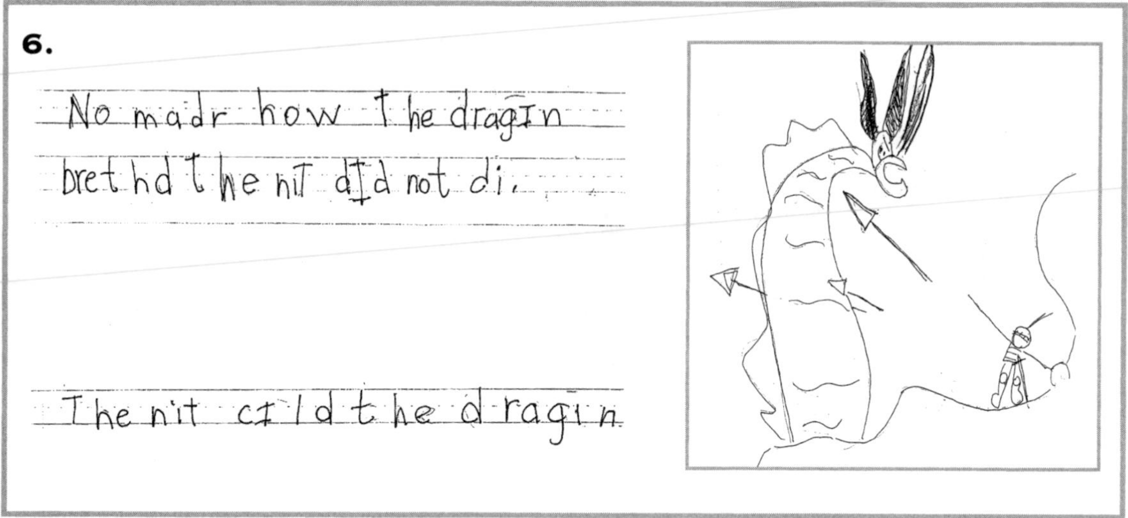

6.
No madr how the dragIn
bret hd the nit dId not di.
The nit cIld the dragin.

7.
Wuns thedragIn wus cIld
the nitcudget the gold.

8.
The nit went into The dragIns
cav.

9.
Wuns he got It onto hIs hors
he left.

10.
Wuns he got bac to the
cassull the cIng gav hIm
a re word a bag uv gold.

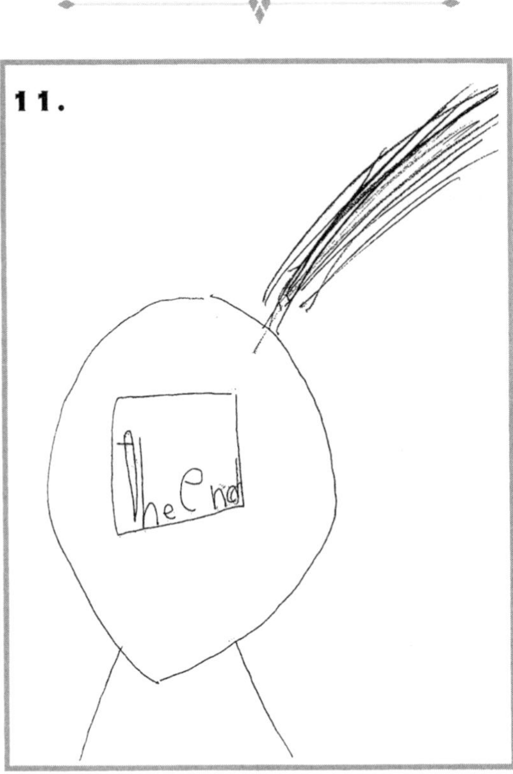

Ideas

Scotty selected a focused topic, a knight's quest for his king. He gives us the setting, the details needed for the story to develop, and a time frame that makes sense. "The nit qast's" central idea is made clear in the written text through details, and enhanced by the pictures. For example, "Thay fout for awrs" is comprehensible. However, when that text is coupled with a picture depicting the battle, the reader gets a vivid image of Scotty's vision. The illustration elaborates the main idea.

What to Say to the Writer

Your idea is so clear in this story. It is clever, makes sense, and I can picture it all the way through.

Organization

This story follows a sensible, chronological sequence. Words such as "then," "when," and "once" link one sentence or short passage to the next, keeping every event in an order. On page 6, two events are described: "No madr how the dragin breathd the nit did not di." Scotty leaves space before beginning the next line,

"The nit cild the dragin," sending a visual message that the two events happened separately. Scotty uses an illustration of the king on his throne receiving the knight at the beginning of the story. For the end, when the knight returns the gold to the king, Scotty draws the same setting, creating a sense of resolution before the tried-and-true final announcement, "The End."

What to Say to the Writer

The way you used words like *next* helped me understand the order of your story. I also like the way you use spaces to let me know where one event begins and another ends. You have a strong beginning, middle, and end.

Voice

"The nit qast" screams with voice. From the title page, where Scotty establishes himself as the author and presents his age ("6 yr 3 months"), to the clever artistic touches, such as turning the "T" in "The" into a sword, to the knight's emphatic response to the king's challenge, this piece is alive. The details in the pictures, details that are not always present in the text, add to the voice too. Notice that the knight is dwarfed by the huge, ferocious dragon as the confrontation begins. As the battle rages, the pictures become more animated, catching the reader up in the life-and-death conflict. The voice is so authentic that we can relate to both characters—the knight and the dragon.

What to Say to the Writer

The dragon was so fierce in this story. I wanted the knight to slay him, but at the same time I felt a little sorry for him. You made the story come alive for me by creating real characters.

Word Choice

Generally, primary students can't capture written words as easily as spoken ones. They tend to choose simple, everyday words because they are safe and easy to spell. So it's refreshing to see Scotty write with such confidence. Again and again, he chooses the perfect word, even if his spelling of it is anything but perfect—for example, "aumedle" is "immediately." What a missed opportunity it would be if Scotty had settled for the simpler synonym *now* because it was easy to spell. Most important at this point is for Scotty to get his ideas down using the best words he knows, not editing himself for correctness. He's chosen precise, evocative words for this piece, such as "a mean fire-breathing dragon" ("a men flyr brethig Dragin") and "He set out on his quest immediately" ("He set owt on his qast aumdele"). Verbs such as *called*, *stolen*, and *fought* add energy and move the piece along.

What to Say to the Writer

Quest, *immediately*, *fought*. These are excellent words to use in this story because they help me see exactly what is happening. It's great to see that you're trying new words as you write. Do you have a favorite?

Sentence Fluency

The sentence patterns and variety in this piece prove that Scotty is a skilled writer. Its natural rhythm makes it easy to understand. Although some sentences are short and choppy, there is good balance of short and long sentences, and they begin in different, interesting ways. For example, page 2 presents five sentences of varying lengths. And, except for the first two, the sentences begin in different ways. Scotty even includes some well-placed dialogue.

What to Say to the Writer

You began your sentences differently and made them different lengths. This is what makes it sound so good when it is read aloud. Good for you!

Conventions

Even teachers who don't work with the youngest writers have little trouble reading "The nit qast." Although it contains many spelling errors, those errors are, for the most part, phonetic ("Thay fout for awrs" is "They fought for hours"), making them easy to understand. Scotty knows to capitalize the first word in sentences and to end sentences with punctuation marks. He even uses space to separate ideas, which is an indicator that he has a rudimentary understanding of paragraphing. Simple things—readable spelling, punctuation marks at the end of sentences, capitals at the beginning, standard grammar—are clearly present. In other words, Scotty uses conventions to guide us through the text. This is their purpose, after all.

What to Say to the Writer

Reading your story was a breeze. You've got punctuation and capitals down. There are some spelling words for us to work on, but I can read them just fine as they are.

PRESENTATION

A piece as sophisticated as "The nit qast" deserves a comment for presentation. It's remarkable that Scotty has drawn pictures that so clearly illustrate each step of the story. His use of perspective adds to our understanding of the text and the pictures. Each page is clear, vivid, and accessible.

WHAT TO SAY TO THE WRITER

Your text looks like a real book. I like how you wrote the text and then added the picture. You made it easy for me to read. Thanks.

All the traits are present in Scotty's remarkable piece, right from the beginning. If we wanted to, we could assess for them and give Scotty specific examples of strengths right along with suggestions for improvement.

Now imagine a different scenario. What if Scotty was in a classroom where the only assessment students received was a single grade, score, or comment? The feedback on Scotty's piece might have been "This is a very cute story" or "Check your spelling, C+." While both of these comments are sound, they don't fulfill one of the core tenets of classroom assessment: it should serve as an instructional tool helping teachers meet student needs. Teachers need *accurate* scores for each student, not necessarily the highest possible scores" (Stiggins, 1994, p. 44). Analytic assessment ensures accurate scores.

By using a common language based on the traits, we create high expectations in the minds of our youngest writers and show them, early on, the writing skills they possess and ways to master ones they haven't yet. The traits empower even the youngest students to say, "Yes, I can" to writing.

In Chapters 3 to 9, I show you how to assess primary writing by providing examples at each point along a continuum of development, describing each example trait by trait and linking the assessment to instructional practices designed to build on what students know.

Nurturing Process Learning

Writing is a complex process. To learn how to do it well takes skill, practice, and courage. Determining which skills to teach young writers and when to teach them is a challenge. Think about driving a car. You need to understand how to work the gas pedal, turn the wheel, and use the mirrors, but there's a lot more to

Get Visual: Create Trait Symbols With Your Students

Libby Jachles of the Brighton School District, Rochester, New York, introduces her students to the traits and helps them remember them by creating visual models. After discussing each of the traits and sharing examples of what they look like in stories and other kinds of writing, she divides the class into small groups and distributes construction paper, pens, and markers. Her directions are simple: "Create a symbol to represent the important thing to remember about each trait. It might be a symbol like a dollar sign, which stands for money, or a red light, which stands for stop." Students approach the task eagerly. Here are some of the results:

When the groups complete their symbols, they share them with the whole class. The class votes on which symbol it prefers for each trait and makes a poster, which is hung on the wall so students can refer to it when they wish.

The poster is especially helpful during peer review as students provide feedback to their classmates about their writing. For example, if one student wants to tell another that her sentence fluency is strong, he draws on her paper. If he likes the paper's idea, he might draw a on a sticky note and affix it to the page. Long before these young writers can write expanded comments, they can use symbols to reinforce each other's writing efforts.

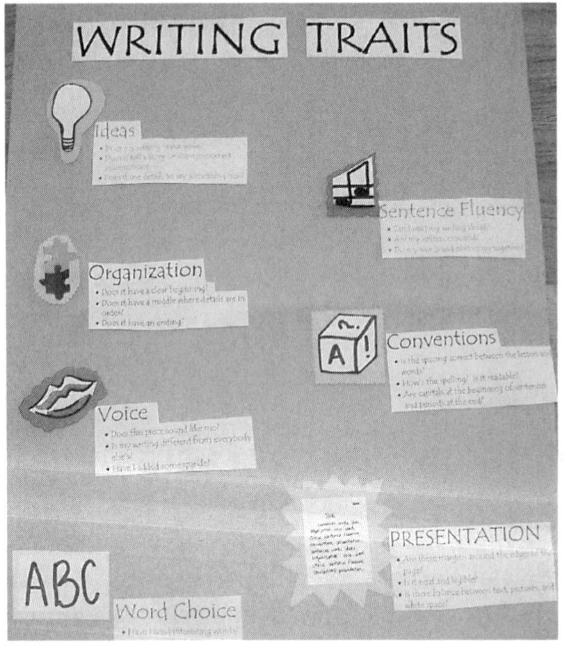

driving than that, right? Just practicing one part of driving does not make you a driver. Driving makes you a driver. The same is true for writing. Worksheets don't create writers. Writing creates writers. Oh, sure, you can use a worksheet now and again to reinforce a new skill, but students become good writers by writing often, on a variety of topics and in a multitude of forms.

Young writers who learn how to ask important questions, consider new ideas, and find unique ways of looking at things are far more successful than those who are given decontextualized tasks and a series of isolated strategies taught through worksheets (Fu and Townsend, 1999). Eager, energetic, and excited primary writers learn about the craft of writing because they have something to say and a real purpose for saying it. For students to become good writers they must do more than practice skills—they must have personal reasons for writing.

In *Writing, Teaching, Learning: A Sourcebook*, Richard L. Graves (1999) reports the findings of Julie Jensen, who asked writing experts this question: "What is the single most important thing that we as a profession know now that we didn't know 30 years ago about the teaching and learning of writing in the elementary school?" Here are summaries of their responses:

- Writing in the early years is a natural gateway to literacy.
- All children can be writers.
- Understanding writing and writers means understanding complex and interrelated influences—cognitive, social, cultural, psychological, linguistic, and technological.
- We write so that both we and others can know what we think.

Indeed, we've learned that writing is a complex process, not easily taught, not easily learned. However, Jensen's survey reinforces the notion that it is a critical part of a student's early literacy. It confirms what most of us observe every day in the classroom: children can write and write well.

Glenda L. Bissex (Jensen, 1999) concludes that this expanded view of writing allows many more children to see themselves as writers—"not only the young poets and storytellers, but the inventive spellers who are working to understand and use our writing system [and also] the children who write about dinosaurs and kittens" (p. 28). No matter what their reasons are for writing—to tell a story, explain, inform, or persuade—if students explicitly think of writing as a process right from the beginning, their writing flourishes. (In Chapter 2, I discuss the writing process over the past 20 years and show what it looks like in today's primary classrooms.)

We must, therefore, resist the urge, even in the primary grades, to place product over process. When we emphasize finishing the work and making it look neat, students don't become writers. They become task-completers. This may be why so many adults claim to be terrible writers. As children, they may have suffered through years of "writing instruction" that was focused on getting it spelled right and getting it done. Our beginning writers deserve better than this.

Is Your Classroom Process-Centered or Product-Centered ?

In a process-centered classroom . . .	In a product-centered classroom . . .
students work on different tasks at different rates.	students do the same tasks.
teachers encourage many short, interesting pieces of writing, any of which may lead to one or two longer pieces over time.	all students complete the same preset writing assignments.
small groups of students work together.	students usually work alone.
writing is shared as it is created.	writing is shared only when finished.
one piece may lead to another on a new topic that is discovered during the writing.	when a piece is finished, students ask for the next task.
failure is an opportunity to stretch and grow.	failure is to be avoided. Emphasis is placed on getting it right the first time.
questions like these are typical: Does this work? What else could I try? Will you help me find a better way to say this? What would happen if I changed it to show . . . ?	questions like these are typical: Is this long enough? Is this what you want? Is this going to be graded?

Ask yourself, If I was a student in my class, which would matter more: 1) writing to get the work finished and turned in, or 2) writing to learn what I want to say and the best way to say it? If your answer is #1, this book may help you a little. However, if your answer is #2, it will help you tremendously because it contains strategies and ideas that support your belief that true learning happens over time and through a process.

Helping young writers understand a general definition of process is a first step to helping them understand writing as a process. From there, we can teach them about the traits because they are a natural fit. Here is a lesson to try early in the year.

MAKING PROCESS LEARNING CONCRETE

When young students get an insider's view of the writing process, they realize that we don't just "write to write." We write to think. And as writing tasks get harder over the years, this understanding helps them stick with it until the work is right.

In this lesson, students create colorful modeling-clay sculptures to experience firsthand what it means to follow a process.

MATERIALS:

- plain white paper plates, one per student
- modeling clay in a variety of colors, enough so each student has several different small balls
- overhead projector or chalkboard
- sticky notes and pencils or pens

WHAT TO DO:

1. After asking students to clear their work surfaces, distribute the paper plates.
2. Pass out at least three small balls of modeling clay of different colors to each student. Provide extra modeling clay in case students want more as the lesson progresses.

Students learn about the concept of process by creating clay sculptures.

3. Review the rules of using modeling clay:
    - Keep it on the work surface.
    - Do not throw it or use it for anything other than this activity.
    - Do not take classmates' modeling clay; if you need more, ask.
4. Ask students to "create something" with their modeling clay. Be intentionally vague.
5. Record on the overhead or chalkboard any questions students have during this stage. They may ask, "What should I make?" "Is this okay?" or "Can I do this?" Refrain from answering by refocusing students on the assignment. Circulate around the room, noticing the different ways students are approaching the task.
6. After 10 to 15 minutes, tell students that time's up.
7. Show them the list of questions you collected and see if they have additional ones to add. They may wish to know why they are doing this task, who will see it, or what it is for. Add those to your list.
8. Tell students that they have two minutes to ADD something to their piece. As students work, write down any questions or comments you hear that reflect how they're feeling, whether it's good or bad. Students may say, "But I like it just the way it is. I don't want to add anything." If they do, remind them that they have to follow the directions and add their comment to your list. Tell them when time's up.
9. Now, tell them they have two minutes to REMOVE something. Continue adding comments or questions to your list as they come up. Tell students when time's up.

10. Give students another two minutes to CHANGE something and stop them when the time is up. Add any new questions or comments to your list.

11. Ask students to come up with titles for their pieces and write them on the plates. Remind them that important words should be capitalized.

12. With the sticky notes in one hand and a pencil or pen in the other, ask students to circulate around the room for ten minutes to observe one another's creations and write substantive comments about each piece, such as "Your elephant is bright and colorful. It makes me happy," "I like how your sun is many colors," or "Your snake seems like it is ready to strike!" Discourage general comments such as "Good job," "Nice work," and "Good for you." If students are unable to write substantive comments, have them tell the sculptor what they think. Model as necessary.

13. Allow time for students to read the comments and share them with each other. Ask them which comments were the most interesting or informative. Return to the master list of comments and questions you created while students were making their sculptures. Guide students through them, emphasizing that there is no one right way to work through a process. Ask, "How did it feel when I told you to revise your work by adding, removing, and changing? Did doing those things help you make your piece better?"

14. As a group, discuss how this activity mirrors what writers do as they write. Let students know that sometimes writers have a great idea and are ready to write without any help. Other times, however, they have to plan, talk, and jot down thoughts before the idea is clear. But either way, they have to jump in and get started. Encourage students to think about how important it was for them to figure out what they wanted to do to their clay sculpture, changing it along the way. Use the term *revision* whenever possible to help students understand that although revision is one of the hardest parts of the writing process, it's necessary to make the writing the best it can be and to make it the writer's own.

15. Discuss the importance of getting helpful feedback. Tell students that throughout the year you will give them the same kind of feedback so that writing will be easier for them.

FOLLOW-UP:

Encourage students to write about what they learned about process and writing from this activity. Then ask them to share their observations as a class.

Using Criteria to Set the Standard

I've found that knowing what "good" looks like helps students succeed in school. When we use criteria to assess their performance in math, science, reading, writing, and other subjects, we show students what they know and can do while pointing the way for further learning. These criteria define what a strong performance looks like and give students important information about how close they are to meeting achievement targets.

Specific, detailed academic criteria have grown out of the performance assessment movement that has swept through our schools over the past 15 years (Stiggins, 1994; Popham, 1995; Wiggins, 1998). For the teaching of writing, researchers such as Paul Diederich (1974) and Alan Purves (1992) established criteria that paved the way for trait-based writing assessment. We owe a debt of gratitude to these scholars.

Improving student writing performance by using the writing traits was documented in a study conducted by Northwest Regional Educational Laboratory, Portland, Oregon, in 1994 (Arter, Spandel, Culham, & Pollard). This study, since replicated by dozens of schools and districts across the country, found that students in writing process classrooms who were taught the explicit language of the traits and given focused instruction in writing using them, created stronger pieces of writing than their counterparts who were not explicitly instructed on the traits. The results of this study mirror the wise words of George Hillocks, Jr. (1986): "Scales, criteria, and specific questions which students apply to their own or others' writing also have a powerful effect on enhancing quality" (p. 249).

Criteria Are Everywhere

Each time we say, "I like pizza" or "It's a good movie," we are using criteria. We make hundreds of casual assessments every day—sorting what we like from what we don't, what works from what doesn't. Chances are, you're already using criteria in your everyday life and don't even realize it. You can describe good weather, a tidy desk, or a favorite movie, right? When I order a steak, I ask for it to be cooked medium—not too rare, not too well done. And when my steak is served, I check it to see that it's been cooked to my liking. That's criteria in action.

We use criteria in the classroom in the same way. From the very first day of school, we make clear what we expect of students in terms of behavior and performance.

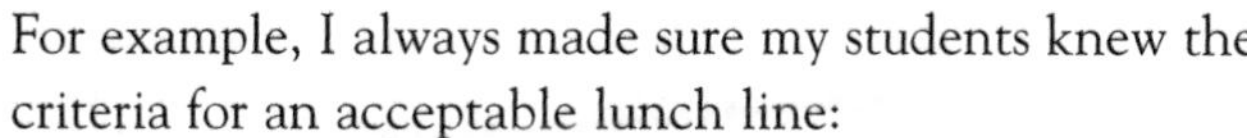

For example, I always made sure my students knew the criteria for an acceptable lunch line:

- It is straight.
- Hands and arms are down straight to the side.
- No one is talking loudly.
- Eyes are facing forward.
- No one is pushing or shoving.

So when I would say, "Your line doesn't look right," my students would apply the criteria and change the line accordingly. In essence, criteria give us the language we need to decide if something is working or not, whether it's a steak, a lunch line, or an organized desk. When my son, Sam, was a first grader, I asked him if he'd had a good day at school. He responded, "No, we would have had to spend a lot more time doing art and less time doing math for it to be a good day." Did Sam understand criteria? You bet! Unfortunately, his criteria and the teacher's didn't match. Although the teacher may have felt the day was a success, her measuring stick was different than my son's, who always thought he should have more time for art.

Effective Criteria

- are written in language students can understand.
- use a common language to build toward deep understanding.
- zero in on what's important and attainable.
- define different levels of performance.
- make it easy to observe and document growth.
- are easy to remember and apply as students learn.
- evolve and are refined over time.

Think about what would happen if we took the time to write down criteria and made them public for students. If, for example, we made a chart with our students, identifying what makes a good lunch line, would they be more likely to apply those criteria after participating in such an activity? Sure they would.

What about my son? If he and his teacher had discussed the learning that had taken place on that day at school, made a list of all the important things they had worked on, noting where he had been successful and where he still needed to work, would Sam have reached the conclusion it was a good day after all, even if there wasn't as much art as he would have preferred? Most likely. When teachers explain their expectations, they are sharing the criteria they use to judge behavior and academic performance, and in doing so they invite feedback from students, creating a context for rich learning experiences. In these classrooms everyone has a clear and common vision of the targets they are trying to hit. It makes a difference.

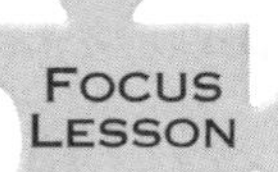

USING CRITERIA TO SHOW WHAT'S IMPORTANT

Here is an engaging lesson, based on the book *Charlie's Checklist* by Rory S. Lerman (1997), that reinforces the use of criteria as a way to clarify what is important. Charlie is a dog looking for new owners. When he puts an ad in the local paper, he gets lots of offers and so he decides to develop a checklist (a set of criteria) to select the best candidate. In this lesson, students develop criteria for the perfect classroom based on what they learn from reading the book together.

MATERIALS:

- a copy of *Charlie's Checklist*
- chart paper and pens

WHAT TO DO:

1. Record on chart paper what students think dogs or other pets need in order to be happy at home.
2. Ask students to help you organize their ideas into five or six categories. For instance, you could have them circle all the ideas about physical comfort in red, ideas about eating in blue, ideas about receiving affection in green, and so on.
3. Divide the class into the same number of groups as categories. Ask each group to continue adding more to its list.
4. Ask each group to create a checklist based on its ideas. Each group should have at least six points—or criteria—on its checklist.
5. Read *Charlie's Checklist* aloud, pointing out when Charlie starts to develop his checklist for selecting new owners.
6. After the read-aloud, compare Charlie's checklist to students' checklists. Ask students to add new points inspired by the story and eliminate points that don't seem to apply any longer.
7. Create a display of all the checklists so that students can see the different criteria that describe what a good home looks like for a pet.
8. Ask students to describe the qualities they think make the perfect classroom. Organize these qualities into categories, such as role of the teacher, role of the students, number of rules, amount of free time, number of toys and games, safety, and so on.

9. Help students create a checklist of the most important qualities to look for in the perfect classroom.

10. Ask the students to help you write a newspaper advertisement seeking the perfect classroom. Use the examples from *Charlie's Checklist* as models.

11. Post the advertisement and checklist, and discuss how students can contribute to making their classroom a productive and joyous place.

FOLLOW-UP:

Have students develop criteria and make a checklist to describe what "good" looks like for another school activity, such as behaving at an assembly or playing a game at recess.

The traits of writing are one set of criteria on which students build successful pieces of writing. In classrooms where the traits are at the center of writing assessment and instruction, the sky is the limit. In fact, I've found that young students who can barely write their name blossom into confident, fluent writers capable of writing several complete, well-written sentences on topics that fascinate them. It's amazing. The sooner we put the traits into the hands of our youngest writers, the sooner they engage in powerful conversations about writing.

USING CRITERIA TO ASSESS PRIMARY WRITING HOLISTICALLY

As discussed earlier, as soon as students begin making marks on the page, they are writing. Using criteria designed to reflect what writing looks like at these early stages is one of the keys to assessing primary work accurately and effectively. The Primary Writing Traits Scoring Guide on page 36 captures the progression of writing skills typically exhibited by primary writers.

Young writers at the "Ready to Begin" stage are not creating letters and words but are drawing and imitating text. As they become capable of writing letters, words, sentences, and paragraphs, they move through levels on the scoring guide. You may find it helpful to compare the levels to progress in baseball:

1. Foul ball—Great. You made contact, and guess what? You get another pitch.
2. First base—You're on your way. Doesn't it feel good to be in the game?

The Primary Writing Traits Scoring Guide

Ready to move to the grades-3-and-up scoring guide!

Ideas
Organization
Voice
Word Choice
Sentence Fluency
Conventions
Presentation

Established  5	The writer shows control and skill in writing standard English text in at least a few sentences.
Extending  4	The writer is creating readable text and trying new, more advanced skills.
Expanding  3	The writer is gaining confidence and showing some skills in creating readable text.
Exploring  2	The writer shows signs of understanding how to create conventional text.
Ready to Begin  1	The writer is attempting to create conventional text.

3. Second base—Halfway to home, and did you know that you can steal bases from here?
4. Third base—You're a few feet from home. So close. Keep your eyes open and your head in the game.
5. Home run—Way to go! You scored. Now see if you can do it again next time you're up at bat.

Home runs are possible, indeed, but do not expect them every time. In professional baseball, after all, a player is considered a contender for the Hall of Fame if he achieves a batting average of .333—not even close to a perfect score. Yet often, in school, many of us expect students to hit a home run on every assignment. This is ridiculous. It will never happen in baseball and certainly not in writing. Every time a student works seriously with paper and pencil it should be considered a win. Every time. We can learn from our students' efforts. We can use what we learn to help them. The Primary Writing Traits Scoring Guide is our scorecard.

Getting Ready to Assess

If we know where our students are on their way to becoming confident, capable writers, we can focus our instruction on what they need to learn most and not repeat lessons and assignments that bog them down. We see tangible evidence of performance each and every time students write, and more important, the students see it, embrace it, and work hard to take steps toward improvement.

If you have any doubts at this point about the power of using writing criteria with primary students, take a look at the next two papers by Ashley, a first grader, whose teacher used the writing traits with students every day. Ashley wrote the first piece at the beginning of the year.

Although this piece is made up of two short sentences, it contains two adjectives, *yellow* and *beautiful*. This is the beginning of word choice. Ashley could have written "I like my blanket" or "My blanket is special," but she didn't because she wanted to give us a clear picture of what is important about the blanket. This is the

ons I had a yelowblankit
it was butifulblankit

"Beautiful Blanket, which first grader Ashley wrote at the beginning of the year, shows evidence of a budding ability to choose strong words.

Wonc u P n a time Ashley went to tan tara. It had a butifl hotel. She had a wondfal time. The water was vere very nise. Ashley had A wund ful time. She met a boy namd Kevin W. he was vere cut all the Babs lovd he But most uv the girls likt his mune.

Chaptr 2 one nate wie Kevin was sleeping I slept in and lefta Note it Sed Dear Kevin I'v Ben waching you sume uv the gils gust whanted your mune. Pleas Becarful why girls like you. Love Ashley. the end

By the end of the year, Ashley writes with confidence and skill, as proven by this piece, "Tan Tara."

direction in which Ashley's teacher will move her—past the mundane, through the obvious, and into the original.

Now be prepared to be dazzled and amazed. Look at what Ashley wrote at the end of first grade (See "Tan Tara," above.)

Clearly, by the end of the year, Ashley has pulled up anchor and sailed past the descriptors on the Primary Writing Traits Scoring Guide. She tells a complete story with interesting ideas and a clear purpose. Her piece contains details that sparkle, and it stays on topic. The organization guides the reader from beginning to end. Passages such as, "Some of the girls just wanted your money. Be careful why girls like you," show insight and convey a distinct voice. This piece has it all. Most students may not go as far as Ashley did in a year, but their steps will be mighty and worthy of our undivided attention. This is what it really means to leave no child behind.

It's fair to assume that primary writers are going to need a lot of attention as they write. To encourage them to take the next step, we must

- talk to them about what they want to say.
- show them what their ideas look like on paper by taking dictation.

- model what we want them to do.
- teach them specific craft skills and provide excellent examples of student work so that they know what they're shooting for.
- ask them questions, lots and lots of questions, especially about the images they see in their minds as they draw and write.

> *"Talk reclaims what we know: Writing is the residue of talk."*
>
> —*Laura Robb*

Talk with primary writers in a way that invites conversation and avoids judgments. The minute we weigh in with words like *good* or *bad*, their thinking stops. Instead, use open-ended comments—"You know a lot about bats. I didn't realize that they hung upside down by their toes. That's an interesting detail" or "Tell me more about baking cookies with your grandpa. I can almost smell them from your picture. What did you do first? Then what did you do?" It's this kind of writing-talk that shows students what is clear about their idea, what isn't, and what they can do next.

Assessment Tips

Here are some tips to help you use the Primary Writing Traits Scoring Guide. Remember, your goal should be to collect data that captures what students do well so they can do it again, and what they're not doing so well so you can help them do better next time. It's not about the numbers or scores; it's about clear communication on writing performance.

- Read all the descriptors from "Ready to Begin" to "Established."
- Read the student's paper or ask the student to read it to you.
- Match the student's piece to the descriptor on the scoring guide that describes it most accurately. Ask yourself, *Can I read this piece with ease on my own or do I need a lot of help from the writer?* If you can read it easily, the piece probably belongs at one of the levels at the top of the guide, but if you can't, it most likely belongs closer to the bottom.
- Point out what is done well. Help students understand what they are doing right, along with areas that need improvement.

The more you and your students use criteria, the easier it will be to notice and celebrate growth.

What You Will Find in This Book

> "*Writing naturally precedes reading. Writing is the gateway to literacy, not reading. Writing is the realm where children can attain literacy first and best feel on top of it—feel ownership and control over the written word.*"
>
> —*Peter Elbow*

Without your help, young writers may not realize that their early attempts at writing—their scribbles, lopsided pictures, imitations of text—are all positive and significant indicators of where they are as writers and where they are going next. What they are able to do on their own may seem insignificant next to what older students can do. Our job is to validate them as writers from the very beginning and find connections to each of the traits in their early attempts to write. Chapters 2 to 9 will help you. Chapter 2 lays a foundation by situating trait-based assessment and instruction in the writing process classroom. From there, in Chapters 3 to 9, you'll find descriptive, detailed, developmentally sound scoring guides for each trait, with sample papers that I have scored, using those guides. They are designed for use with our youngest writers; they're teacher-tested and primary writer–approved. You'll also find plenty of trait-specific lessons, activities, and suggestions for picture books for teaching writing.

These chapters are laid out so you can jump right in. You'll find everything here you need to use the traits for assessment and instruction with primary students. Teaching students how to write is some of the most significant work we do as educators. When we use the traits to teach writing, we give our students the vocabulary and tools for understanding our lessons and directing their own learning. What could be more important?

◆ CHAPTER 2 ◆

Blending the Writing Process With the Traits

for the Beginning Writer

Based on her piece on the next page, I can tell Kayla understands that writing is about thinking, collaboration, and feedback. In other words, she understands it's hard work. It is indeed challenging for students to express their ideas through stories, information, and pictures. But insight like Kayla's can help a young writer go from making rudimentary representations of text to competently writing traditional letters, words, and sentences. Breaking the writing process down into manageable steps also helps. Adding the traits does too. In fact, the writing process and the traits support one another well.

First you think, then you
write. Then you write some
more. Finally, you get to read
it to someone and make it
better. Then you turn it in
but sometimes it comes back
anyway.
Kayla
Grade 2

Second grader Kayla shows insight on the writing process.

Think of the traits not as a set of discrete lessons to be taught each day, but a way of thinking, shaping responses to writing, and talking about the writing. The traits *are* the writing process at the revision and editing stages. They don't stand alone in the writer's world; they shouldn't be taught in isolation; they shouldn't be portioned out by grade level.

Everywhere I travel, I am asked the same question: "Can I teach just one or two traits to my primary students? All seven of the traits seems like a lot." The answer is an emphatic No. We're teaching our young students to write, not to trait. Remember this. The CliffsNotes of this text is only one sentence: We're teaching writing.

Not only can primary writers learn to write, they can learn to write well. Don't sell them short. If we give them tools, they will soar. Students can learn their limitations from us, or they can learn their possibilities. It's up to you which vision becomes a reality in your classrooms. But, as Kayla explains, it will take practice: "First you think, then you write. Then you write some more."

Understanding the writing process, how it became the foundation for writing instruction, how it applies to our youngest writers, and how it connects to the traits of writing is the focus of this chapter.

The Writing Process and Its Impact on Today's Writing Classroom

In the early 1960s the National Council of Teachers of English commissioned a study to find out what was known about the teaching of writing. The report, "Research in Written Composition" by Braddock, Lloyd-Jones, and Schoer (1963), found that there was "only a rudimentary understanding of teaching writing. Some terms are being defined usefully, a number of other procedures are being refined, but the field as a whole is laced with dreams, prejudices, and makeshift operations" (p. 5). They found that the teaching emphasis was on grammar, conventions, and on the modes of writing (narrative, descriptive, expository, and persuasive). The university writing classes of the 1960s were the training grounds for future teachers, so this narrow view of writing was perpetuated through the 1970s and '80s. A few teachers during this time were fortunate enough to attend one of the fledgling training courses that advocated a process methodology, a multiple-step approach that included prewriting, revising, and editing. These courses sprang up in the 1970s, primarily through the National Writing Project at the University of California, Berkeley, and its professional development network, which now includes 50 states, Washington, D.C.; Puerto Rico; and the U.S. Virgin Islands.

Arthur Applebee (1986) sums up the 1970s and '80s as a time that produced a "groundswell of support for 'process approaches' to learning to write" (p. 95). Teachers expressed interest in them, but the availability of published support materials was limited. As a result, Applebee found that teachers struggled to put process approaches to teaching writing into practice. In fact, he found that students rarely wrote more than one draft, added or deleted details, or reorganized text.

With landmark works in the mid-1980s such as *A Writer Teaches Writing* (1985) by Donald Murray, *Writing: Teachers and Children at Work* (1983) by Donald Graves, and *The Art of Teaching Writing* (1986) by Lucy Calkins, the professional literature took a huge step toward showing teachers how to take a process approach to writing instruction. Examples of effective instructional strategies infused these books, allowing teachers an insider's view into the writing-process classroom. The authors based their ideas on the notion that young students should think of themselves as writers who draw upon different strategies for different writing purposes. They did not view the writing process as a series of linear steps; instead, they viewed it as highly flexible and recursive.

In the 1990s refinements to the teaching of the writing process proliferated. Significant books included *What a Writer Needs* (1993) by Ralph Fletcher and *A Fresh Look at Writing* by Donald Graves (1994). Calkins's *The Art of Teaching Writing* was updated. For better or worse, publishers jumped on the bandwagon and produced a plethora of curriculum materials.

The '90s also became the decade of educational standards and writing benchmarks, which were recommended and, in some instances, demanded at the national and state level. The IRA/NCTE Standards for the English Language Arts (1996) validated teaching writing process by embedding it in its core list: "Students employ a wide range of strategies as they write and use different writing process elements appropriately to communicate with different audiences for a variety of purposes" (p. 25).

More authentic forms of performance-based writing assessments began to emerge for measuring how well students were meeting standards in Texas, California, New York, and Florida. These new assessments, which required students to produce a piece of writing based on a prompt, were a welcome addition to traditional norm-referenced tests, which were made up of multiple-choice questions related to writing. These first large-scale writing assessments were scored on a holistic scale, meaning the raters gave one score to the entire piece, focusing a great deal on conventions and correctness rather than the creation of insightful, imaginative text.

The Rise of Analytic Assessment

As early as 1985, however, a few states, such as Oregon, started implementing an analytic scale based on six individual characteristics of good writing: ideas and content, organization, voice, word choice, sentence structure, and conventions. Other states followed this lead.

Today most states use a rubric to assess student writing samples for multiple characteristics in writing (Thomason & York, 2000)—a significant shift. The new generation of writing tests encourages students to use the writing process to generate text, and since the papers are assessed for several qualities, or traits, from a standardized scoring guide, teachers who are eager for their students to score well are beginning to align their teaching with the tests. Many classrooms are using the writing process and the writing traits on a regular basis.

How the Traits Developed for the Primary Grades

Initially, the traits were conceived strictly as an assessment tool for grades three and up and for use with texts of at least one well-developed paragraph. Primary teachers did not have a scoring guide that matched the developmental needs of their young writers, who were learning how to make letters, words, and sentences, precursors to stand-alone paragraphs. This fact became clear to me in the early 1990s when I noticed an increasing number of frustrated primary teachers attending my workshops and seminars, many of whom had been tapped to be raters for the Oregon state writing assessment, administered to all third graders.

As a rater myself, and later as a director of writing assessments in states across the country for the Northwest Educational Laboratory, I read thousands of papers written by third graders, which was difficult because many of them were made up of only a sentence or two and were, frankly, incomprehensible. We often marked the papers as too short to score, and sent them back to the teachers and students without additional comment. It made most readers, including myself, wish we had a developmentally appropriate and accurate way to respond to the work of the youngest writers.

As a result, in the mid-1990s, the first primary writing scoring guide for the traits was created by the professional staff of the Assessment Program at Northwest Regional Educational Laboratory. We took our cue from districts, such as Juneau and Homer, Alaska, that had been working on their own primary scoring guides for the traits and generously shared their work. The result of our collaboration was implemented widely, and over the next years, the guides were revised several times reflecting teacher, administrator, parent, and student feedback. Since then, in my new career as an independent consultant, guest teacher, and author, the continuing refinement of this scoring guide to support the youngest writers has taken priority. The Primary Writing Traits Scoring Guide on page 36 and the individual trait scoring guides on pages 70, 104, 140, 174, 209, 245, and 278 represent my most current thinking.

So how has all this history impacted the everyday lives of today's primary students? In my experience, these students seem to be

- writing more than ever before.
- writing for a variety of purposes and in many formats.
- writing at least one grade level higher than primary students were 12 to 15 years ago.

Thomas Newkirk of the University of New Hampshire (Jensen, 1999) states, "I would say that the single most important thing we have learned is the systematic way children learn about written language from a very early age . . . We now expect primary children to write and share writing where 15 years ago this would have been a novelty" (p. 27).

> *"Studies of how writers actually work show them shuffling through phases of planning, reflection, drafting, and revision, though rarely in a linear fashion. Each phase requires problem solving and critical thinking."*
>
> *—National Writing Project and Carl Nagin*

WRITING PROCESS IN ACTION

One thing is for sure: you can't turn the writing process into a recipe. Attempts to do so fail because writing is recursive, not linear (Hairston, 1999). That means you can't ask students to brainstorm on Monday, draft on Tuesday, revise on Wednesday, edit on Thursday, and turn in a final copy on Friday. You won't coax the best writing from your students if you do, so please don't. The steps in the process should not dictate what writers do; the writing should.

The writing process is just that, a process. Its beginning, middle, and end flow like a river, always going somewhere but often taking its own sweet time to get there. We need to show primary students what it's like to be a writer and how to think aloud on paper. We need to open the door to possibilities in writing, giving students topic choices, teaching them skills, showing them how to work through problems, and allowing them time to arrive at solutions. We need to show them the steps that successful writers follow so they can follow those steps in their own work.

Primary classrooms should be places where there are writing demonstrations and discussions every day about what comes next and why. They should be places where there's a strong connection between reading and writing, as students look to mentor texts as models. They should be places where teachers and students interact using trait language to question if the work is clear and focused, if it is organized so the reader can see where the idea is going, if the voice is truly the writer's, if the words are accurate and precise, if the sentences flow smoothly, and, of course, if conventions are used correctly.

Steps of the Writing Process

The writing process can be broken down into teachable and manageable steps, which, as I mentioned earlier, need not be followed in lockstep fashion, especially by primary writers.

- Prewriting: The writer comes up with ideas for the work. Predominant trait: ideas

- Drafting: The writer gets the ideas down in rough form. Predominant traits: ideas, organization
- Sharing: The writer gets feedback on the draft from a reader or listener. Predominant traits: ideas, organization, voice, word choice, sentence fluency
- Revising: The writer makes reflective choices based on the first five traits—ideas, organization, voice, word choice, and sentence fluency.
- Editing: The writer "cleans up" the piece, checking for correct capitalization, punctuation, spelling, paragraphing, grammar, and usage. Predominant trait: conventions
- Publishing: The writer goes public. Predominant trait: presentation

Every time our primary writers put pencil to paper, we want them to realize that they have choices—that the writing process is a series of flexible steps for them to use to help them write well. The next section describes the steps in detail and how to teach them to primary students.

PREWRITING

All writing begins with having something to say, so helping young writers figure out what they want to say is time well spent. No trait will be more in play here than ideas. Drawing upon experiences, observing what's going on around them, and asking questions are essential to prewriting at this level. And young writers will usually not approach prewriting systematically. A kindergarten teacher friend of mine says it this way: "I see writers circling the writing first—doing things to get ready: sharpening pencils, straightening their desktops, fussing with clothes, listening to music, reading, fiddling with their paper, staring out the window—circling the act of writing until they are ready to pounce."

Prewriting Questions

Before they begin to draft, encourage primary writers to ask themselves:

- What do I want to write about?
- Do I have enough information to start?
- Where could I go to get more information?
- What does my reader need to know?
- What could I say that only I can write about?
- What do I want readers to learn?
- What is the purpose of my writing? To tell a story? To inform? To explain? To persuade?

"If the children in our classrooms don't care about their readers, how can they develop as writers? They can't because they won't care about what they're writing, and they won't want to revise."

—Mem Fox

Some teachers give students a topic and a sentence starter, such as "Pets" and "My favorite pet is a (an) __________ because __________," with the hope that the writer's ability to come up with and flesh out topics independently will grow over time. It won't. Let's be clear right from the start: if you want children to learn to write, you need to give them pencils and let them write. When we don't give students the opportunity to make their own writing decisions—to think for themselves—we limit their ability to become independent.

Whether they're selling wrapping paper at the school fundraiser or helping to prepare the nursery for a new baby brother, children come to care deeply about their work when we give them authentic tasks. And an authentic writing task means having a real audience. Mem Fox, author and primary literacy expert, is a great proponent of having real audiences for writing. She believes, and I agree, that when students have real audiences, they invest more heavily in writing (1993). When students think someone else—the principal, their schoolmates, their parents—might read and react to their writing or if they think it will be hung on the bulletin board, they do their best work.

Primary students can create lists, letters, captions on pictures, stories, explanations, brochures, notes of appreciation, directions, and descriptions—all very authentic forms of writing for real audiences. You can help students find ideas for writing by

- talking about topics that are interesting to them.
- asking questions to help them clarify what they want to say.
- reading aloud fiction and nonfiction on a variety of topics.
- asking questions to help them discover details about topics.
- wondering aloud as you consider new ideas.
- creating lists of possible ideas for writing.
- sharing your own writing so they see how a more experienced writer chooses topics.
- showing them how other writers draw on personal experience as a source of details.

- having them keep writer's notebooks to capture possible topics, favorite words, interesting details, and observations about life.
- asking them to share what they are thinking with you and/or classmates.
- teaching them to look closely at picture books for clues about where the writing is headed.

Get Started With Writer's Notebooks

Give students writer's notebooks to capture, in pictures and words, what they care and wonder about. Urge them to keep their notebooks handy at all times and record ideas often so that when it's time to come up with an idea for writing, they'll have lots of material from which to draw.

Keep your own writer's notebook. As new thoughts strike you, write them down and discuss them with students. This way, you can show them what it's like to see the world through the eyes of a writer.

Children are naturally curious about things they observe in their world. Ralph Fletcher (1996) calls the thoughts they propose to themselves, "fierce wonderings." He says, "It's important to pay attention to what haunts you, what images or memories keep running around in your mind even when you try not to think about them" (p. 17). We can teach students how to tap their wonderings for writing ideas.

I keep a writer's notebook of my wonderings, use it for ideas for my own writing, and share it with students as a model. Here are some of my latest wonderings: "Do cats smile? When I look at my cat, I think she is smiling, but then I wonder, what is she smiling about?" "Why do some states have Daylight Savings Time and others don't?" "How does my TiVo DVR pause live TV?" "Why do hot-water pipes freeze faster than cold-water pipes?" "Are we sure that slugs don't feel anything when we kill them with salt?" Imagine the possibilities for writing!

In prewriting, we help students figure out possibilities for writing. Students who routinely complain, "I don't know what to say," don't yet understand that seemingly insignificant things lead to very significant writing. They are waiting for that one important topic to materialize magically. Recently, when his teacher asked him what he was going to write about, first grader Jesse said, "I'm not sure. The pictures are still in my head. I'm waiting for them to pop out." We all know that students like Jesse can sit there for years, waiting. So, we have to talk, draw, and write with them to show them that good writing ideas come from our experiences, and that little observations about everyday life can make interesting topics.

FOCUS LESSON

MODELING HOW TO FIND A TOPIC

If you believe that all children are writers, you also believe each has stories to tell, thoughts to share. It's just a matter of coaxing them out. You can teach students where ideas come from through modeling. In this lesson, students come up with four different ways of writing about a simple, everyday event.

MATERIALS:

- overhead projector or chart paper and pens

WHAT TO DO:

1. Ask the class, "What has happened so far today that we could write about?" and list all the things students say. Make sure you get down what they observed and learned. You may start with an observation about yourself. "Remember when we were reading *Double Trouble in Walla Walla* and I laughed so hard I started to snort? And then Carlos joined in and had to hold his sides because they hurt from laughing? I love it when a story makes me feel that way."
2. Once you've picked a topic to develop, have students draw and caption it on their own. Encourage them to re-create the topic visually: "Let's draw a picture of what that looked like and see if we can do it so clearly it makes us laugh all over again. I'll come around and help you caption your pictures with the words you want to add."
3. Once students have completed their drawings, bring the class back together and create a list of new topics inspired by the original topic: "Let's make a list of all the other times you can remember laughing hard in and out of school." Post the list so students can refer to it for future writing topics. Encourage them to add to the list as they think of new ideas. We want writers to know that good topics don't just happen; they evolve over time.
4. Using the list for inspiration, come up with a story idea by walking students through a series of questions: "Could we write a story that had someone laughing in it? Who would be in this story? What would he or she be doing? What would happen?" Display the story elements or key details that surface from this discussion so students have material to draw from in case they choose to develop the story later.

5. If students decide to develop the story, be sure they have all the information they need to address the topic accurately and completely. Ask, for example, "Does anyone ever wonder why people say laughing is good for you? What do you suppose happens to the human body when we laugh? What muscles does it take to laugh? Does the brain like it when we laugh? How would we find out the answers to our questions? Who might know?" Although we know young students won't be using the media center to do extensive research, they can ask an adult or older student their questions. They can make a phone call, look up simple facts, and report back what they find.

Prewriting with primary students should be fun. Exploring possible topics, considering what they already know, figuring out what they need to know, narrowing the ideas, reflecting on personal experience, drawing what they see in their minds—young writers can do all of these things. And in the process, they discover what they have to say about what matters to them.

Drafting

If we've done our work well in prewriting, then, like racehorses at the starting gate, students will be champing at the bit to get started. They see the idea in their mind and want to get it down on paper quickly, before it fades. This is drafting—getting the idea down. The result could be:

- a simple drawing or squiggles that stand for an idea.
- imitative text running across the page that only the writer can "read."
- a drawing with a caption.
- a short word or phrase that suggests the topic.
- pictures from magazines, newspapers, and Web sites.
- an oral explanation told to you or the entire class.
- conventional text.

No attempt to write here should be discouraged. Whether capturing an idea with sentences, words, or even pictures, students are writing. And they are often euphoric when they start—"Look at me! I'm doing it!" It's empowering.

Just as important, each child is thinking deeply. As they compose, students are answering important questions, such as:

- How do I get started?
- Do I have everything I need? Paper, pencil, markers, word lists, pictures, background information, and so on?
- Should my picture look like this or something more like this?
- What's important to say or show here?
- Should my words say this or something more like this?

To get the ideas flowing, let students work at their own pace and in their own way. As you circulate through the room, nudge students by asking them to tell you about what they're doing and if they need help. Encourage students to share their ideas with their peers as they draft, to bring the ideas to life. They can think aloud: "Should I add a rain cloud and thunderbolt to show it was a big storm?" "Maybe I'll add the sound of the thunder right up here by the cloud." "I am hiding under the table during the storm. How do I say that?"

If you hear interesting bits of conversation though students seem perplexed about how to add the ideas to their drawing or writing, stop and show them how. Use trait language: "Do the words *tremble* or *shake* describe how you felt as you crouched under the table? That's word choice that might work." You can even jot a word or phrase down on a sticky note and leave it for the student to consider using later.

Here's a dialogue between first-grade teacher Karen Davidson and one of her students that demonstrates how to validate a student's draft and encourage him to write more:

Karen: Tell me what you are saying here.

Joel: It says, "Maximilian was a stinky, bratty little brother."

Karen: *Stinky* and *bratty*—great word choice. Sounds like you have your hands full with Maximilian. Can you draw and write more about a time he did something that really bugged you?

Joel: Okay. You know, he really smells like rotten bananas when he comes home from day care.

Karen: Looks like you know what to write already and have some great words to use. I'll be back to see what else you've drawn and written about your little brother. I'm just starting to get a picture of him.

When primary students are drafting, discourage editing. Tell them that spelling, punctuation, and capitalization can wait; for now, they should just focus on ideas and their order. You can always help them fix the conventions later. Reassure them that this is what writers do. They get it down first, then go back and look at it for correctness.

I learned this important lesson a few years ago when I was working with first graders in the International School in Beijing, China. These top-notch students were bright and eager. The staff urged me to make my demonstration lesson rigorous since the average child was working at what they identified as second-grade level.

I started by reading *Feathers and Fools* by Mem Fox (1996) to the students. The children sat mesmerized as the story fell from my lips, a feast of rhythm and cadence, each sentence honed to perfection. When I finished the story, we talked animatedly and enthusiastically about how Fox uses peacocks and swans to stand for, among other things, different groups of people who don't like or understand each other. The students' understanding of the story was sophisticated.

I then asked the students if they would like to hear the story again, only this time from the author herself. I explained that I had a tape recording of Mem Fox reading the story. "Yes!" they replied. "Yes, let's hear it."

I told them, "As you listen, write down any words or phrases you hear that you really like." And then I played the tape.

The students listened intently, dropping their heads to write a word or two now and then. The teachers at the back of the room nodded and smiled as they watched how seriously students took the task. By the end of the story, every student had written down several things. I turned off the tape and turned to them, eager to hear what they had chosen. "Mem Fox has shown us what good writers do to create pictures in our minds, hasn't she? Let's share the words and phrases she uses to do that. Who wants to go first?"

No hands went up. The students looked down at their desks—not a single one would make eye contact with me. I could feel the tension mount in the room; something had gone terribly wrong. Why wouldn't anyone speak? I walked over to the first desk and saw that the student had written *the*, *of*, *day*, *one*, *go*, and *and*. The next student had chosen similar words, and so had the next. Not a single student had chosen the beautiful, interesting words. They had all opted, instead, for the simple words they could spell. I suspected that over-teaching of conventions had taken a serious toll on these students.

We had to regroup. I asked students to call out their favorite words and phrases

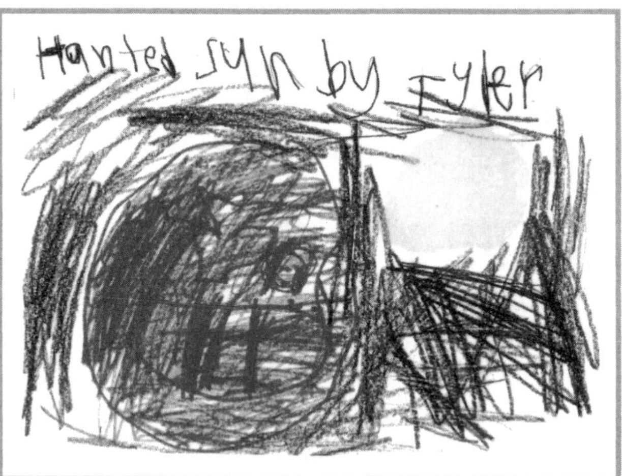

After listening to Mem Fox's *Feathers and Fools*, Tyler chooses "Haunted by the sun" as his favorite example of word choice from the book.

Another student selects "and sharpened arrows" as a memorable passage from Fox's book.

"Shall we be friends?" was the standout phrase for another student.

from the story. One by one, tentative little voices began to chime in: "Magnificent peacocks. Once my mom took me to the zoo, and there were peacocks. They were really beautiful." "Heart raced." "Great strength, I like that one." "Shall we be friends? That's the best." I wrote each on the overhead projector as fast as they were spilling out. In just a few minutes, we had more than a dozen words and phrases.

"Now," I said, turning off the overhead, "it's time for you to write again. Try writing down the words or phrases that you still hear. I want you to come up with at least three favorites." I gave students paper, markers, scissors, tape, and glue and asked them to illustrate their choices. Students happily wrote, talked, and drew, and in the end they'd created several pages illustrating favorite parts of the text. We bound their book and put it in the library alongside the original text.

Later, as the teachers and I talked about the lesson and about student writing in general, they expressed concern that their students were so bound to conventions. They resolved to temper their lessons on spelling with time spent on word choice, ideas, and voice. When I returned the next year, these same students were writing freely and with more confidence.

Sharing

Many students don't enjoy sharing their writing, especially if they think it isn't very good. However, it's important for students to get feedback on their drafts from you and their peers so they know if their ideas are clear. And, if they're lucky, they'll get substantive suggestions for making their writing better.

One way to encourage young writers to take this risk is to share your own writing and ask for feedback. Write a piece that needs a lot of work on ideas, organization, voice, word choice, or sentence fluency. These are the revision traits, the areas where writers need the most help making their ideas clear before they edit. If your example has short, choppy sentences, read it aloud and ask students what you should do to make the sentences sound better. Or maybe your example doesn't have a clear idea—it jumps around from elephants to baseball and winds up describing matzo-ball soup. Ask student to tell you the main idea, and if they have trouble, ask them to focus on their favorite part. Then, in the next draft, show them how you can take that one idea and make it the focus of a whole piece of writing with lots of interesting details.

Focusing on one trait makes it easier for students to see what's working and what isn't. It helps them make specific observations and questions, which in turn helps the writer make revision decisions. If you throw too many traits out there at once, it's like cramming too many people in a canoe—you are bound to sink. As a rule of

thumb, ask students to read their work to you and then pose a trait-specific question:

- What a great idea. How ever did you think of that? (ideas)
- It looks like you are starting with what you know about turtles. Which fact should come first? (organization)
- Will you read this to me? Oh, yes, when I close my eyes, I can hear your voice in your words. (voice)
- Show me your favorite word or phrase. Want to know mine? (word choice)
- I can feel the words pouring out of you. What part do you think sounds the smoothest? (sentence fluency)

Sharing doesn't need to take a lot of time. You can simply ask, "Tell me what you have done here." Then listen. Nod and smile to validate that the response works for you. Or if you don't understand the student's response, say so, and ask clarifying questions. Maybe all the student has done is drawn an outline for a picture. Fine. Or perhaps she has written one word. Good start. Let the student tell you what she is doing and what she is trying to do, and acknowledge the effort it took to get there. If the writer is ready to revise, leave her with one trait-based idea to consider. Just one. When we honor what students have done, rather than asking for too much or cajoling them into doing things that they are not equipped to do, we propel kids forward.

Revising

Primary writers don't always revise because they are focusing on basic skills: mastering left-to-right directionality, letter formation, spacing between words, and so on. The first two levels on the Primary Writing Traits Scoring Guide on page 36, Ready to Begin and Exploring, describe many writing behaviors that young writers exhibit before they are able to revise.

When students reach the Expanding stage, they begin to appreciate the role that revision plays in making their writing more powerful and interesting. They learn to do simple things—change a word, add a detail, lengthen or shorten a sentence. From there, their interest in revision increases because they begin to see its power to improve their writing.

Because few of us had teachers who showed us what revision looks like, it's not surprising that many of us are uncomfortable teaching it. For so many teachers in school, revision was taught as correcting the writing, following the rules of standard

English. We know now that correcting is editing, but we didn't back then. Thanks to the work of writing process gurus like Donald Graves and Donald Murray, we realize that revision means just what it says: "seeing again." That means working with the idea until it is clear, organizing with a sense of order, selecting words that are accurate and specific to the topic, making sure our voice is appropriate for the audience, listening for the flow of the words and sentences, and changing them when the melody breaks down. But fixing spelling, using punctuation, writing upper- and lowercase letters properly, using grammar correctly, and indenting in all the right places—that's editing.

> *"We must speak to our students with an honesty tempered by compassion: Our words will literally define the ways they perceive themselves as writers."*
>
> *—Ralph Fletcher*

Don't ask students to revise if they are not ready. Creating basic text can be taxing enough when you are just learning. Asking youngsters to make changes that are too sophisticated for them is the fastest way to get them to throw in their writing towel. Remember, it's about the process, not the product. If the student doesn't score above a 2 on the Primary Writing Traits Scoring Guide on page 36, don't push revision.

When Students Are Ready to Revise

There are effective ways to ease primary writers into revising. For instance, if they have generated text, encourage them to add favorite words from the word wall or illustrate the piece. Students will revise when getting something written down gives way to wanting to get something really good written down. And when that happens, the power of modeling cannot be overstated. Show students what revision looks like using your own work and talking through your writing decisions.

Focus Lesson

Modeling Revision

Focusing on one trait gives students a powerful mental model to apply to their own work. So here is a simple lesson you can use to model revision at the word level.

Materials:

- overhead projector and pens

WHAT TO DO:

1. On the board or overhead, write a poorly written short paragraph that repeats words, such as:

   > "I love spring. Spring is the best. Spring is fun and I love it. When I think about spring, I think about all the fun things about it."

   Read your piece aloud. Students may giggle because they recognize that using the same word over and over isn't effective. Great. That's what you are hoping for.

2. Ask, "Boys and girls, did the words I used in my writing help you to picture this time of the year?" They will most likely tell you—in their own words—that because you used *spring* so often, without the use of specific, supporting details, they found the paragraph distracting and not very visual.

3. Ask, "What does the word *spring* make you think of?" On the board or overhead, make a list of all the ideas students contribute: Spring is when

   - the flowers start to bloom.
   - the grass turns green.
   - the cows have little baby calves.
   - I get to play baseball.
   - the days start getting longer.
   - *American Idol* is the best show on TV.
   - we can go outside to play again.
   - I can get my bike out and ride to my friend's apartment.

4. Move students through a series of questions, such as:

   - What does spring smell like? (fresh, wet, warm, tingly)
   - What does spring taste like? (cake with gooey frosting for my birthday in April; barbecued hot dogs at the t-ball game; sandy, like when we go to the beach for spring break)
   - What does spring feel like? (breezy, hot and cold, windy, itchy, sunny, rainy)

5. On the board or overhead, revise your short paragraph, thinking aloud as you go. Explain which words and descriptions you're going to use and which you will save for later. Walk the walk: Show students that you consider their ideas,

but reserve the right to decide what's best for your next draft. Explain to students why you are following their advice sometimes but want to make your own decisions at others. That way, you link sharing and revision in students' minds and reinforce process over product.

Your next draft may look more like this: "Spring is barbecued hot dogs at the t-ball game and baby calves taking first steps in the open, grassy fields. Spring is when the air smells like the beach and freshly mown grass. Spring is birthday candles and gooey chocolate frosting. I love spring."

6. Ask students if they feel the second version is better than the first and why. Use phrases that reinforce the word-choice trait such as "painting a picture," "creative use of everyday words," "sensory images," and so on.

When you model revision for your students, you read your work aloud, ask for feedback, question yourself, and then work to clarify the odd bits that don't make sense while seeking new ways to say what's on your mind and in your heart. Lessons don't get more important than that, do they?

Sometimes revision means letting the piece sit for a day or two so you can come back to it with a fresh eye and ear (Angelillo, 2005). I'm always amazed at what a little time and distance do to help me see what needs improvement in my own writing. Primary students need this same opportunity to let their ideas germinate.

When students are ready for specific feedback, confer with them. Always begin with something you notice the student can do, something that is working well, and then move on to what is yet to be learned. For instance, you might notice that the picture and the text support each other well. Compliment the writer; this is a huge deal. After that, you can point out something that needs attention, such as sentences that begin the same way, but don't start with criticism. In this all-important battle to help students see themselves as writers, we must take time to recognize the knowledge and skills they bring to the writing table. It's always easier to work on problems if you have already established that there are strengths.

To the untrained eye, the pieces to the right don't look all that different. But they show that this writer is

A simple sentence and outline drawing provides a starting point for this young writer.

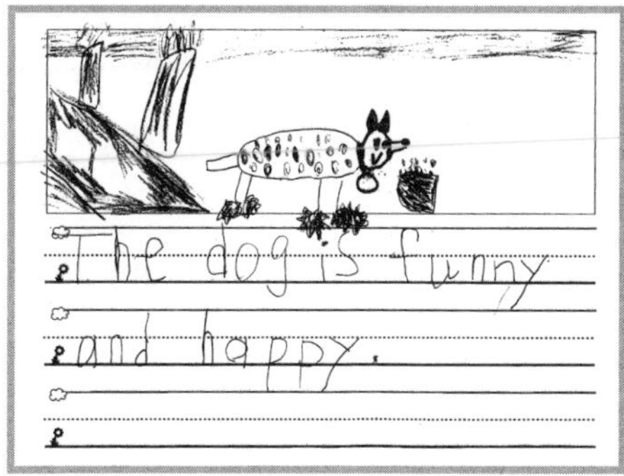

By adding detail to the text and picture, the writer demonstrates a successful attempt to revise.

beginning to revise. Notice that the first picture of the dog is a simple outline? You can tell it's a dog, and that's good. But what kind of dog? What does this dog really look like? We don't know from the picture or the text. In the second picture, the dog has fur, detail in the face, and the setting is beginning to take shape. Yes. This kind of revision is natural, logical, and exactly what we hope for as students begin to see what is possible.

In students' work, no matter how rough, look for early indicators of a sense of time, such as verb tense or the words *now* or *later*. Perhaps the writer has attempted sentences, played with new words and sound patterns, or reinvented old ideas in new, quirky ways. These are entry points to support the revision process. Notice what students are trying to do and praise it. Celebrate small victories. Stretch their thinking; encourage them to be patient and keep at it. If you have questions, begin them with "I wonder." Tread carefully because the message we send to our youngest writers can determine how willing they are to move their work forward and take ownership.

Below are some simple questions students should ask themselves as they revise their work for ideas, organization, voice, word choice, and sentence fluency. You can give students individual questions or clusters of questions, depending on their levels and needs. You can, of course, also revise the questions to be developmentally appropriate.

Ideas

- Does my writing make sense?
- Do I know my topic?
- Is my writing interesting?

Organization

- Do I start off strong?
- Is everything in the right order?
- Are similar things together?

Voice

- Can you hear me in the writing?
- Can you tell I care about this idea?
- Have I added some sparkle?

Word Choice

- Do these words sound and feel right?
- Have I tried new words?
- Have I painted a picture?

Sentence Fluency

- Can I read my writing aloud?
- Do my words and phrases go together?
- Have I tried to use sentences?

Editing

Unlike revision, editing is about cleaning up the text to make it readable. When we assess for it, we look for skill with spelling, punctuation, capitalization, grammar and usage, and paragraphing. In other words, we look at whether the piece meets the conventions of writing.

> *"No one in real life fills in ditto sheets. Filling in the blanks doesn't foster fluency, higher-level thinking, or the creation of extended texts. Ditto sheets are nothing but the frustrating one-way streets of writing."*
>
> *—Mem Fox*

Conventions must be learned one at a time, and students must apply them to their own work. When we teach conventions, it's important to avoid the red pencil. Instead, demonstrate the kinds of things students should be looking for in their text; show them how to use conventions well, and let them make those changes themselves. It may be tempting to turn to worksheets, but just as it is true that students learn to write their ideas more clearly by writing, they learn to edit by editing both their own work and the work of others. Until we insist students do their own editing, and learn to do it well, the only person in the classroom getting better at editing is the teacher.

The first step in teaching editing skills to primary students is to identify which skills they already have and which ones they don't by using the Primary Scoring Guide: Conventions on page 245. Otherwise you run the risk of giving them editing activities they don't need or are too challenging for them. Below are some writer's questions to share with students to help them understand conventions. Post these under the heading "Editing Questions," clearly separating them from the revision questions listed in the last section.

Conventions

- Is the spacing correct between the letters and words?
- Is my spelling readable?
- Does my punctuation and capitalization make sense?

What Primary Students Know About Conventions

When students are not using conventions to help readers understand the writing, they fall at the bottom of the Primary Scoring Guide for conventions. When they can spell simple words correctly, use basic punctuation marks such as periods, and differentiate between upper- and lowercase letters, they fall in the middle range. When their spelling is accurate even on a few challenging words and their basic capitalization and punctuation usage are correct, they are at the top of their game. You may even see paragraph-indenting and standard grammar in the writing. See Chapter 8, page 261, for a complete list of editing skills to teach to primary writers.

Setting the Stage for Teaching Conventions

Remember the two rules of thumb for teaching conventions to primary writers:

1. Teach skills one at a time and in the context of their own work.
2. Let them do the editing, no matter how simple.

The research on this is clear: students learn conventions when they apply them to their own writing (Weaver, 1979, 1996; Noden, 1999). It's most effective to isolate the skills; teach students to edit for simple things first, such as capitalizing the first word in a sentence, and build toward more complex skills, in the context of their own work, such as indenting paragraphs. So, out with the worksheets and black-line masters and in with editing practice on their own work. Over the years this approach will create skilled, polished self-editors.

Sadly, teachers work many hours editing student papers, only to find that students do less and less editing on their own over time, not more. Moreover, if we edit for them, they don't internalize skills or apply them consistently every time they write. The only way to help students gain skill in conventions is to show them how to edit, one skill at a time, and hold them accountable for using that new knowledge when they make final copies.

When first grader Kelly was writing a story, her teacher overheard her calling the mark at the end of her sentence a "dot." Curious about Kelly's choice of word, the teacher asked, "Tell me about what you have done here at the end of your sentences?"

Kelly responded, "Oh, that. Well, it's what you told us to do. We're supposed to put a dot at the end of every sentence, right?"

"Good for you," the teacher replied. "You know that we put punctuation at the end of a sentence to give the reader a place to pause, but it's called a *period*, Kelly, not a *dot*."

Kelly, full of writer's indignation, retorted, "Nuh, uh. It's a dot. You know, like on the Internet—'dot com'?"

Now this is a child who is on her way to owning conventions.

A child may actually be able to put capitals on the first word of ten sentences on the worksheet, but the more impor-

> *"For too long teachers and editors have stood guard over conventions, as if they were esoteric knowledge available only to the few. Seldom did children see their teachers demonstrate how they used conventions where they belong—in writing—or ponder how to use a convention to say something more clearly or more effectively."*
>
> *—Donald Graves*

tant question is, Can this same child actually write a sentence? And if she can, does she put a capital at the beginning? Does she know how to use space between words in the phrase or sentence? This is where our time should go when teaching conventions—not in isolated skill-and-drill exercises, but making sure students can create text that shows what they know about editing. I dream of the day when parents' typical response to their children's writing is, "This teacher is doing a wonderful job teaching writing because my child likes to write and he is learning how to edit his own work."

Ideas for Creating a Conventions-Ready Classroom

- Post easy-to-read conventions rules with examples so that students can refer to them as they write.
- Create a poster of editing symbols for use by students as they edit. (See page 261.)
- Create an editing center with highlighter markers, paper, pens, pencils, tape, scissors, and copies of the student-friendly guide to assessing conventions. (See page 273.)
- Use word-processing software that allows students to highlight problems in spelling, capitalization, and punctuation as they draft.
- Make personal word lists and dictionaries to assist students with spelling.
- Keep simple style guides handy for reference. My favorites are published by Great Source.

PUBLISHING

When a piece is ready to be published, we turn our attention to the presentation trait. Neatness and readability matter most here. What we're looking for is writing that looks finished. Think of it this way: When we stay at home on a Saturday night, we don't put on our best clothes, shine our shoes, and make sure all our accessories match. But if we're going out to dinner, we make sure we look put together. This is presentation.

Publishing primary work means letting go of perfection. It teaches students that real audiences can and will react positively to their ideas, even if their writing isn't flawless. Since many primary writers struggle with fine motor skills, they know they have a long way to go to get that perfectly slanted handwriting, lovely curving letters, and clean, crisp margins. But they work at it when they know that their work is going public. Boy, do they. Students who know that someone other than the teacher will be reading and reacting to their writing crank it up a notch. They spend more time on the pictures, too, adding a dash of color here, filling in detail there. They think about what the reader sees on the page and work for a positive response. As a result, they take great pride when their work goes public, whether it's perfect or not.

Empower your students to say to themselves, "I am a writer" by publishing what they write. Let them know that you see them as writers too. Below are some publishing questions to help students with presentation. Post them prominently so students can refer to them when working on their own or in groups.

PRESENTATION

- Is my paper framed with open space?
- Is there balance between pictures and text?
- Is it neat and legible?

Publishing your primary students' writing can be as simple as

- posting the finished piece in a heavily traveled area of the classroom.
- putting it in a portfolio or writing folder as an example of "best work."
- adding it to a class book.
- sending it home.
- posting it on a bulletin board in one of the school's common areas.

Rick Hanks, who is the principal of Palmer Way Elementary School in National City, California, knows the power of publishing for his young writers. Look at the pride on the face of this girl (left) as she shows what she has done.

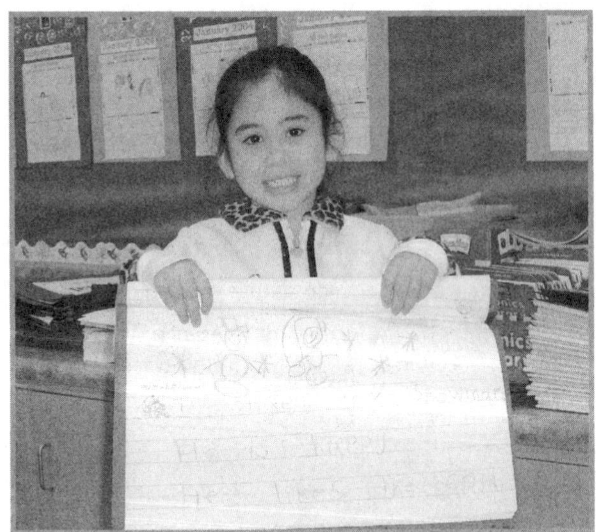

A proud kindergarten student at Palmer Way Elementary School shows off her work.

In this school, at the principal's request, the work of every student, all 700 of them, is on display. As you walk into a classroom, the first thing that catches your eye is the writing—it's everywhere. And as you stop to look more closely, students cry out, "Look at mine. It's over here. Let me show you." There is an amazing sense of pride among these young writers. From the kindergarten, where students read each other's stories from big books, to the second grade, where students collaborate on a class newspaper, evidence of writing and sharing pour out of every door. We need to do more publishing, more bragging, more public flexing of our students' writing muscles. It gives kids writing power, and that's a very, very good thing.

Final Reflections

Students learn what we show them. If we take the time to model the writing process and share writer's secrets, they will get an insider's view of what they are expected to do and have a better chance of doing it for themselves.

As tools for assessment and instruction in the writing process, the traits give us a much-needed vocabulary for showing young writers what they are doing well and what comes next. Students and their teachers can work with the traits in the primary classroom to move writing ahead by leaps and bounds. It's measurable, it's teachable, and it's doable.

The following chapters focus on what is important for students to learn about writing. Each one explains a trait, shows examples of how to use it for assessing student work, and provides focus lessons and activities for strengthening writing in that trait.

CHAPTER 3

Inspiring Ideas

Many primary students know, long before they are able to write extended text, that finding an idea is the writer's job number one. And great teachers take every opportunity to help students build on that knowledge, encouraging them to see the world through a writer's eyes and capture little bits of life that inspire ideas.

Rex Payumo and Rocio Huh are just such teachers. Their first graders notice everything that goes on around them. When Rex and Rocio wear new clothes, the kids comment. A new haircut is the subject of questions as soon as the teachers walk in the door. So, on the day Rex and Rocio hung a poster with all words covered except for one, *ideas*, the students' curiosity was piqued.

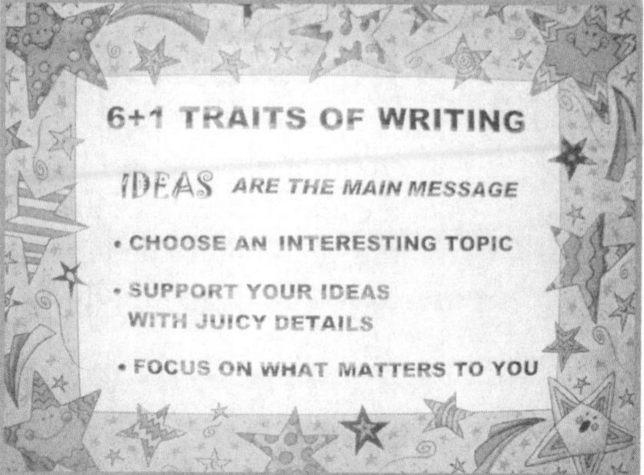

First-grade teachers Rex Payumo and Rocio Huh cover the definition of the ideas trait to pique students' curiosity and encourage dialogue.

Rex and Rocio told the students they would be learning a new vocabulary based on the seven traits of writing, and they would begin with *ideas*. They pointed to the exposed word on the poster and asked students to guess the definition under the paper. Here are some of the definitions students wrote down:

- Ideas are things that help us think.
- I think ideas are places to make storys intrustimg.
- I think ideas are good qestens.
- I think ideas are seckrits.
- I think ideas are stuff you now.
- Ideas means stay on a main idea and use what, who, why, how, when, where in your writing.
- I thing idea means what you come up with.
- Ideas mens you are thinking obaot wo yor wrkeing on

Indeed, ideas are all these things. They are the result of the writer's thinking aloud on paper and are then developed into the content of the piece. By defining the ideas trait in their own words, the first graders in Rex and Rocio's classroom are well on their way to understanding the importance of learning to write well.

The Challenge of Teaching Ideas

It seems in every school I've ever visited a teacher asks how to help students find interesting ideas for writing. Typically, when teachers hand students topics, the writing turns out flat and uninspired. But when they leave students to come up with ideas on their own, the writing is often broad or ordinary. Or worse, students don't come up with ideas at all.

We need to show students how to spot good ideas in their own writing, in others' writing, and in their lives. The observations, stories, questions, and comments that young writers have about life is great fodder for ideas. And they come fast and furious sometimes. "Teacher, do you know what my Uncle Frank did last night?" "Teacher, I put my gym shoes in the microwave and they blew up—*ka-blewy*!" "Teacher, do elephants get hiccups?" "Teacher, my sister says your hair is bleached. Is that true?"

As we teach students to look at the world through a writer's eyes and validate what they see, they become skilled observers, marvelous storytellers, and conscientious recorders of information. They think actively about how the world works, what issues matter to them most, and what beliefs they hold. In fact, I believe that the desire to capture what they think drives primary students to do the hard work of learning to write—of moving from pictures to letters to words to sentences.

When they are in classrooms where the traits are part of the writing process, students internalize the criteria for clear ideas. As they spend time thinking about and working on the ideas trait, and you spend time supporting them and providing practice opportunities, they move from writing about general thoughts to specific ones. They notice what others overlook. They describe bits and pieces of life, the ordinary, in extraordinary ways. Once this happens, primary writers find out they have important things to say. Then they bring their ideas to life.

Ideas: A Definition for Primary Students

The ideas trait is about the writing's overall message and meaning. It is about the content of the writing. Ideas are strong when they are clear and focused, and move from the general to the specific. Though their texts may not be lengthy, young writers convey ideas by

- drawing pictures with bold lines and lots of color.
- experimenting with letters and words.
- captioning pictures they create themselves and gather from sources.
- talking about what happened to them or their characters.
- asking questions and making lists about things that interest them.
- noticing significance in little things and events.

Assessing Student Work for Ideas

The Primary Scoring Guide on page 70 helps us describe how primary writers capture ideas in writing. Use it to assess individual pieces of writing, as follows:

STEP 1: Collect student papers you want to assess for ideas.

STEP 2: Photocopy the Primary Scoring Guide: Ideas since you'll want to write on it and highlight key words as you go.

STEP 3: Read the scoring guide's descriptors for each of the five levels, from top—5: Established—to bottom—1: Ready to Begin. Each descriptor shows how writing typically reveals itself at that level. Also, notice that the descriptors parallel one another from level to level. For example, the first descriptor for each level deals with having a clear and coherent topic.

STEP 4: Read one of the student papers carefully, paying attention to everything on the page, both pictures and text.

STEP 5: Look at the first descriptor for each level and determine the one that most closely matches the paper. Work your way through the rest of the descriptors for each level, checking off the appropriate ones. Each level has a point value; average the total to determine the piece's overall score in ideas. The process will get easier, faster, and more accurate as you practice.

Scoring Guide

Ready to move to the grades-3-and-up scoring guide!

The Primary Scoring Guide

Ideas

Established 5	____ The idea is clear and coherent. ____ The text is a well-developed paragraph. ____ Elaboration through interesting details creates meaning for the reader.	____ The writer shows understanding of the topic through personal experience or research. ____ Pictures (if present) enhance the key ideas but aren't necessary for comprehension.
Extending 4	____ The writing works by itself to explain a simple idea or story. ____ The writing is made up of several sentences on one topic. ____ Key details begin to surface.	____ The writing makes sense, but some information may be missing or irrelevant. ____ Pictures and text work harmoniously to create a rich treatment of the topic.
Expanding 3	____ The idea is written in a basic sentence. ____ A simple statement with somewhat detailed pictures captures the topic.	____ Basic details are present in the text; the illustrations work to enhance the main idea. ____ The text contains real words. ____ Text and picture are understandable to the reader.
Exploring 2	____ One or more ideas are present in the most general way. ____ Letters and words can be picked out as clues to the topic. ____ The drawing helps to clarify the idea.	____ The text is composed of simple, recognizable letters with some early attempts at words. ____ The reader gets the basic idea but needs the writer's assistance to comprehend it fully.
Ready to Begin 1	____ The piece conveys little meaning. ____ Real-life objects show up in drawings. ____ Drawings may not be completely recognizable.	____ Letters are not consistent or standard. ____ An oral reading by the writer is needed to understand the message.

Sample Papers to Assess for Ideas

Assessing your first few papers may be challenging and time-consuming. It's important, however, and the payoff is great. Invest your energy in understanding the different performance levels for each trait. The better you know the scoring guides, the more skilled you'll be at assessing papers.

The five papers that follow represent a wide range of skills in the ideas trait. Review the scoring guide on page 70, read each paper closely, assess the paper, and then read my descriptor-by-descriptor evaluation of the piece to see how our findings compare. Do the sample pieces reflect the writing of students in your classroom? Try out the scoring guide on your students' work after you've practiced on these.

PAPER #1
"SCRIBBLE FACE"

Time to Assess

PAPER #1
"SCRIBBLE FACE"

This is a paper by a truly emergent writer. If I asked the student to read it to me, I might get one story today, another tomorrow. The ideas are virtually nonexistent as the student tries to capture them on paper. The descriptors at the 1: Ready to Begin stage match this student's writing performance.

- The piece conveys little meaning.

  There is a drawing of a face, but most of the "text" is made up of scribbles, making the meaning impossible to decipher.

- Real-life objects show up in drawings.

  The writer has drawn a face. It's simple but clearly present. This is the beginning of an identifiable idea.

- Drawings may not be completely recognizable.

  A drawing of a face is clear and central, but other representations are incomprehensible. This piece is a mix of scribbling and a roughly drawn face.

- Letters are not consistent or standard.

  No conventional letters appear in this piece. The writer uses drawings to stand for ideas.

- An oral reading by the writer is needed to understand the message.

  The writer would most definitely need to read this piece aloud for the reader to understand the intention.

Paper #2
"I like to spend time swinging"

Time to Assess

PAPER #2

"I LIKE TO SPEND TIME SWINGING"

This piece is probably about swinging on a swing set, based on what the writer says and depicts. The text stops in the middle of the last word, but the picture helps to complete the thought. Unlike "Scribble Face," there is some early text here with a picture that supports it. Therefore, the descriptors at the 2: Exploring level match this student's writing performance.

- One or more ideas are present in the most general way.

  The simple text, which needs interpretation, is combined with the picture to convey a simple idea, swinging.

- Letters and words can be picked out as clues to the topic.

  Some of the words, like "lik" and "spend," are easy to read. However, without the picture, the reader wouldn't know what the piece is about since it stops at the most critical word: swinging.

- The drawing helps to clarify the idea.

  Thank goodness for the picture, which adds a vital piece of information— a detail that makes the idea clearer.

- The text is composed of simple, recognizable letters with some early attempts at words.

  "Tim" for "time" is close to standard spelling. But "wi" for "swinging" is a stretch for even the most experienced reader.

- The reader gets the basic idea but needs the writer's assistance to comprehend it fully.

  Part of the picture is very clear and matches the text, but the circle and ovals near the center need interpretation.

PAPER #3
"I AM GOING TO BE BATMAN FOR HALLOWEEN"

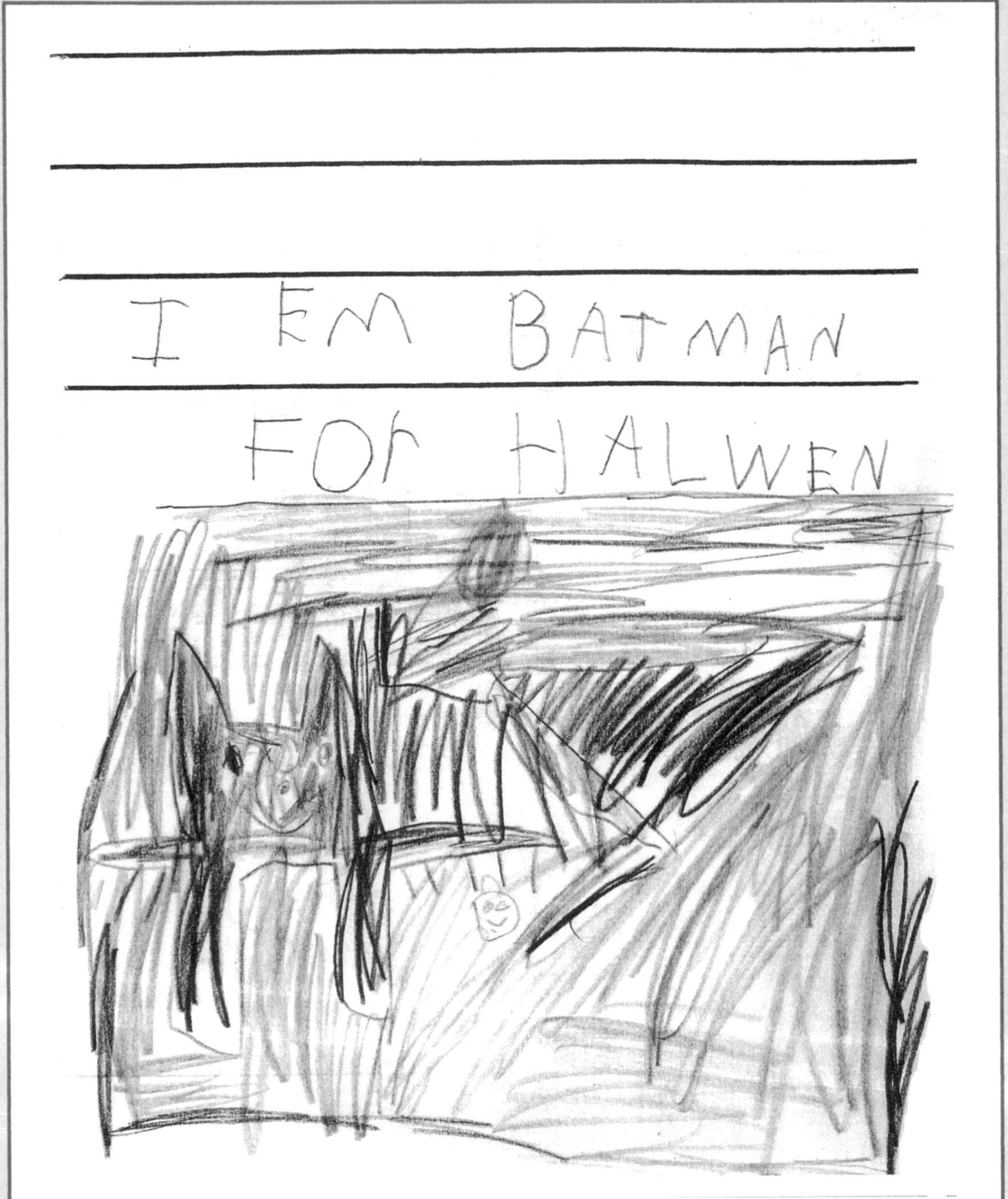

Time to Assess

Paper #3

"I Am Going to Be Batman for Halloween"

Although it may seem this writer didn't spend much time on this picture, he gets his message across. What distinguishes this piece from the last is a complete sentence that captures a complete thought. With "Swinging," the reader must fill in key words. In "Batman," it's all here. I score this piece at the 3: Expanding level.

- The idea is written in a basic sentence.

  "I am Batman for Halloween." There it is. Whether the intention is to talk about the future or serve as a caption for the illustration, the idea is essentially clear.

- A simple statement with somewhat detailed pictures captures the topic.

  The statement and illustration add up to an idea the reader can figure out without help from the writer.

- Basic details are present in the text; the illustrations work to enhance the main idea.

  The illustration in this piece supports the main idea but doesn't replace the text. The reader needs both picture and text to get the main idea.

- The text contains real words.

  "I", "Batman", and "for" are spelled correctly, and the others are very close. "HALWEN" is easy to recognize.

- Text and pictures are understandable to the reader.

  The text and pictures help the reader understand what is being communicated in a basic way, but there is no elaboration.

Paper #4
"There are lots of stars"

Thar aR los of
StRS. The StRS ar
Yollow. The StRS ar
upin The Sky.

Time to Assess

Paper #4

"There Are Lots of Stars"

This text contains multiple simple sentences on the same subject. The picture matches the text very well. The difference between this piece and "Batman" is that the writer expands on the idea. The descriptors from the 4: Extending level match this text.

- The writing works by itself to explain a simple idea or story.

  The three statements convey three different pieces of information about the topic that are comprehensible without the illustration.

- The writing is made up of several sentences on one topic.

  The writing stays on one topic and is made up of three complete simple sentences. This is no small feat for a young writer.

- Key details begin to surface.

  The writer demonstrates accurate knowledge about the subject. The reader finds out that stars are abundant, yellow, and found in the sky.

- The writing makes sense, but some information may be missing or irrelevant.

  This is a sensible piece. The reader may wish for more details, but as it stands, the writing is clear. This writer has stuck with the topic.

- Pictures and text work harmoniously to create a rich treatment of the topic.

  The stars, positioned in a contained space under the text, give the piece a sense of completion.

Paper #5
"I do not think I would like camping . . . "

I do not think I would like camping because I would be itchy and I could get muddy. if it rained I could catch a cold and rain would put the fire out. That is why I do not like camping.

Time to Assess

Paper #5

"I do not think I would like camping . . ."

"Camping" is a complete, cohesive paragraph, unlike "Stars," which is a series of short sentences. The writer doesn't just present an idea, but elaborates on it with confidence and clarity. In other words, he owns it. This piece deserves a 5: Established.

- The idea is clear and coherent.

  The writer explains why camping would not be enjoyable for him, giving the reader a complete idea. He offers more than one detail on the topic.

- The text is a well-developed paragraph.

  The accumulation of details over the three sentences makes the idea clear. The last sentence sums it all up: "That is why I do not like camping."

- Elaboration through interesting details creates meaning for the reader.

  Being itchy, getting muddy, catching a cold, and losing a fire to rain are all good reasons to dislike camping. This litany of discomforts creates a strong impression of a miserable experience and also gives the reader a sense of the writer.

- The writer shows understanding of the topic through personal experience or research.

  The ideas here are unquestionably the writer's. Not all kids would mind getting muddy, for instance, but this writer clearly is not keen on the idea. The reader understands that his estimation of camping is based on experience, especially with being uncomfortable.

- Pictures (if present) enhance the key ideas but aren't necessary for comprehension.

  The reader doesn't need the picture to understand the writer's message completely. It appears that the writer's time was spent primarily on the text and the drawing was a quick addition.

The 6+1 TRAIT model not only helps you pinpoint where students are on the road to becoming strong writers, but also provides you with language to guide them to improve. So as you use all the Primary Scoring Guides, think about how to use their descriptors to convey information about your students' writing.

Conference Comments

Here are some responses for students who are well on their way to applying the ideas trait in their work.

- I love this piece. It makes sense to me.
- Thanks for writing this down so I can see what you think.
- The way you drew this helps me make a picture in my mind.
- This picture of a spider web looks just like ones I have seen in real life.
- You've used color and detail to make your picture clear.
- How did you ever come up with such a clever idea?
- What is your favorite part of this piece?
- You've got my interest. Tell me more!
- This idea is crystal clear. You are a glorious writer.

Teaching With the Ideas Trait

Writing must make sense; that's what the ideas trait is all about. To help your students reach that goal, this section provides lessons and activities organized into categories:

1. Finding the Right Topic
2. Selecting Interesting, Relevant Details
3. Making the Content Clear

But before I discuss specific strategies, I want to share some general thoughts on teaching with the ideas trait. In some ways, ideas is the most essential trait. Without an idea, after all, writers don't need to worry about the other traits. Students must figure out what they want to say in writing. Here are some considerations to keep in mind as you help them to do that:

> *"Assessment must promote learning, not just measure it."*
>
> *—Regie Routman*

- Tap into their imaginations and experiences so they have topics that matter to them.
- Ask questions about drafts that lead them to see possible directions their writing can take.
- Listen to them talk about their writing. You'll discover so much about their intentions.
- Play music, display art, and read wonderful books to show students that ideas can be shared in a variety of ways.
- Use language from the Primary Scoring Guide on page 70 to help students improve their ideas.
- Sing "The Ideas Song" together regularly. Primary students enjoy learning about the traits and remember key qualities of the traits when core ideas are set to music. You'll find other trait-focused songs on pages 118, 154, 188, 224, 264, and 291. Post them all and let students sing them as they write.

The Ideas Song

(sung to the tune of "Row, Row, Row Your Boat")

Write, write, write your thoughts.
Make your ideas clear.
Tell the reader what you know
And what you hold most dear.

> "*Children are our most important evaluators . . . When a child can say with some degree of specificity, this is good because . . . then we know that child is becoming a better reader and a more independent writer.*"
>
> —*Donald Graves*

- Use the student-friendly scoring guide on page 99. When students are developmentally ready for the guide, give them photocopies of it, discuss the descriptors at each level, and have them use it to assess their own and classmates' writing. As you discuss the ideas trait, make sure students can see the difference between ideas that are just starting to gel and ideas that are completely formed.

The following pages present focus lessons and activities that help primary writers get started. Many of these ideas are the brainchildren of process-focused, trait-focused teachers from across the country. I'm grateful to them for contributing their experiences. We all benefit from them.

Finding the Right Topic

What to write about? Many teachers struggle with helping students answer that question. Although it may be tempting to give students a steady diet of specific topics for writing, resist. Writing assignments that don't require creativity or thinking are largely meaningless. In fact, if the goal is to help students become true writers who figure out independently what they want to say, they are even detrimental.

> "*Writers learn by working through all their struggles—including selecting topics and being stuck sometimes—as well as by the writing they accomplish.*"
>
> —*Carol Avery*

Instead of telling students what to write, prompt them to consider the possibilities. There's a big difference between "Today we are going to think about all the things that have to do with this cold winter we've been experiencing, and then write about them" and "Today we are all going to write a snowman story together. Our snowman's name should go in the first line. So what shall we name him?" It's tempting, I know, but we handicap our students when we deny them the chance to hunt for their topics.

Tips for Students Working on Ideas

- Pick an idea that interests you.
- Of all the ideas you have, name the main one.
- Keep your idea in focus; don't add ideas that aren't related.
- Add details that only you could write.
- Answer questions that you think your reader may have.
- Write about what you know or want to know.

Once students have something, anything, down on paper, you can scaffold their learning—observe and comment to help them see the possibilities for their work. Let's take a look at some lessons and activities that give students the tools to find topics.

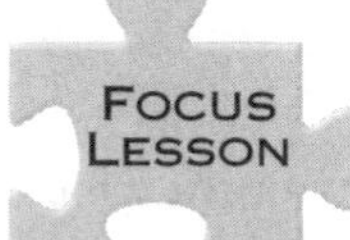

WHAT'S SO SPECIAL?

Sometimes the most powerful ideas come from our everyday lives. It may not seem that way when our days are made up of running kids around to soccer practice, returning phone calls, picking up dry cleaning, making the bed, and cleaning the cat box. Who would want to read about those things, right? But don't overlook them. You might find a diamond in the rough:

- The cashier at the dry cleaners may be studying at night to become a pharmacist.
- There may be a new high-tech process for recycling used kitty litter.
- Making the bed is a ritual that many cultures have shared for centuries, from ancient China to modern America.

Essential Terms

Assignment: A teacher-directed writing task.

Prompt: A trigger designed to help students begin to explore a topic for writing.

Topic: The main idea for writing that either the teacher assigns or the student selects.

- The next time you return a phone call, you may dial incorrectly and wind up calling . . . Well, who do you think's on the other end of the line?

Dr. Samuel Johnson (1905), one of the great literary figures of the eighteenth century said, "The two most engaging powers of an author are to make new things familiar and familiar things new" (p. 86). Mem Fox's *Wilfrid Gordon McDonald Partridge* (1989) illustrates this idea. Young Wilfrid meets an elderly woman, Miss Nancy, who has lost her memory. As he shares special objects with her that he has collected over the years and explains why they are important to him, Miss Nancy recalls her own precious memories. Fox's book inspired this lesson in which students come up with ideas for stories by seeking out treasured objects from their lives.

MATERIALS:

- a copy of *Wilfrid Gordon McDonald Partridge*
- a basket or other container with at least six treasured objects from your life
- one treasured object that each student brings from home
- writing paper and pencils or pens

WHAT TO DO:

1. Gather a collection of treasures from home—everyday things of little monetary value that matter to you. Pick things because of the person who gave them to you, the place you got them or they were given to you, or the time you got them or they were given to you. A thank-you note from a student, a rock from the beach where your family spent vacation, a ticket stub from a favorite film, the collar of a beloved dog, or a newspaper clipping announcing the birth of your youngest child are all good choices. Put the objects in a basket or other container and bring them to school.
2. Sit the children in a circle, and show them the objects one by one, taking a minute or two to explain why each one is a treasure. Then invite the children to tell you about things they have tucked away in their desks or in hiding places at home that are special to them. Remind them that the object itself might not be very valuable, but the memory it conjures is, indeed. Tell the students that the story behind each special object is the source of good ideas for writing.
3. Ask the students to bring a treasured object of their own to school. Send a note to the parents with guidelines for helping their children choose, such as this one:

Dear Parents:

Your child is on the hunt for new ideas for writing. Will you help your child select an object that will be a starting point for a piece of writing? This object should

- be personally meaningful to your child.
- have a story behind it (perhaps how your child got it and why it is special).
- be of little monetary value (in case it gets lost).
- be easy to carry.

The object could be a refrigerator magnet from a special vacation, a rock from the front yard where your child learned to ride a bike or shoot baskets, a ticket stub from a favorite concert or sporting event, a picture of someone or something important, a card or letter from a special person, or a CD with a song that brings back a significant memory. We're going to be writing stories about why these objects are special. The object will be returned to you by the end of the week.

Thanks for your help. I look forward to sharing your child's writing with you once the project is complete.

Sincerely,

4. Read *Wilfrid Gordon McDonald Partridge* to the class, pausing to show the pictures. When you are finished, ask the students to tell you some of the things that Wilfred treasures and why they're important to him.
5. Ask students to take out the object they brought from home. Those who forgot an object should draw a picture of something they value.
6. Put the students in small groups and let them share their objects and thoughts on why they chose them. Remind students to take turns and listen carefully. Encourage shy students to listen to what other children have to say to get ideas for writing.

7. Ask the students to return to their desks and tables and give them paper. Tell them to describe their object and why it is important to them. Students who aren't yet writing a lot of traditional text can draw the object. As they compose, encourage students to talk to one another. As you circulate among the students, help those who aren't writing by transcribing what they say.

8. When the students are finished, hang the papers up in a display area with Fox's book right alongside. Later, gather the papers into a class book for students to look at in their free reading time.

Other Activities for Finding the Right Topic

Fun With Funnels

Metaphors can make sophisticated concepts easier for young students to learn. With that in mind, bring a funnel to class and ask students if they know what it is. Write *funnel* on the board. Explain that a funnel is used to move liquids and other pourable materials from one container to another. Maybe students have seen their parents use a funnel to put gas in the car, or a waitperson use one to pour salt into a shaker. Explain that writers use a funnel too. When writers get an idea, they need to put it in an imaginary funnel to make it smaller, more specific, and easier to write about.

Give students a sheet of paper, have them roll it into a funnel, and tape it together. Give them broad ideas, such as "My Bike," "Bats," or "The Internet." Ask them to picture it going in the wide end and coming out the narrow end as a focused topic, such as "The day I crashed my bike into Uncle Dorien's prize geraniums," "How bats use radar," or "The best site on the Internet to find the winner of *American Idol*." Have them call out the new topics. As students write, encourage them to always use the writer's funnel to focus their ideas.

> *"What a waste of precious time such exercises [worksheets] seem when one thinks of children's great capacities to wonder, to conjecture, to imagine alternative realities and take on others' perspectives."*
>
> *—Danling Fu and Jane Townsend*

Ideas Are Everywhere

Create a writing center for your students to visit. For kindergartners the rules for the writing center might be as simple as:

- Go there at least once a day.
- For at least five minutes, write about something you see, smell, hear, or touch in or outside the room.

- Draw and write about something that interests you for at least five minutes. If you draw, include at least one alphabet letter, maybe even try for words.

Students who write every day develop the ability to capture ideas. They don't wait for topics to be assigned or to appear magically.

Picture This

Find a picture from a magazine showing a person expressing a strong emotion: happiness, sadness, anger, fear, worry, and so on. Put the picture up for all the students to see and ask them to tell you the person's story: Who is the person and why is he or she feeling the emotion? Jot down responses on the overhead and have students use them as starting points for stories about the person.

Narrow It Down

Like "Fun With Funnels," this activity helps students move from a general topic to a more specific one. Ask students to call out topics, such as "Animals," "Friends," "Sports," and so on. Display one of the topics, then ask students to narrow it down. For example, if the topic is "Animals," students may respond, "Dogs." Write that down, then ask them to narrow it down again. This time they may say, "German Shepherds." Write that down and ask them to continue narrowing the topic until you come to an idea that is focused enough to write about, such as "The time my German Shepherd scared off a burglar," "Why German Shepherds make good buddies," or "How to take care of a German Shepherd puppy." Be sure students see how the topic became more manageable with each refinement. Encourage them to narrow down their own writing topics.

Selecting Interesting, Relevant Details

When we explore a topic in depth, ideas for writing emerge. If the topic is the cold winter we're having, maybe one student will investigate how much colder it is this year than last by comparing simple weather charts. Another student may choose snowflakes as a topic, and research how they are formed, why no two of them are alike, and how many of them are in one foot of snow. Another student may want to write a story about what happened at home during a power failure caused by a blizzard. The possibilities are endless when we present a big idea and teach students how to find writing topics within it.

Once students have a topic, let them develop it by adding interesting, relevant details. Resist giving them worksheets, sentence starters, and meaningless assignments. Like all writers, they need to pick up the pencil and write. Just as the miller's daughter couldn't spin straw into gold in *Rumpelstiltskin*, primary students can't spin golden ideas if all we give them is straw as raw material. When students learn how to get inside topics and find the rich details, they begin to spin golden ideas.

Try the following lessons and activities with your students to help them weave interesting and relevant details into their writing.

FOCUS LESSON

CAN YOU SEE IT?

Primary students are very observant. Ask any teacher who has missed a shirt button, worn mismatched socks, or lost an earring—kids are always the first to notice. Looking for the details that others might overlook is an important skill. This lesson focuses on developing that skill for writing.

MATERIALS:

- unlined paper
- crayons, markers, pens, and pencils

WHAT TO DO:

1. Have students close their eyes and tell them they are going to draw what they see in their mind. Let them giggle and wiggle a bit as they do this, but no peeking!
2. Ask them to picture the way they look by asking themselves questions such as:
    - What color is the shirt you have on today? What about your pants or dress? Are there any patterns or textures in them? What kind of shoes are you wearing? Are you wearing any jewelry?
    - What color are your eyes? What color is your skin? How tall are you compared to everyone else in the class? Are you the shortest, the tallest, or somewhere in the middle?
    - What color is your hair? Is it curly? Straight? Neat? Messy? Is it parted? If so, to which side?
    - Picture one place in our classroom. Maybe it's a bulletin board, our pet iguana's terrarium, the view from the window to the street, or your favorite place to sit and read. Imagine you are there now, or imagine it as a photograph. What do you see?

3. Let students open their eyes. Ask them to compare what they imagined to what they now can see.

4. Tell them to draw a picture of themselves in the place they chose. Urge them to show as many details as they can so the reader of their picture will know exactly who and where they are. As they draw, encourage them to share ideas with classmates but keep their piece unique.

5. When everyone has finished, hang their pictures up along the wall or across the board. Give the students sticky notes and ask them to identify the person and place in each picture. They may write, "Devon at the writing center" or "Katrina and her book on the reading rug." Jot down the captions for students who aren't writing yet.

Other Activities for Selecting Interesting, Relevant Details

I'm Making Dinner . . .

This game has been around forever for a reason: it's a lot of fun and it can help young writers discover details about a topic. Begin by asking, "I'm making dinner and what do I need?" Then come up with a word that begins with the letter A, such as *apple*. Write the word on the board and select a student to do the next letter. Have the whole class recite, "I'm making dinner and what do I need?" The selected student answers with a B word—"B, *bologna*—then onto the next student and letter until everyone has had a turn and you have recorded a word for each letter. Ask students to pick their favorite two or three and write them in their notebooks. Tell them to record at least three details they know about each word so they can use them later in writing. They may write, "Bologna: round, tasty, pinkish."

Drawing the Idea

Select a common activity, such as grocery shopping. Ask students to draw a picture of what that activity looks like. Help them set the scene by asking, for example, "What is the name of this grocery store? Who are you with? Who else is around? Are you happy to be there? Are you taking your time or rushing? What aisle are you in? What do you see as you look straight ahead? What about to the left and the right of you? If you reached out to touch something, what would it be? Is music playing? Can you hear anything else? Do you have a cart? What's in it?"

Special-education students draw their ideas about going to the playground. Note the variety of interpretations.

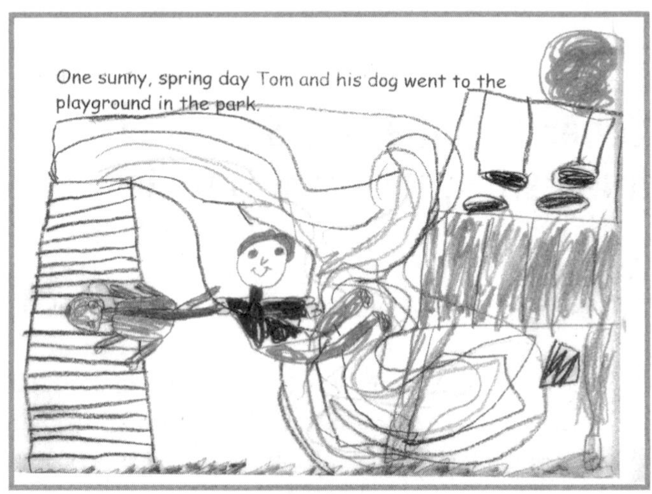

Questions like these give students ideas for details. Collect all the pictures and show them to the class one at a time, pointing out that even though everyone wrote about the same idea, each person did it differently. The examples on page 92 are from second-grade special-education students who know how to use details to elaborate on a main idea.

Making the Content Clear

Having an idea and developing it with details is a good start, but really strong writers go one step further—they make their idea clear. They tell readers everything they need to know to make sense of the writing. Here are some ways to help your students realize and apply this important notion.

FOCUS LESSON

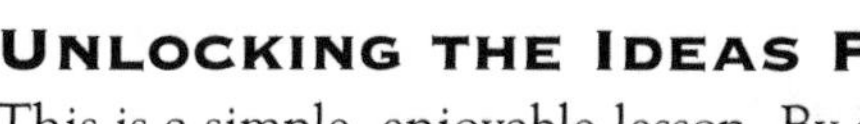

UNLOCKING THE IDEAS PUZZLE

This is a simple, enjoyable lesson. By assembling puzzles, students realize the importance of putting small pieces together to create a big picture. In other words, they learn a powerful metaphor for selecting details that support, clarify, and communicate a main idea.

MATERIALS:

- 5 or 6 jigsaw puzzles (about 100 pieces each) with student-friendly images, such as animals and famous buildings. I've had good luck finding them at garage sales.
- overhead transparencies and pens
- teacher note pad to record comments
- writer's notebooks

WHAT TO DO:

1. Set up an area in your classroom to work on the puzzles. Divide your class into groups of three to four students and give each group a disassembled puzzle. Do not show groups the box covers.

2. Ask the students to spread out the puzzle pieces. To help them get started, tell them to separate the edge pieces (especially the four corner pieces) from the center pieces.
3. Before they start assembling the puzzle, ask each group to find clues on individual pieces, such as the eyes of an animal or a part of a door, to help them determine the image. Write these clues on the overhead transparency.
4. As students work on the puzzle, circulate through the room and write down key comments students make as they arrive at the final image, such as "Oh, look at this. It's the headlight of a car," "This looks like a red nose. Do you think it's a clown?" and "Here's another flower. It *must* be a garden."
5. When groups are finished, show them their predictions of the final images and compare them to the images on the box covers. Ask students to tell you at what point they recognized the image. At the beginning, when they had the border together, or much later?
6. Tell students that writing is a lot like assembling a puzzle. Writers need many details to create a clear picture for readers, and the details have to be arranged in the right order.
7. Ask students to write in their notebooks about how the ideas trait is like a puzzle.

Other Activities for Making the Content Clear

Questions, Anyone?

Get into the habit of recording on the board questions that arise during reading time. If students are reading an article about fire ants, ask them what they want to know that is not covered in the article. Do fire ants sleep at night? Do they get married? How long do they live? Record these questions on the board. When the list grows to ten questions, ask students to select one and send them on an "information scavenger hunt" using grade-appropriate encyclopedias, Internet sites, textbooks, nonfiction trade books, knowledgeable adults, and so on. Some students might even be able to interview experts from the community. Write the answers students find next to the original questions and talk about how this strategy can be used to enhance the content of their own writing.

Can You Tell What Happened?

Tell students in great detail about something that happened to you—maybe the time you got stuck in an elevator for hours, ran out of gas, or lost your luggage while traveling. Jot down all the important details except for one. In other words, intentionally leave out a bit of information essential for the story to make sense. For example, if you're writing about being stuck in an elevator, you might exclude the fact that you hit the alarm button for help. When the students notice that your written version doesn't make as much sense, discuss the importance of not only using details, but also using them logically so they add up to a complete idea. Record what students tell you to add to make your written version complete.

Picture Books to Strengthen Ideas

Reading to and with students is one of the most rewarding and effective ways to teach about ideas. When students look to fiction and nonfiction of professional authors, they discover strategies for finding interesting topics, selecting details, and making ideas clear for use in their own writing. Here are some titles to share with primary writers to boost their understanding of and appreciation for the ideas trait.

All the Places to Love

Patricia MacLachlan
HarperCollins, 1994

In this book, the young narrator takes you on a journey to the rural farm where he grew up. Sensory details enrich lovely passages, such as "My grandmother loved the river best of all the places to love. *That sound, like a whisper,* she said"; " . . . gather in pools where trout flashed like jewels in the sunlight"; and " . . . the birds surrounded us: raucous black grackles, redwings, crows in the dirt that swaggered like pirates." Can't you see those fish and birds? Read this book to students and ask them about their most vivid thoughts of home. Remind them that their writing, too, can create pictures in the reader's mind.

Baghead

Jarrett J. Krosoczka
Alfred A. Knopf, 2002

"On Wednesday morning, Josh had an idea. A very big idea. A very brown idea. A very big, brown, bag idea." So begins this story that demonstrates the power of a good idea. Chronicling the day Josh wears a paper bag over his head, the author presents interesting, original details in a book that's sure to make your students smile and want to write. *Baghead* is a good model for organization, too, because of its cause-and-effect structure.

Edward and the Pirates

David McPhail
Little, Brown, 1997

Edward enjoys reading all kinds of books, but he's especially fond of adventure stories. One night, after reading a book about pirates, Edward finds himself surrounded by them. The pirates demand the book of Edward so they can find their buried treasure and will make him walk the dreaded plank if he doesn't hand it over. When Edward realizes that the pirates can't read, he offers to tell them the story, leaving readers to figure out where the pirate treasured is buried. "Some pirate treasure has never been found . . . " This final line is a great starting point for students who want to write their own pirate stories.

I'm in Charge of Celebrations

Byrd Baylor
Simon & Schuster, 1986

This joyous celebration of the earth shows how to find ideas for writing in everyday life. The narrator announces, "Last year I gave myself one hundred and eight celebrations—besides the ones that they close school for." In prose that reads like poetry, she highlights some of her favorite self-proclaimed holidays: green cloud day, dust devil day, and triple rainbow day. Primary writers who fall in love with this book can make lists of their own celebration days as possible topics for writing.

The Perfect Pet

Margie Palatini
HarperCollins, 2003

The pet battle begins! Elizabeth desperately wants a pet, any pet. But there's one little problem: her parents don't. Elizabeth has some tricks up her sleeve to win her parents over, though, including waking them from a dead sleep and begging for a pet. When she finally finds the perfect pet, a bug named Doug, her parents are relieved. Or are they? This upbeat book will inspire kids to write about persuading a parent into getting them a pet, or anything else, for that matter.

Sidewalk Circus

Paul Fleischman and Kevin Hawkes
Candlewick Press, 2004

In this wordless picture book, a girl waits for the traditional circus to come to town, while another circus is happening all around her. Where a sign advertises a "Tightrope Walker," a construction worker carefully walks across a steel beam. "Goliath the Strongman" is a delivery man, carrying a heavy load on his back. "Fantastic Feats of Juggling" are demonstrated by a cook flipping pancakes. Students look for the details from daily life that match the announcements.

What You Know First

Patricia MacLachlan
HarperCollins, 1995

Written from a child's point of view, this story reminds us of how it feels to leave somewhere we love and to hold memories in our hearts. " . . . I'll try hard to remember the songs, and the sound of the rooster at dawn, and how soft the cows' ears are . . . " Illustrated with detailed woodcuts, it provides an example of how to gather ideas for writing from our lives, a good lesson for any writer.

When Sophie Gets Angry—Really, Really Angry . . .

Molly Bang
Scholastic, 1999

Sophie, like the rest of us, gets really, really angry—until "she wants to smash the world to smithereens." But luckily, she doesn't. Bang emphasizes that people behave and think in their own way when they're angry, and sees the value of overcoming anger to move to a more positive place. Events that conjure up feelings of anger and other emotions are good topics for writers of any age.

Who Is the Beast?

Keith Baker
Harcourt Brace, 1990

"The beast, the beast! We must fly by! We see his tail swing low and high." So begins this richly illustrated story of the search for an animal hiding in the deep, dark jungle. Is it the tiger whose tail swooshes through several pages? Is it one of the birds hiding in the lush landscape? Your students will be surprised and delighted to find out that the beast is actually . . . them, readers of this delightful book! Baker provides a fine example of how simple details can add up to a big idea.

Whoever You Are

Mem Fox
Harcourt Brace, 1997

Mem Fox's timeless book assures us that no matter who we are and where we live, there are people who are just like us. As this idea plays out, in details showing all the ways humans are similar, Fox treats us to poetic rhythms and cadences. At the end, she tells us, "Joys are the same and love is the same. Pain is the same and blood is the same. Smiles are the same and hearts are just the same—wherever they are, wherever you are, wherever we are, all over the world." Read this important book aloud and invite students to talk about the similarities of people in their town and around the world. Ask students to draw pictures of their school, houses, and favorite activities, and caption them. Then find a school in another part of the world (through a reputable international pen-pal Web site such as www.epals.com) and send these pictures to students there to connect with another culture.

For a complete list of picture books that align with each of the traits of writing, see my book *Using Picture Books to Teach Writing With the Traits* (Scholastic, 2004). Organized by trait, this teacher-friendly text contains more than 200 annotations of picture-book titles and more than 30 ready-to-use focus lessons.

Final Reflections on the Ideas Trait

Ideas may well be the most important trait because all writing begins with having something to say. Students will always be working on ideas because they must tackle them every time they write. The journey toward writing that has clear ideas is a series of steps and missteps, making the scope of this trait intimidating to students and teachers. But by examining ways to find topics, use details effectively, and make content clear, you give students tools to make great progress.

Once the idea begins to crystallize, students need to consider how to organize their thoughts, which is the focus of the next chapter. Like two legs of the same pair of pants—separate but dependent—ideas and organization are intrinsically linked.

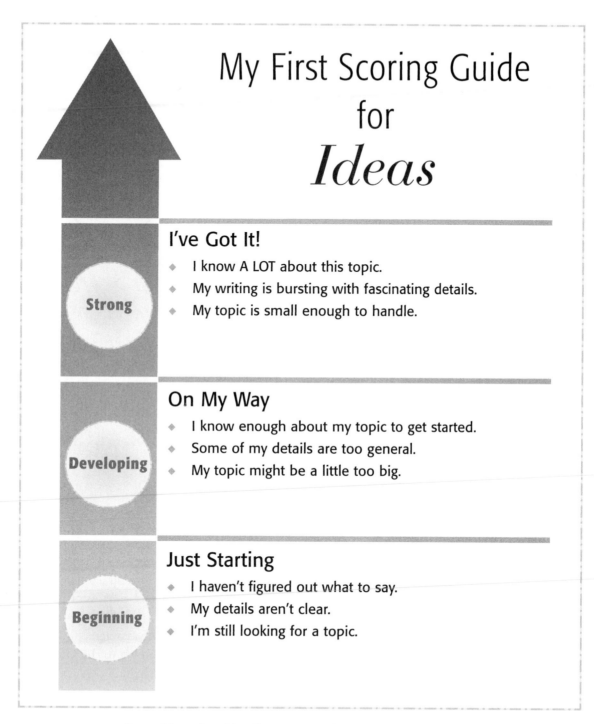

My First Scoring Guide for *Ideas*

I've Got It!

- I know A LOT about this topic.
- My writing is bursting with fascinating details.
- My topic is small enough to handle.

On My Way

- I know enough about my topic to get started.
- Some of my details are too general.
- My topic might be a little too big.

Just Starting

- I haven't figured out what to say.
- My details aren't clear.
- I'm still looking for a topic.

Share this student-friendly scoring guide with students when they are ready to assess their own and their classmates' writing for ideas.

CHAPTER 4

Shaping Organization

The piece shown on the facing page was written by Sergei, a kindergarten student. It reads, "I came from Russia. I'm 5." Tony Boyland learned this when he asked Sergei about the piece in a conference. Sergei went on to tell Tony that he is five now but came to the U.S. from Russia when he was much younger. He separated these two ideas with his own version of a paragraph marker—a line—in an effort to make it clear to the reader that coming to the United States and turning five happened at different times. This is a helpful organizing technique. It is also an important moment to celebrate. Our role as teachers is to reinforce intelligent decisions like these.

Sergei's piece, which says "I came from Russia. I'm 5," shows early signs of organization.

Structuring information so that it makes sense to the reader is what the organization trait is all about. This trait works hand-in-hand with the ideas trait because it is the ideas, after all, that are moved around and grouped as sensibly as possible to convey a clear message. When I asked primary students for their definition of organization, this is what they wrote:

- Organization is a filling cabinet.
- Organization is the opposite of my room.
- Organization is like if you put evrething to gether
- Organization is like a recipe to me.
- Orginizatoin means that after you'v written your story you check it over, and make sure you didn't wright the first thing thin as the fourth thing you did.
- I think ornization is hot dish.

Hold it. Hot dish? Organization is "hot dish"? I had to ask the student for a little more information on his definition. His reasoning was sound. When he watches his mom prepare lasagna for potluck dinners, she follows steps: first she adds the pasta, then the meat, then cheese, then all of those ingredients again in the same order and tops off the dish with seasoning. This is exactly what good writers do. They organize parts of their writing into one delectable whole. The child who wrote "I think organization is hot dish" has that figured out.

Organization: A Definition for Primary Students

Think of organization as the skeleton that holds a building together–the concrete foundation, the steel beams, the weight-bearing timbers. When the building is finished, the skeleton isn't visible. What you see instead are the shapes of the rooms, the finished walls, the windows, the light fixtures. But the building is solid because of its sturdy framework. You know it works. Same goes for writing. If you look closely at the work of even emergent writers, you may see signs of organization:

- several pictures on the same topic, in sequential order
- information grouped by circling, highlighting, and drawing lines between connected thoughts
- beginnings
- connecting words such as *and, but,* and *so*
- sequencing words such as *first, then, later*, and *the end*
- a sense of time through a sequence of events
- labels, titles, captions
- lists

The Challenge of Teaching Organization

We know that students struggle to organize their texts, but often this is the result of the kinds of assignments we give them, formulas such as writing a topic sentence—for example, "I'm going to tell you the three reasons why pizza is my favorite food"—followed by three paragraphs that describe each reason in detail. But formula writing doesn't work because, as Tommy Thomason and Carol York (2000) point out, it "reads like what it is: the literary equivalent of a paint-by-numbers set" (p. 21). Few published authors use the three-paragraph-essay approach to organization. They understand that formulas usually cramp their style and lead them to cramped writing.

The alternative to formulas is not simple, but it works: primary writers who read and are read to a lot know what effective organization looks like even before they are able to create conventional text themselves. And when teachers share models of effective organization, students develop a repertoire of techniques to apply when they write. Use well-written picture books, early chapter books, magazine articles, and nonfiction books on content area topics to show students the organizational craft behind the words. Teach them to question how the author begins the text. How does she move the reader from one idea to the next? Are there surprises? How does the piece end? Are stories organized the same way as informational text? Once students see how authors organize, they can apply strategies those authors use to their own writing. See page 129 for a list of picture books to consider for building students' awareness about organization.

Assessing Student Work for Organization

The Primary Scoring Guide on page 104 helps us describe how primary writers organize their writing. Use it to assess individual pieces of writing, as follows:

STEP 1: Collect student papers you want to assess for organization.

STEP 2: Photocopy the Primary Scoring Guide: Organization since you'll want to write on it and highlight key words as you go.

STEP 3: Read the scoring guide's descriptors for each of the five levels, from top—5: Established—to bottom—1: Ready to Begin." Each descriptor shows how writing typically reveals itself at that level. Also, notice that the descriptors parallel one another from level to level. For example, the first descriptor for each level deals with the inclusion and quality of the piece's title.

STEP 4: Read one of the student papers carefully, paying attention to everything on the page, both pictures and text.

STEP 5: Look at the first descriptor for each level and determine the one that most closely matches the paper. Work your way through the rest of the descriptors for each level, checking off the appropriate ones. Each level has a point value; average the total to determine the piece's overall score in organization. The process will get easier, faster, and more accurate as you practice.

Ready to move to the grades-3-and-up scoring guide!

The Primary Scoring Guide
Organization

Established 5	____ The title (if present) is thoughtful and effective. ____ There is a clear beginning, middle, and end. ____ Important ideas are highlighted within the text.	____ Everything fits together nicely. ____ The text slows down and speeds up to highlight the ideas and shows the writer's skill at pacing. ____ Clear transitions connect one sentence to the next.
Extending 4	____ The title (if present) comes close to capturing the central idea. ____ The writing starts out strong and includes a predictable ending. ____ The writer uses a pattern to spotlight the most important details.	____ Ideas follow a logical but obvious sequence. ____ The writing's pace is even; it doesn't bog the reader down. ____ Basic transitions link one sentence to the next.
Expanding 3	____ The simple title (if present) states the topic. ____ The piece contains a beginning but not a conclusion. ____ The piece is little more than a list of sentences connected by theme.	____ There is basic order with a few missteps. ____ There is more text at the beginning than in the middle or end. ____ Sentence parts are linked with conjunctions (*but*, *and*, *or*).
Exploring 2	____ The piece has no title. ____ Letters or words are used as captions. ____ Simple clues about order emerge in pictures or text.	____ The arrangement of pictures or text shows an awareness of the importance of structure and pattern. ____ Left-to-right, top-to-bottom orientation is evident. ____ No transitions are indicated.
Ready to Begin 1	____ Letters (if present) are scattered across the page. ____ No coordination of written elements is evident. ____ Lines, pictures, or letters are randomly placed on the page.	____ Lines, pictures, or letters are grouped haphazardly. ____ There is no sense of order.

Sample Papers to Assess for Organization

The student papers that follow represent a range of skill in the organization trait. Review the scoring guide on page 104, read each student paper closely, read my descriptor-by-descriptor evaluation of the piece, and see what you think. Do you agree with my assessment of each writer's work? Do these pieces reflect the kind of work you see in your classroom?

If you wish, go back to the scoring guide in Chapter 3, page 70, and score these pieces in ideas. You may see quite a difference between what you give them in ideas and what you've given them in organization. This is when the versatility of analytic assessment shows itself, when students do well in one trait but not so well in another. These gaps inform our teaching.

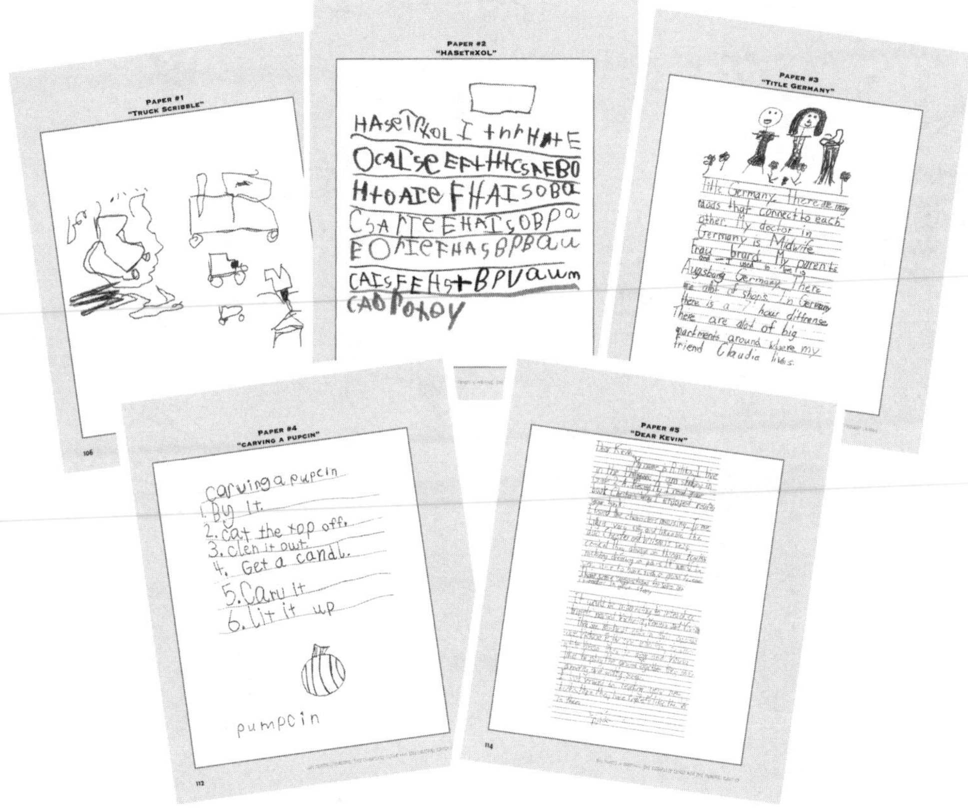

Paper #1
"Truck Scribble"

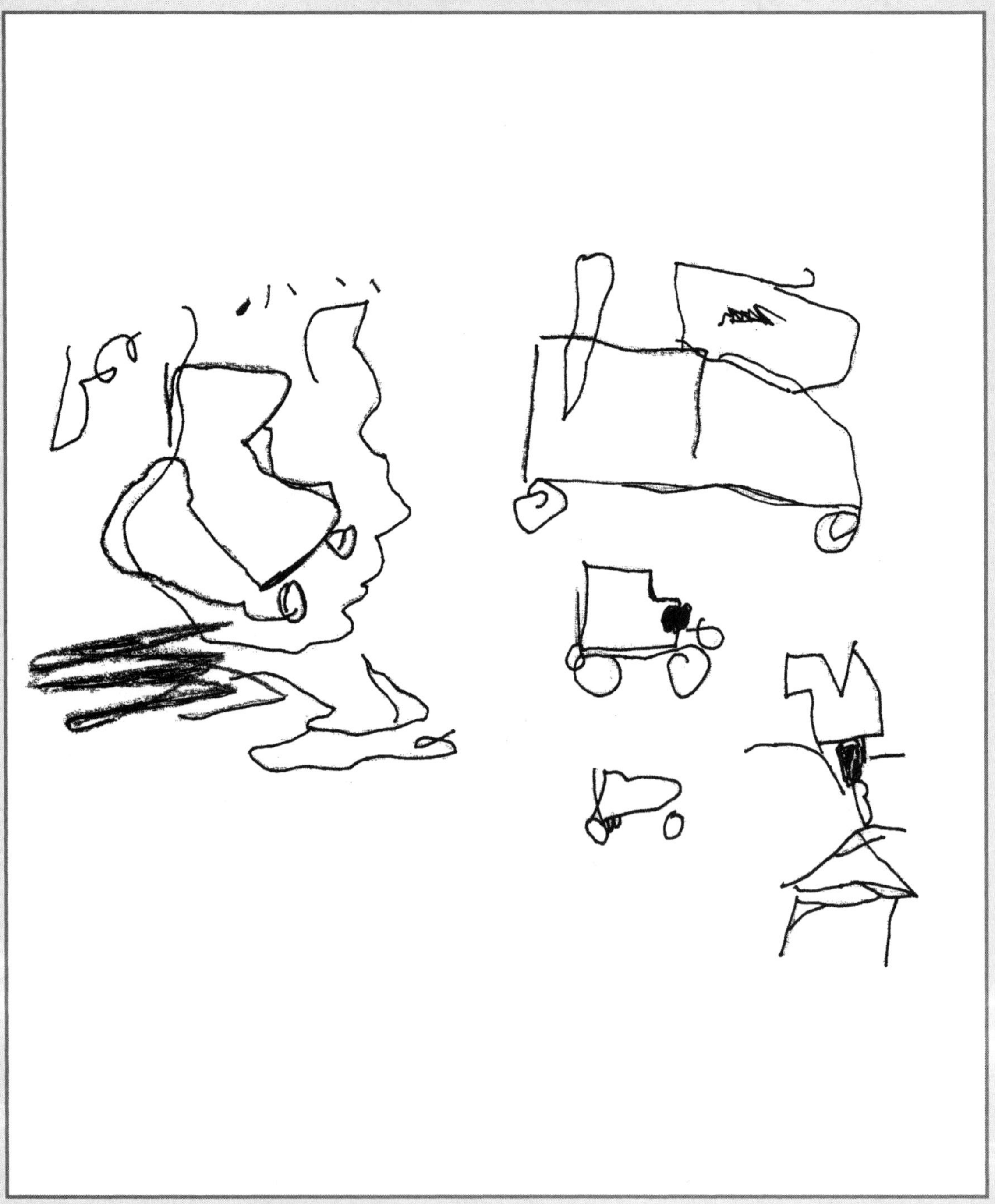

Time to Assess

Paper #1
"Truck Scribble"

This young writer has given us one familiar image, a truck, but the rest of the marks are indecipherable. The piece doesn't have any sense of order. Clearly, it is at the 1: Ready to Begin stage in organization.

- Letters (if present) are scattered across the page.

  There are no letters on the page. The simple line drawings are randomly placed.

- No coordination of written elements is evident.

  Only lines, scribbles, and a drawing of a truck make up the writing. No letters or captions are present. The reader gets no sense of how these marks work together.

- Lines, pictures, or letters are randomly placed on the page.

  When the paper is turned around, it looks about the same. The truck is the only feature that provides a clue to the intended orientation.

- Lines, pictures, or letters are grouped haphazardly.

  The marks are isolated; there is no evidence of connections between them. Each picture stands by itself.

- There is no sense of order.

  The reader's eye is drawn to the whole piece at once, not from one section to the next. The piece is made up of a random set of marks.

Paper #2
"HASeTrXOL"

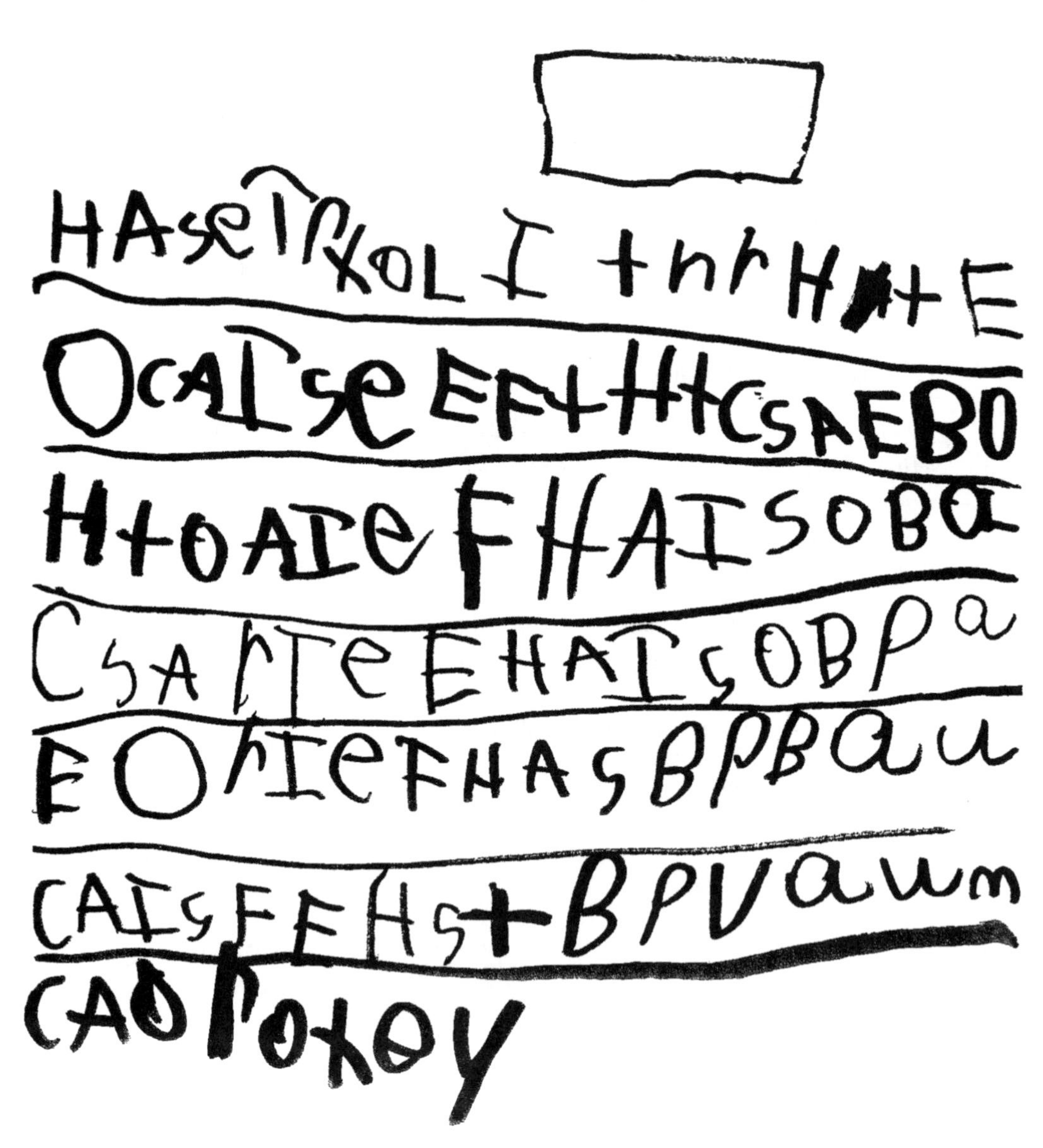

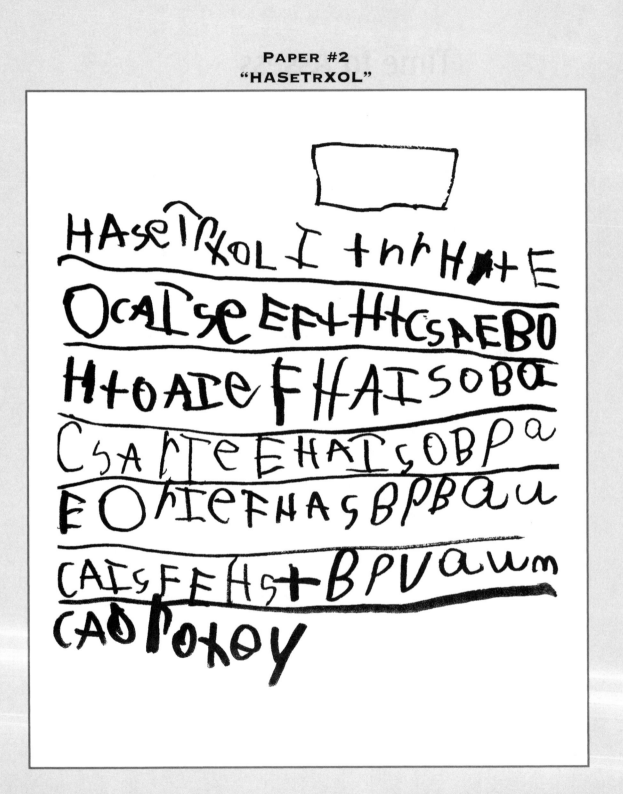

Time to Assess

PAPER #2
"HASETRXOL"

This piece is an excellent example of how a writer's ability to organize can be further along than the ability to capture ideas. The letter strings, separated by lines, show elements of organization, but no meaning can be gleaned from them without the student's translation. This is a strong 2: Exploring in the trait of organization, but only a 1: Ready to Begin in ideas.

- The piece has no title.

  No title is present. There is a box at the top which indicates that the writer understands the need for a title, but it's empty.

- Letters or words are used as captions.

  There are no illustrations, so there is no need for captions.

- Simple clues about order emerge in pictures or text.

  Bingo. This piece gives the reader two clues: the line to separate one "sentence" from the next and the use of color to distinguish different sections of writing.

- The arrangement of pictures or text shows an awareness of the importance of structure and pattern.

  Another direct hit. The writer separates letter strings with different-colored lines to indicate that each line of text is a related but separate idea.

- Left-to-right, top-to-bottom orientation is evident.

  The letter strings, although random collections of upper- and lowercase letters, are written left to right, top to bottom. The writer is mimicking how text looks and is laying out the letters clearly.

- No transitions are indicated.

  Each line of text stands alone, with no signals as to how they connect.

Paper #3
"Title Germany"

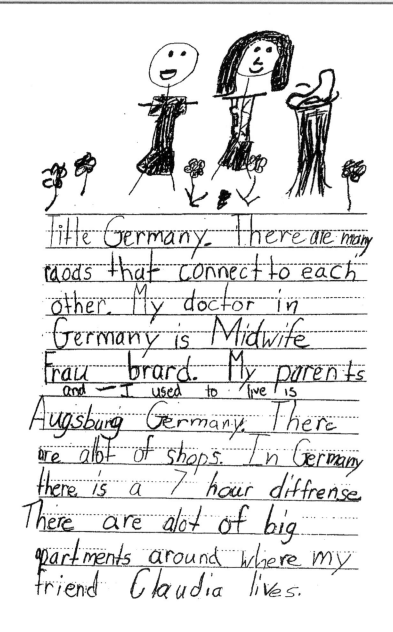

Title Germany. There are many
raods that connect to each
other. My doctor in
Germany is Midwife
Frau brard. My parents
and I used to live is
Augsburg Germany. There
are alot of shops. In Germany
there is a 7 hour diffrense.
There are alot of big
apartments around where my
friend Claudia lives.

Time to Assess

Paper #3
"Title Germany"

Each of the details in this piece is about the main topic, Germany. However, none of those details connect to one another in a logical sequence. We can take the first sentence, "There are many raods that connect to each other," and put it at the end or somewhere in the middle. Take the last line, "There are a lot of big apartments around where my friend Claudia lives," and move it anywhere in the text. This is true for all the sentences. They are unified only by topic, not by a logical sequence of ideas. This piece would score a 3: Expanding in organization.

- The simple title (if present) states the topic.

  "Title Germany." Can't state the topic much more directly than that!

- The piece contains a beginning but not a conclusion.

  The writer provides an opening sentence, but it does not set the tone for the piece as a good beginning should. It is a sentence, like all the others in the piece. The same is true for the last sentence. The piece contains six sentences about Germany, but no clear beginning, middle, or end.

- The piece is little more than a list of sentences connected by theme.

  This piece is a list of things the writer thinks about the topic. The writer unifies the piece around a theme, Germany, but does not sequence any of the details.

- There is basic order with a few missteps.

  The order of the sentences is random. If those sentences are moved around, the same meaning comes through.

- There is more text at the beginning than in the middle or end.

  The writer has not provided any clues about why the ideas are in this particular order.

- Sentence parts are linked with conjunctions (*but, and, or*).

  Each sentence stands alone without conjunctions to show how one point relates to the next.

Paper #4
"Carving a Pupcin"

carving a pupcin

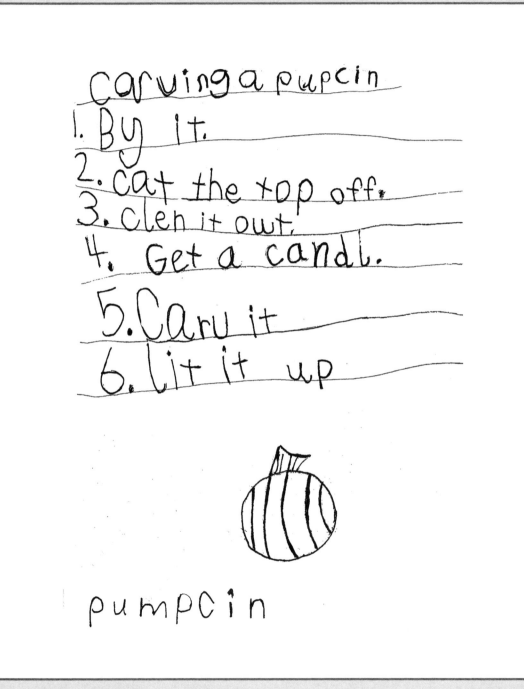

1. By it.
2. cat the top off.
3. clen it out.
4. Get a candl.
5. Caru it
6. lit it up

pumpcin

Time to Assess

Paper #4
"Carving a Pupcin"

This paper is a successful attempt at what I think the writer of "HASeTrXOL" was trying to accomplish. This student uses lines to separate individual ideas—specifically, steps in pumpkin carving—but adds numbers to guide the reader. He also begins each line with a verb, includes a title, provides a captioned illustration, and uses conventional English, which allows us to appreciate the flow of ideas. The piece is clearly more organized than the earlier examples and therefore scores a 4: Extending in organization.

- The title (if present) comes close to capturing the central idea.

  The idea is clear from the beginning because of the title, "carving a pupcin." The reader recognizes immediately that it is a how-to piece.

- The writing starts out strong and includes a predictable ending.

  The play of ideas is strong throughout this piece. Each line stands alone yet connects to the next, from beginning to end.

- The writer uses a pattern to spotlight the most important details.

  The step-by-step approach leads the reader through the text with ease.

- Ideas follow a logical but obvious sequence.

  The six steps make sense. Of course, we would cut the top off the pumpkin before cleaning it out, and of course we would clean it out before lighting it.

- The writing's pace is even; it doesn't bog the reader down.

  Each statement takes a single, sensible step toward the final one: "lit it up."

- Basic transitions link one sentence to the next.

  The numbers link the ideas. They clearly lay out the order in which to carve a pumpkin.

PAPER #5
"DEAR KEVIN"

Dear Kevin,
My name is Ritika. I live in the Philippines. I am studying in Grade 2-A. Recentlly I read your book Chester's Way. I enjoyed reading your book.
I found the characters amusing. To me Lilly is very silly and likeable The duo Chester and Wilson is very comical They always do things together including dressing in pairs. It would be very nice to have such a good friend.
I have some suggestions for some new characters in your story

It would be interesting to introduce triplets named Victoria, Venesa and Vivian They are identical only in their appear-erce. Victoria is the one who love to dance while Vivian likes to sing and Venesa likes to play the drums Together they mae a merry and witty group.
I look forward to reading your new books. Hope they have triplets like the Vs in them

Love
Ritika

Time to Assess

PAPER #5
"DEAR KEVIN"

"Dear Kevin" unfolds in a natural, lovely way. A logical progression, free of forced transitions, makes it a pleasure to read. This piece receives a 5: Established in organization.

- The title (if present) is thoughtful and effective.

  "Dear Kevin" is a letter, so no title is needed.

- There is a clear beginning, middle, and end.

  The writer starts out with a personal introduction and shares specifically why she enjoyed reading Chester's Way. She goes on to suggest new characters for future books. The conclusion ties back to the most important point in the letter, the triplets. Great work.

- Important ideas are highlighted within the text.

  A simple but well-crafted topic sentence begins each paragraph, such as "I found the characters amusing" and "I have some suggestions for some new characters in your story." These provide a road map for readers as the ideas unfold.

- Everything fits together nicely.

  The writer uses important details to explain her main idea—her reaction to the book. She remains faithful to her main idea.

- The text slows down and speeds up to highlight the ideas and shows the writer's skill at pacing.

  The ideas unfold evenly in the first two paragraphs and are given the same level of importance. The writing picks up steam toward the end when the writer makes a plea for Kevin to include Victoria, Venesa, and Vivian in his new book.

- Clear transitions connect one sentence to the next.

  "Recently," "To me," and "I look forward" link sentence to sentence. By avoiding more common transition words, such as next and finally, the writer makes the piece a pleasure to read.

Assessing for organization can be tricky. It's easy to be dazzled by the primary writer's ability to present events in order—and, for very early writers, that is a major accomplishment. But more advanced writers are capable of so much more. Save your loudest applause for the writer who is clearly thinking aloud on paper; taking some risks to structure his or her piece to fit an idea, not follow a formula. Lucy Calkins (1998) explains the role of organization this way: "Writing allows us to turn the chaos into something beautiful, to frame selected moments, to uncover and celebrate the organizing patterns of our existence" (p. 8). Discovering those patterns is a key.

Conference Comments

Here's what you may say to students who are working well with the organization trait.

- This was the perfect way to begin (or end) the piece.
- Step-by-step is a clear way to show how to do something in order.
- Because one thing happened all the other things followed. Nice thinking.
- Your captions help me see how your pictures go together.
- What is going to happen next? I can hardly wait to find out.
- I was surprised by your ending. I didn't see it coming!
- The way you arrived at the solution to your main character's problem makes good sense.
- The way you put the events in order by time works well.
- You grouped your pictures to show how they fit together. Nice work in organization.
- You've left breadcrumbs to help me find my way through your paper easily, thanks.

Teaching With the Organization Trait

Organization may very well be the hardest trait for students to master. Over the years, I've noticed that no matter how high students score in other traits, their scores in organization lag behind. This may be because many young students lack exposure to a full range of quality fiction and nonfiction. Often they are fed a steady diet of one particular genre, such as fairy tales, so they don't hear, see, and internalize the structures of other genres.

Now that you've seen firsthand how to assess for organization and understand what primary students can do, take a look at the organization lessons and activities grouped in the following three categories:

1. Bold Beginnings
2. Mighty Middles
3. Excellent Endings

Before doing so, however, here are some ideas for introducing organization:

- Provide lots of models to show students how authors showcase their ideas through good organization.
- In conferences, small-group discussions, and whole-class discussions on specific pieces of writing, ask students questions such as, "What comes next?" "And then?" "How can you build a bridge from this sentence to the following one?" "What's the most important part of your piece?" "How does this compare with that?" "What's the last thing that happened?" "How do those two ideas connect?" and "What does this have to do with that?" Use answers to help students with organization.
- Give students chances to think about cause-and-effect relationships in everyday life. For example, if students are working with modeling clay and they don't put the lid on tightly, it dries out. This may lead students to apply a cause-and-effect structure in their next piece of writing, especially if you help them make a connection.
- Use art, music, math, and science to show how organization appears in other areas of everyday life. For example, song lyrics are often organized by stanzas; in science, students use sequential steps to conduct experiments; in

written responses for mathematics, students must logically explain how they got their answers.

- Use language from the Primary Scoring Guide on page 104 in your day-to-day teaching so that students internalize it and apply it to improve the organization of their writing.
- Sing "The Organization Song" often to remind students of the trait's key qualities.

The Organization Song

(sung to the tune of "Mary Had a Little Lamb")

Writing has a good beginning,
strong conclusion,
and builds bridges.
Writing has a good beginning.
The order just makes sense.

Post the lyrics of the "The Organization Song," along with the other trait songs that you introduce, where students can refer to them whenever they wish. (See pages 83, 154, 188, 224, 264, and 291 for the other songs.)

- Use the student-friendly guide on page 133. When students are ready, give them photocopies of the guide, discuss the descriptors at each level, and have them assess their own and classmates' writing. As you discuss the organization trait, make sure students have the guide in front of them so they can see the difference between a paper strong in organization and a not-so-strong one.

"First sentences are doors to worlds."

—Ursula K. Le Guin

What follows are some ideas that teachers use to help primary students organize their writing. You may be surprised that many of them don't require students to use paper and pencil. Instead, they rely on everyday materials such as cartoon strips and everyday activities such as lining up from tallest to shortest, youngest to oldest. The reason: to teach students basic principles of organization.

Once they understand those principles, it is easier for them to apply them in writing. Lessons and activities like these teach students how to organize long before they can write extended text.

Tips for Students Working on Organization

- Start with a brilliant beginning. Make it enticing.
- Build a mighty middle. Make it powerful.
- Create an excellent ending. Make it memorable.
- Tie the details together so they fit and flow.
- Give your piece just the right title.

Bold Beginnings

When a paper begins, "I'm going to tell you about . . . " readers hit the snooze button. But when it begins "Bang! I woke up and wondered what on earth was going on," readers pay attention. They want to know where the writer is going. What follows are a few of my favorite techniques for helping students start their stories and informational writing with a bang.

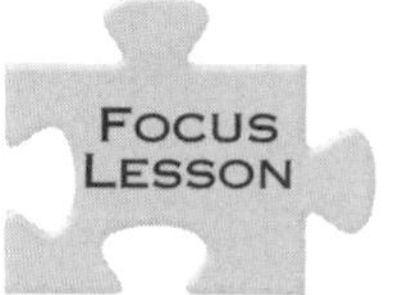

Ring of Leads

A collection of interesting leads can inspire writers who are looking for ideas. In this lesson, you and your students create leads, write them on cards, organize the cards by technique, and place them on a loose-leaf ring for easy access.

Materials:

- 30 to 40 index cards and pens or pencils
- a 2-inch loose-leaf ring
- an overhead transparency of the techniques and examples below

What to Do:

1. Write the following techniques for creating bold beginnings on the front of individual index cards, then write or draw the examples on the back.

   Lights, Camera, Action: The writer makes something happen.

   Example: "For the last time," my dad said. "Put your gum here."

Single Word: The writer sets off an important word by itself and follows it up with more information.

Example: Gum. Gum was everywhere. It was in my hair. It was in the carpet. It was on my pillow.

Fascinating Fact: The writer presents an intriguing piece of information.

Example: I blew a bubble bigger than my brother's head.

Imagine This: The writer captures a moment in words or pictures.

Example: The gum made my bangs stick straight out from my head.

Or a picture of a person with gum in his or her hair.

It's Just My Opinion: The writer states a belief.

Example: Kids should be able to chew gum any time they want.

Listen Up: The writer describes a sound.

Example: *Smack*, *snap*, *slurp*.

I Wonder: The writer asks a question or a series of questions.

Example: Have you ever wondered how many pieces of gum will fit into the human mouth? Five? Ten? More?

2. Arrange students in groups of three to four. Give each group a card.
3. Have a member of each group read the technique and the example. Then tell groups to come up with another example.
4. Ask groups to write the new examples on the cards. Encourage students to add pictures if they think it will clarify the message.
5. Prepare an overhead transparency of the original list of techniques and examples. Read one at a time and ask groups to share their new lead and the technique on which it's based. Be sure all groups have a chance to share.

6. Collect the cards and punch a hole in the top left corner of each for binding with the loose-leaf ring. Put this ring of leads in the writing center as a resource for students when they can't think of a way to begin future work.

7. Encourage students to add techniques and examples to the ring as they think of them.

8. See page 126 for Endings That Work, a variation of this lesson.

Ch ch ch do you know
what that sound is it is Sicors
cuting. Dot dot dot do you know
what that is gloo. We did a
lot of that today because we
made big bugs. befor we did that
we drew a Picher of what we
were going to make. on Turs day we
are going to make the bugs Mrs.
Voss siad.
I am going to make a Dragen
fly. Ch Ch Ch and Dot Dot
Dot!

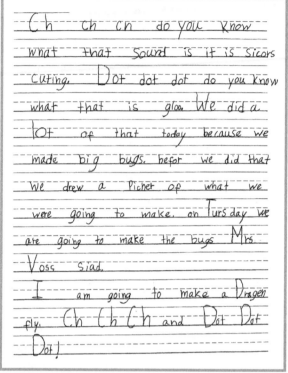

Courtney's piece grabs the reader's attention largely because of her use of onomatopoeia in the first line and throughout.

Other Activities for Writing Bold Beginnings

My Life Story

Tell students that a famous movie producer is going to film their life stories. Ask them to draw the picture of the opening scene of the movie, using whatever materials they wish: paper, pencils, markers, pictures from magazines, paint, chalk, and so on. Remind them that good autobiographies don't always start with the subject's birth. Sometimes they begin with an important event in the subject's life, a strong belief that has guided the subject, or a description of a meaningful person or place. From there, have students share their pictures with the class, and see if volunteers wish to act out one or two of them.

Getting Hooked

Bring in a video or DVD of a movie or TV show that students like that is age appropriate. Show just the first minute or two and ask students to tell you if it has a good opening. Maybe there was something funny right at the beginning. Or perhaps a character said something that piqued their interest. Or maybe thrilling colors and graphics hooked them. Discuss different ways movies and TV shows begin and the implications for writing.

What I Saw First on My African Safari

Tell students they are going on an imaginary ten-day African safari. They will see many animals, from the tall, elegant giraffe to the majestic, fierce lion. Tell students to close their eyes, picture themselves in their big tent, and visualize all the things around them: sleeping bags, lanterns, boxes of food, cameras, water bottles, clothes, first-aid kit, and so on. Invite them to call out what they see as they go deeper into the scene. Record what they say on a chart. Now ask students to imagine waking in the morning, stretching, and opening the front of the tent. Have them call out what they see first and record what they say on the chart. After imagining ten days of waking up in Africa, let students pick their favorite image and draw a picture of it. Caption the pictures and hang them in chronological order on a bulletin board titled "What I Saw First on My African Safari."

Mighty Middles

There are many ways to help students organize the bodies of their papers. They can put ideas in chronological order or in order of importance. They can compare and contrast ideas, examine cause-and-effect relationships, or predict what happens next.

The purpose for writing should drive decisions about organization. In stories, chronological order is usually helpful. In essays, however, key points listed in order of importance may be more useful.

What follows are ideas for helping primary students build mighty middles. Each requires a different level of writing ability, so for inexperienced students, select those that are designed to teach the concept of organization and move gradually toward ones that require paper and pencil.

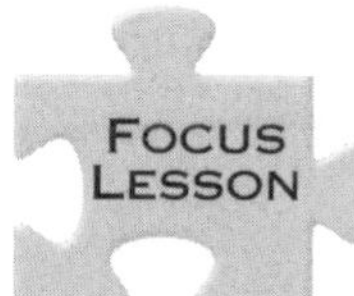

Shopping Spree

Grocery stores are organized logically. Each aisle is clearly marked and stocked with similar items so that shoppers can easily find what they want—from soup to nuts. Here students categorize real grocery items and learn an important lesson in organization.

> *"The trick is not a great beginning but a great middle."*
>
> *—Thomas Trebitsch Parker*

Materials:

- several bags of items from the grocery store in at least five categories: canned goods, cereal, soda, candy, crackers and chips, condiments (ketchup, pickles, mayonnaise), paper goods (towels, plates, toilet paper, facial tissues), and storage materials such as aluminum foil, plastic wrap, and sandwich bags. Bring in empty boxes and cans or items that have not been opened.
- construction paper and markers
- drawing paper

What to Do:

1. Spread out the groceries in a common area.
2. Divide the class into five teams. Tell the first team they have three minutes to sort the groceries into piles according to categories of their choice. They could sort the groceries by color, size, shape, material, weight, cost, and so on.
3. Call time and ask a team member to tell the class what categories the team chose and why. Record the team's categories on the overhead or board.
4. Tell the second team to sort the groceries a different way, give members three minutes to sort, and then ask them to share their categories with the class. Record their categories on the board or overhead next to the first group's.
5. Rotate through the teams, letting students sort and re-sort the groceries in different ways. Write down each group's categories until you have one set from each team.
6. Tell each team to draw a picture of their organizational plan. If they chose to organize the groceries by packaging—cans, boxes, jars, bottles, and so on—they may draw a picture of those different types of packaging. Ask them to write a caption for their picture that describes their organizational method.

7. Post the drawings with the stack of grocery items underneath them.
8. Encourage students to think of different ways to organize their writing by classifying and ordering the details in interesting, unusual ways.

Other Activities for Writing Mighty Middles

Back Atcha

Tell students you are going to start telling a story. When you stop and say, "Back atcha," the student you point to must continue the story by adding a sentence or finishing the last sentence another way. The only rule is that nobody can use the phrase "and then." For instance, if you start the story by saying, "I looked under my bed, and I saw a bug. It was huge," the student may respond, " . . . but kind of cute. It was green and purple and fuzzy and it looked like it came from outer space." That student then sends it back to you by saying, "Back atcha." Continue the story, keeping ideas flowing in a sensible order by sending it out to other students until you decide to end it. Back Atcha is a good way to practice using transition words and phrases.

Cut It Out

As a class, brainstorm words that suggest the passage of time, such as *while, after, first, then, later, next, suddenly,* and *last.* Then give magazines to small groups and ask members to cut out examples of those words and create posters from them. Ask students to title their posters and hang them in the hallway or in another public place for schoolmates to use as a reference in writing.

It's Your Life

Tell students they are going to create a time line of their lives. Start by having them list important events in their lives and order them chronologically. Entries may include their birth, the birth of younger brothers and sisters, major moves, getting or losing a pet, the first day of school, losing a tooth, learning to ride a bike, making a new friend, and winning a ribbon or award. Encourage students to include milestones, too, such as the day they realized they were tall enough to see themselves in the bathroom mirror. Give students long pieces of butcher paper and markers. Then help determine which events to include and how to organize them.

Better Organization Through Graphic Organizers

By ordering information numerically, students practice organizational skills.

T-charts, Venn diagrams, and semantic webs are excellent for helping students organize their thinking before they write because they give students a plan for unfolding their ideas. In the photo to the right, students organize and report their data in numeric order. They apply a preplanned structure to their writing.

While graphic organizers can be very helpful to young students just getting started, take this word of warning: Don't rely on them too heavily or they become a crutch for students. Each piece of writing requires the writer to consider the best form, not just plug in a convenient one. Knowing how to organize is a thinking skill, make no mistake about it.

Excellent Endings

Wrapping up a piece of writing is a challenge. Ask any writer. That's probably why a lot of young students cap theirs off with something like, "Now you know three reasons why hippopotamuses are ferocious," "I hope you liked my story," or the perennial favorite, "The end." Indeed, as I sit here writing this chapter, I have no clue whatsoever how it will end—maybe with a story, a quotation from someone I admire, a piece of writing from a student. Time will tell. What's fortunate for me, though, is I know I have choices other than, "Now you know all the reasons primary students should learn the traits," "Thank you for reading my chapter," and "The end."

I learned how to write endings by looking at what other writers did and deciding what worked well for me as the reader. But we can also actively direct students to examine endings and the elements of endings. In this section, you'll find a lesson and activities to inspire primary writers to wrap up their writing so that it lingers in readers' minds.

> *"The ending is far more than the final ribbon that adorns a piece of writing, the rhetorical hairspray to keep everything in place. The ending may well be the most important part of a piece of writing."*
>
> —*Ralph Fletcher*

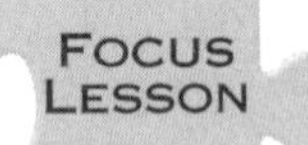

ENDINGS THAT WORK

Is there anything more satisfying than a story with a good ending? In Barbara Abercrombie's *Charlie Anderson* (1995), the reader gets not one, not two, but three. Charlie Anderson, a very fat, gray-striped cat, has it made. He gets to live in two houses with two families who love him. During the day, he eats and sleeps at one house, leaving at night for the second. But neither family knows it is sharing the cat. Both families think "their" cat is out hunting when he's not at their house, and it's only through a creative surprise ending, which works on several levels, that the truth is revealed.

MATERIALS:

- a copy of *Charlie Anderson*
- an overhead projector and pens

WHAT TO DO:

1. Ask, "What are some of the things authors do to signal to readers that they are wrapping things up?" Write students' ideas on the overhead. Their list may include "The End," "Thank you for reading my story," or "And then I woke up and it was only a dream." They may also come up with more original ideas such as, "Now you know three reasons why I don't eat green food." Discuss how effective each of these endings is and how important it is to conclude writing with a powerful thought, an image, or an idea that makes the reader think.
2. Show students *Charlie Anderson* and tell them it has three endings and one of them is a surprise.
3. Read the book aloud, pausing to show the pictures. When you come to the end, read the last three pages—the three endings—and let the last one sink

in. Then ask, "Did this ending surprise anyone? Where in the story did the writer give us a little hint that set up this ending?"

4. Discuss how there's usually a clue to surprise endings earlier in the text so that the ending, while a surprise, makes sense. For example, early on, Abercrombie explains that Elizabeth and Sarah often visit their dad and stepmother in the city. So, when the story ends with the conclusion that the cat *and* the girls are lucky to have two families who love them, the reader thinks, "Oh, yeah!" This ending reveals the theme: There are other ways to love and be loved outside of a traditional family. Although primary writers most likely couldn't create endings as powerful as Abercrombie's, it's never too early to point them in the right direction.

5. Revisit the book's other two possible endings. In the first, the problem of who owns the cat is diplomatically resolved by renaming him Charlie Anderson, a combination of the names he was called by each family who thought he was exclusively theirs. The second ending deepens the reader's experience with the story. It becomes personal when one of the girls asks Charlie Anderson to declare which family he loves best.

6. Read the story again, focusing on the three endings. Pause after each, letting the artistry of the writer sink in.

7. Encourage students to look at the endings in other high-quality books. Do the authors wrap up the story convincingly, dig deep, or work with a big idea?

Other Activities for Writing Excellent Endings

Knot Just an Ending

Bring two strands of beads into your classroom, one with a knot at the end and one without. Tell students that the strands stand for their writing and the beads stand for the ideas in their writing. Point out that the first strand has a knot at the end to keep the ideas in place. Hold the second strand up so the beads slip off. Tell students that when they write, they need to include a good, solid ending so the ideas don't slide off—in other words, so they stay strong and connected in their reader's mind. Remind them to always make "a final knot" to hold their ideas in place.

Zoom In and Zoom Out

Ask students to imagine that they are holding cameras with powerful zoom lenses. Have them hold their cameras up to their eyes, focus on a subject, and tell you what they see as they zoom in. Have them zoom in closer and focus on one tiny detail and describe it. If they are photographing a desk, they could focus on a blemish in the wood finish, a chewed pencil that is lying on top, or a dent in the leg. Tell them that a focused detail can make a good ending. By being very specific, readers can picture the ending in their minds right along with you.

Now ask students to zoom out to get a picture of the classroom, school, and whole neighborhood. Maybe they can see cars along the street, the flower beds at the entrance of the school, the playground equipment in back, and the houses surrounding the school. Tell students that they can use this wide-angle view to end their writing, too. Sometimes writers close by leaving the reader with a big picture of the idea. Ask students to look at a story or piece of informational text they are working on and try both techniques. Which one works best?

Endings That Work

Using the format for the lesson Ring of Leads on page 119, help students create a collection of endings to use as a reference as they write. These endings may include

A wise thought: *Getting into your sister's stuff can turn into a big problem.*

A surprise: *When I opened the box, the frog was gone.*

A quote: *"Don't come in here. I mean it," yelled my sister.*

A tie-up: *None of us will ever forget that day.*

A question: *"What on earth happened here?" my sister cried.*

A challenge: *"Jeremy, you clean this up, or I'm telling Dad," cried my sister.*

A sign of what is to come: *I knew my sister would get even one day.*

A laugh: *My brother will never forget that day!*

Picture Books to Strengthen Organization

There are many picture books that provide excellent models of well-organized text. Look for books that contain a clear structure (thematic, chronological, compare-and-contrast, cause-and-effect, and so on), smooth transitions, and strong beginnings and endings. Some of my favorites are:

Alphabet City

Stephen T. Johnson
Viking Press, 1995

Alphabet books are excellent for teaching students how to organize their ideas, and there are many fine ones available. This one shows that letter shapes can be found in the details of everyday life. Ask students to find letters around the school, on the playground, or at home. Then have them bring those letters back to the class and create new texts organized like Johnson's. (See sample right.)

This piece was inspired by Stephen T. Johnson's *Alphabet City*.

Dear Mr. Blueberry

Simon James
Margaret K. McElderry Books, 1991

This book is organized around a series of letters between Emily, a young girl who thinks she has a whale named Arthur living in her pond, and her teacher, Mr. Blueberry. Mr. Blueberry is understandably skeptical and points out that whales live in salt water and couldn't possibly live in her pond. Unaffected by Mr. Blueberry's response, Emily continues to write to him about Arthur's activities. This enjoyable book shows young writers how letters are organized and may inspire them to start up their own correspondence about a topic of their choice.

DON'T Take Your Snake for a Stroll

Karin Ireland
Harcourt Children's Books, 2003

Students will love this hilarious book filled with over-the-top characters, language, and reasons to avoid taking wild animals places they don't belong. For instance, Ireland tells us not to take your moose to the movies because the people sitting behind him will have a hard time seeing over his antlers. Her simple organizational pattern, focusing on one animal at a time, is a cinch for students to replicate. Encourage them to write their own silly reasons to avoid taking wild animals—or other things—to places they don't belong.

Henry Hikes to Fitchburg

D. B. Johnson
Houghton Mifflin, 2000

This is a book about Henry David Thoreau, his friend Bear, their trip to Fitchburg, Massachusetts, and their two very different routes to getting there. Henry walks through the countryside, stopping to enjoy its beauty as he goes. Bear, however, decides to travel by train and must work to earn the fare. The book traces each character's journey and ends with the two of them meeting in Fitchburg, where Bear says, "The train was faster." But Henry replies, "I know, I stopped for blackberries." Students compare and contrast the two characters' approaches to travel—and to life—and apply what they learn in their own writing.

I Love Going Through This Book

Robert Burleigh
Joanna Cotler Books, 2000

"I love going through this book. Just watch me do it. No matter how long it takes, I'm going all the way through it!" So begins this book about books: a perfect introduction to organization. In his lively, rhyming text, Burleigh teaches readers that a book's pages swing open, smell good, take you to new and wonderful places, and finally come to an end. This is *the* book to use to help students understand how books are organized and how they open doors to worlds.

Old Henry

Joan W. Blos
Mulberry Books, 1987

You can't miss with this picture book. Old Henry doesn't keep his yard or house neat, opting to feed the birds and read instead. The neighbors give him a very bad time—so bad, in fact, Old Henry is forced to move away. At the end of the book, however, he writes the mayor, agreeing to care for the property if he is allowed to return. The reader is left with Old Henry's letter on the book's last page, a logical point for students to write their own responses to Henry, either inviting him back or telling him to stay away. This book is excellent for showing how the choice of ending influences the way readers understand the story's main idea.

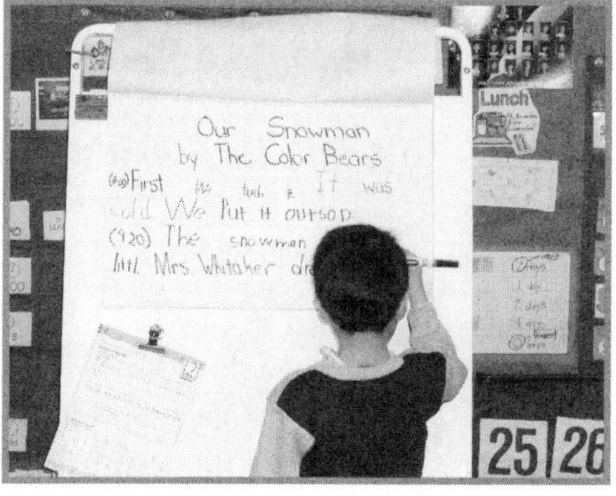

The Paperboy

Dav Pilkey
Orchard Books, 1996

The paperboy wakes while it is still dark, puts on his shoes, and goes to work. At the end of his route, he crawls back into the warmth of his bed, just as the rest of the world is waking up. Following a simple, chronological order that students will easily grasp, this award-winning picture book is a stellar example of good organization.

It is fun to build a snowman. First I made a large snoball, a medium snowball and made a small snowball. Then put the large snowball on the bottom, then stacked the medium snowball, then stacked the small snowball on. Next I put a carrot for the nose, and for eyes and the muoth I used rocks. finaly I put on a scarve for his neck, stick for his arms., button for his tummy and hat. My snowman is the best.

Raymond Briggs's *The Snowman* motivated students to write how-to pieces on building a snowman.

The Snowman

Raymond Briggs
Random House, 1978

This carefully sequenced story of a young boy who goes on a magical adventure with his snowman friend is not only a children's classic but an excellent example of organization. A wordless picture book, the piece unfolds logically through the detailed illustrations. The book is available on video with a wonderful musical soundtrack that creates a memorable story experience for children of all ages. Share the book and video with your students and have them create how-to pieces on building snowmen, like the one on the previous page.

Subway Sparrow

Leyla Torres
Farrar, Straus and Giroux, 1993

An English-speaking girl, a Spanish-speaking man, and a Polish-speaking woman have a hard time understanding one another on the subway as they seek to free a trapped sparrow. One at a time, they try different ways to capture the bird. Finally, they work together to find a solution. They cover and catch the bird with a beautiful scarf and take it off the car to the subway's exit. This is a sweet, sweet book with a smooth pace from beginning to end.

What's Up, What's Down

Lola M. Schaefer
Greenwillow Books, 2002

Divided into two parts, this book asks, "What's up?" from the perspective of a mole under the earth who looks at roots, grass, trees and, finally, open sky, and, "What's down?" from a perspective that starts above the planet and ends at the ocean floor. The organization of this book is simple yet logical, making it easy for students to create their own *What's Up, What's Down* books.

Final Reflections on the Organization Trait

Organizing a piece of writing requires some head scratching, but the payoff is great. Encouraging students to write often, pay close attention to models, and try many different techniques will increase their ability to organize their writing. And that's a worthy goal for us, their writing teachers. Don't be afraid to tackle this trait with creativity.

Expect students to organize their ideas with an eye toward style and clarity, but leave the door open for some surprises along the way. In other words, keep in mind the sage advice of author and teacher Tom Romano: "Form should be a voice giver; not a voice taker" (p. 59), which leads us to the next chapter, "Sparking Voice."

My First Scoring Guide for *Organization*

I've Got It!

- I have a bold beginning, mighty middle, and excellent ending.
- My details are in the right places.
- My ideas are in an order that really works.

On My Way

- I've made a good attempt at a beginning, middle, and ending.
- Most of my details fit.
- The order of my ideas makes sense.

Just Starting

- My writing doesn't have a clear beginning, middle, or ending.
- My details are jumbled and confusing.
- I have "stuff" on paper, but it's not in order.

Share this student-friendly scoring guide with students when they are ready to assess their own and their classmates' writing for organization.

CHAPTER 5

Sparking Voice

A. J., the seven-year-old son of my good friend Bridey, has a vivid imagination. After dinner recently, he announced that he was going upstairs to his room to write a story about his mom. Half an hour later he emerged, waving his piece. "Here you go, Mom," he said. "You've always wanted to meet George Clooney. So I wrote this story for you." Bridey and I giggled together as we read what A. J. wrote.

The Girl

Wonce upun a time
a Girl named Bridey
Was Walking to the coffie
shop. of corse she
got a moca molt frapach
no. So she went to
go set down at a tabl
Then she saw Gorge
cloony.
lattar she rote
a secret Love
letter. Gorge
Dident no hoe It
was from

Sind ?

because all It said Was
Sind ? Gorg Was cenfuse
latter Bridey went
shoping for an new
dres. The she went to
his hose and asket to
go out on a Date.
he said yes.
She was happy!

So they wenon a Date!
And they lived happil
efer after! ♡

There is a strong connection between A. J.'s confidence in writing and his voice in writing, as proven by this piece, "The Girl."

What is the source of such energy and originality? Obviously, A. J. has listened carefully as his single mom has shared with friends how perfect life would be if she could only meet George Clooney. That idea had been running around in his active mind for several years, and on this particular evening, for no reason other than a sheer desire to write, A. J. decided to put it down. The result is more than satisfactory; it is evidence that A. J. is a highly skilled writer. He uses writing not only to succeed in school assignments but to make sense of the world, to capture his thoughts, and to connect with his mom on a very sweet, personal level.

Writing is a priority in A. J.'s second-grade classroom. His teacher, Chris Poulsen, offers diverse and open-ended writing tasks that demand thinking. On any given day you're likely to see students talking, drawing, and writing to create stories, informational pieces, and journal entries.

Recently, Chris put a piece of candy on everyone's desk and told students to write a persuasive piece to convince her and the rest of the class why they deserve to eat the candy. As students wrote and then read their papers aloud, she asked the class to rank how persuasive each one was on a scale of 1 to 10. She told the class, "Whoever gets a 10 may eat the candy first."

> *"Who can confidently say what ignites a certain combination of words, causing them to explode in the mind? Who knows why certain notes in music are capable of stirring the listener deeply, though the same notes slightly rearranged are impotent? These are high mysteries."*
>
> —E. B. White

The amount of energy these students put into their writing was amazing. Their arguments were sound and often hilarious. One student wrote, "I should get to eat my candy because I will need the energy when I get home to mow the lawn, rake the leaves, walk the dog, feed the cat, change the fish water, play with the hamster, and listen to my little brother yell until he gets what he wants." Needless to say, he was among the first to eat the candy. In time, all of Chris's students learned to write persuasively. They also learned a valuable lesson about writing with voice.

Because A. J. writes every day, he doesn't see it as an isolated activity and applies what he knows about writing to nonwriting situations. For example, I have witnessed him practicing his persuasion skills on his mom by trying to talk her into letting him stay up later, play catch, or get pizza for dinner. Indeed, A. J. uses his most convincing voice to get his way.

A. J.'s brother Dominic, who is in fourth grade, isn't so lucky. In his class, thinking is not encouraged. Topics are handed out. There is no fun. Dominic talks about writing as a chore to be crossed off the list: "We're doing a narrative. The next paper is an expository." Yawn. It rarely occurs to Dominic to write outside of class for any reason. Sadly, when Dominic does write, his pieces lack the luster and energy of his brother's. His work is mechanical, voiceless.

Sometimes teachers tell me that they don't quite understand the voice trait. They think it is "touchy-feely" and, therefore, hard to assess and teach. But I've found that the opposite is true for students. When I ask even primary students which trait is their favorite, hands down it is voice. Some first graders described voice in the following ways:

- Voice: I think it means like extrodarary. Fabulus. Amazing.
- The voice means icsbresibing [expressing] your voice And shoinge your felings.
- Voice means when you feel like you got to shout it out.
- Voice is like my solo its my time to shine.
- Voice means to me that you can soooooooooooo much hear the other person's voice in the writing.

Every student comes to school with voice. Their voices may vary tremendously, from quite forceful to quite delicate, but all students have them. And some students—lucky ones—are aware of the extent to which voice in writing influences readers because of books that have been read to them. Their favorite authors have touched them through humor, sadness, anger, and other emotions. Reading has set the stage for their understanding the importance of addressing an audience. So take comfort in knowing that an awareness of voice is in all our students to varying degrees. Our job is to draw out that awareness—draw out their voices—through high-quality assessment and our teaching. That's what this chapter is all about.

> *"Voice is the quality, more than any other, that allows us to recognize exceptional potential in a beginning writer; voice is the quality, more than any other, that allows us to recognize excellent writing."*
>
> *—Donald Murray*

Voice: A Definition for Primary Students

Sparkling, confident, unquestionably individual. These are words that describe a piece of writing with voice. Voice is the writer's passion for the topic coming through loud and clear. It's what keeps us turning the pages of a story long after bedtime. It's what makes an essay about camels fascinating, even though we didn't think we cared all that much about camels. Voice is what primary writers use to assert their own way of looking at an idea. You'll find it in scribbles, in their letter strings, in their sentences, and in their continuous text. Voice can permeate writing, regardless of where the writer falls on the developmental continuum. Primary writers are well on their way to applying voice when they

- have something important to say.
- create drawings that are expressive.
- find new ways of expressing familiar ideas.
- capture a range of emotions, from gleeful to poignant to frightened.
- offer sincere thoughts.
- are confident that what they say matters.
- demonstrate awareness of an audience.
- are willing to take a risk and try something that no classmate has tried before.
- apply original thinking.

The Challenge of Teaching Voice

Too many of us confuse voice with personality. Voice is not personality. Voice is the writer's ability to express personality in language, for a particular purpose and audience. There is a difference.

Writers have many voices and they learn to summon the right one to suit the purpose of a piece of writing. For instance, if a young writer is telling a lively, imaginative story, she might use a "creative," "lighthearted," or "entertaining" voice. If the same student writes a piece about the properties of water, she might use an "authoritative" or "knowledgeable" voice. Same child, different purpose, and therefore different voice. So when we assess a paper for voice, we are definitely not assessing the student's personality. We are assessing her ability to bring the topic to life through the use of a carefully chosen, one-of-a-kind, can't-be-duplicated language that helps her achieve the purpose for the writing.

Furthermore, primary writers who know their audience fine-tune their voice accordingly. A. J., for example, used a voice that he probably wouldn't use in a letter to the custodian to request the repair of a wobbly desk. Writers learn to ask, "Who is the audience for this piece?" The answer helps them find a voice that will bring the piece to life for the reader.

Donald Murray (1996) tells us, "It is the voice that attracts us to the story and makes us believe or not believe it. Voice is the magic that is hard to describe, but it is the most important element in the story, the music that supports and holds the story together" (p. 91). I couldn't agree more. Voice is a complex quality of writing, difficult to describe and, therefore, difficult to teach. However, voice is the driving force behind effective writing, so the sooner we introduce it to students, the better.

Assessing Student Work for Voice

The Primary Scoring Guide on page 140 helps us describe how primary writers bring voice to their writing. Use it to assess individual pieces of writing, as follows:

STEP 1: Collect student papers you want to assess for voice.

STEP 2: Photocopy the Primary Scoring Guide: Voice since you'll want to write on it and highlight key words as you go.

STEP 3: Read the scoring guide's descriptors for each of the five levels, from top—5: Established—to bottom—1: Ready to Begin. Each descriptor shows how writing typically reveals itself at that level. Also, notice that the descriptors parallel one another from level to level. For example, the first descriptor for each level deals with the extent to which the writer "owns" the topic.

STEP 4: Read one of the student papers carefully, paying attention to everything on the page, both pictures and text.

STEP 5: Look at the first descriptor for each level and determine the one that most closely matches the paper. Work your way through the rest of the descriptors for each level, checking off the appropriate ones. Each level has a point value; average the total to determine the piece's overall score in voice. The process will get easier, faster, and more accurate as you practice.

Ready to move to the grades-3-and-up scoring guide!

The Primary Scoring Guide

Voice

Established 5	___ The writer "owns" the topic. ___ The piece contains the writer's imprint. ___ The writer is mindful of the piece's audience and connects purposefully with the reader.	___ The tone is identifiable–bittersweet, compassionate, frustrated, terrified, and so on. ___ The writer takes real risks, creating a truly individual piece of writing.
Extending 4	___ The writer takes a standard topic and addresses it in a nonstandard way. ___ The writer tries a new word, interesting image, or unusual detail. ___ The writing speaks to the reader in several places.	___ The writing captures a general mood such as happy, sad, or mad. ___ The writer begins to show how he or she really thinks and feels about the topic.
Expanding 3	___ There are fleeting glimpses of how the writer looks at the topic. ___ Touches of originality are found in the text and pictures. ___ There is a moment of audience awareness, but then it fades.	___ BIG letters, exclamation points, underlining, repetition, and pictures are used for emphasis. ___ A pat summary statement conceals the writer's individuality.
Exploring 2	___ The piece is a routine response to the assignment. ___ The writer copies environmental text but also adds an original bit. ___ The text connects with the reader in the most general way.	___ The drawings begin to reveal the individual. ___ The barest hint of the writer is in evidence.
Ready to Begin 1	___ The reader is not sure why the writer chose this idea for writing. ___ The writer tries to copy without purpose what he or she sees around the room.	___ No awareness of audience is evident. ___ The piece contains very simple drawings or lines. ___ Nothing distinguishes the work to make it the writer's own.

Sample Papers to Assess for Voice

Here are five papers that illustrate different performance levels in voice. Review the scoring guide on page 140, read each student paper closely, read my descriptor-by-descriptor evaluation of the piece, and see what you think. Do you agree with my assessment of each writer's work? Do these pieces reflect the kind of work you see in your classroom?

You can also practice scoring for voice using your students' papers. Keep your eyes open for remarkable moments in even a writer's earliest work. Many students have voice before they demonstrate skills in other traits.

If you wish, go back to the scoring guides in Chapters 3 and 4 and score these pieces for ideas and organization. (See pages 70 and 104.) By scoring multiple traits at once, you build a profile of students' strengths and weaknesses, which can be invaluable in planning your work.

PAPER #1
"ALPHABET SEMICIRCLE"

Time to Assess

Paper #1
"Alphabet Semicircle"

This piece has no voice. The alphabet follows the circle, but why? This piece shows some strength in organization because the letters run in sequence and fit inside the circle, but the voice has yet to show itself. The paper receives the lowest score, 1: Ready to Begin.

- The reader is not sure why the writer chose this idea for writing.

  Without a doubt, there is an idea behind this set of alphabet letters and the quartered circle. But without the writer to explain it, the reader can't decipher it.

- The writer tries to copy without purpose what he or she sees around the room.

  The writer presents two very common things, the alphabet and a circle. No original thinking here. This writer is on the verge of doing something original but isn't there yet.

- No awareness of audience is evident.

  The writer shows no understanding of what the reader needs to know to make sense of this piece.

- The piece contains very simple drawings or lines.

  The drawing is clear, but not detailed enough for the reader to feel anything. With more detail, the reader would make a stronger connection to the writer's idea and purpose for writing.

- Nothing distinguishes the work to make it the writer's own.

  Alphabet, circle, lines—most students can create these. There is nothing here that distinguishes this student from others.

Paper #2
"JacobH Helps me"

Time to Assess

PAPER #2
"JACOBH HELPS ME"

The writer of this piece communicates a sincere thought, "Jacob helps me." Without elaborating, he clearly attempts to write with feeling. The reader gets a glimpse into an important relationship in this student's life. This piece receives a 2: Exploring in voice.

- The piece is a routine response to the assignment.

  It's possible this writer was given a prompt, such as "Write about a person who cares about you" or "Tell about an influential person in your life," and the writer responded with "Jacob helps me." Nice, but even if the writer came up with the idea without being prompted, he does not achieve a distinct voice.

- The writer copies environmental text but also adds an original bit.

  The writer may be answering the simple question "Who helps you?" The answer, "Jacob," is the individual response.

- The text connects with the reader in the most general way.

  This is a straightforward statement with no elaboration whatsoever.

- The drawings begin to reveal the individual.

  The characters pictured are probably Jacob and the writer. However, the writer gives no clues to confirm this. They are outlines of rather generic-looking people.

- The barest hint of the writer is in evidence.

  This piece connects the author and Jacob with one honest statement. To hear his voice, we need details, elaboration, examples, and precise word choice.

Paper #3
"Wah-hoo"

Name____________________________

Wah-hoo I made it I mad it to Sacent grade.

At first I was shy but after a wile I got yost to it

Time to Assess

PAPER #3
"WAH-HOO"

Excited to leave first grade and head for second, this student gives us an exclamation followed by a clear message, using repetition for emphasis. Then she tells us a little about herself. I give her paper a 3: Expanding in voice. It's easy to feel this writer's joy.

- There are fleeting glimpses of how the writer looks at the topic.

  The writer expresses her happiness about moving on to second grade, but the text is short. It's truly a glimpse.

- Touches of originality are found in the text and pictures.

  The beginning, "Wah-hoo," is a standout moment. It gives the writing life.

- There is a moment of audience awareness, but then it fades.

  Stronger at the beginning than at the end, this piece does not sustain the voice. In the last sentence, the writer explains that she was shy and now is used to "it." What does that mean? She's used to school? Being shy? The reader is not sure but knows a change has taken place.

- BIG letters, exclamation points, underlining, repetition, and pictures are used for emphasis.

  The repetition of the phrase "I made it" calls attention to the point that the writer is moving on to second grade.

- A pat summary statement conceals the writer's individuality.

  "I got yost to it" is a missed opportunity for more voice. If the writer reads the piece later, perhaps she will add details so that it ends with as much voice as it begins with.

PAPER #4

"I FEEL SAD"

I feel sad when my dad has to leave. When my dad has to leave I cry with lonely tears. my face gets wet and I frown. ~~and~~ I yell because I miss my dad so much that I want to stay with him.

Time to Assess

PAPER #4
"I FEEL SAD"

The genuine emotion this writer feels about being separated from her father touches me deeply. Her voice becomes strong as she moves from the telling statement "I feel sad when my dad has to leave" to the showing statement "I cry with lonely tears." This piece receives a 4: Extending in voice.

- The writer takes a standard topic and addresses it in a nonstandard way.

  Being separated from an important family member is a topic that lends itself to strong voice. This writer expresses a range of emotions.

- The writer tries a new word, interesting image, or unusual detail.

  The phrase "lonely tears" conjures a powerful image.

- The writing speaks to the reader in several places.

  "I cry with lonely tears. My face gets wet and I frown. I yell because I miss my dad so much that I want to stay with him." The middle of the piece is extraordinary, although the end is not.

- The writing captures a general mood, such as happy, sad, or mad.

  There is such a sweet sadness to this piece. The father and daughter clearly have a positive relationship; most readers hate the fact that the two must separate.

- The writer begins to show how he or she really thinks and feels about the topic.

  There is little question that this writer has a strong attachment to her father and misses him deeply. This piece is honest and communicates real feelings.

PAPER #5
"OCEAN"

~~powam~~ poem   My Choice | Ocean ~~[illegible]~~ ME! → topic

"Do you know who my best friend was before the water went away?" "Well, you would think that my friend was human, but rally he was... the Ocean when ever I have a drink of water I can always hear him blowing big waves, And whenever I take a bath I can always see his face, But, when I dram I can always see his blue and wavey heart waving like the waves, but I'm all alone now that the water went away but whenever It rains I can always hear him say "You're always in my heart, You're always in my heart!"

Time to Assess

PAPER #5
"OCEAN"

Oh, yes! This writer captures our attention right away by telling us his best friend is the water, but the water has gone away. From beginning to end, this piece is strong in voice. It unquestionably deserves the highest score, 5: Established.

- The writer "owns" the topic.

  The writer uses what he knows about water to bring his unique perspective to the piece. His comfort level with the topic reveals itself from the first line.

- The piece contains the writer's imprint.

  We may not know this young writer personally, but we know him through his ideas, his organization, and most particularly his voice. I'm sure his lucky teacher didn't even have to check the name on the paper—this writer's voice screams it.

- The writer is mindful of the piece's audience and connects purposefully with the reader.

  The references to things we all understand—friends, big waves, baths, rain, and so on—help the reader to connect. Each of these things is described uniquely, showing the writer cares that the reader "gets it."

- The tone is identifiable–bittersweet, compassionate, frustrated, terrified, and so on.

  Imaginative with touches of whimsy and melancholy, this piece is memorable long after one reads it. The tone lingers in the reader's mind and heart.

- The writer takes real risks, creating a truly individual piece of writing.

  Writing about a friend is fine, but choosing the water as the friend and using sensory details creates layers of meaning.

I've found that when it comes to voice, sometimes teachers give more credit to students than they deserve. They don't want to give a piece a 1 in any trait, but especially voice because it feels negative, like an attack on the student's character. Objectivity, however, is what makes the assessment work for students. How else will they know where their work stands? Think of it as a "1 and a hug." When you assign a score of 1 you are saying, "Thanks for getting this down. Good for you for getting started. Now where do you want to go from here?" And when students get high scores that pinpoint strengths, they learn what is working well so they can repeat it in the future.

One of the simplest checks for voice is to gauge how eager writers are to share. Do they enthusiastically ask you to read their work? Do they volunteer to read it to the class? If so, chances are the voice is strong. When students feel the power that the voice brings to their writing, they can't wait to share. It's an early sign that all is well.

Conference Comments

Here's what you may say to primary students to support signs of voice in their writing.

- I have never thought of it this way. Your voice is really coming through here.
- No question that you are the author of this piece. It sounds like you.
- I bet your mom really enjoyed this letter. I can tell it was meant for no one else but her.
- I want to keep reading because I'm so interested.
- What an unusual description of your dog. In all my years of teaching, I've never seen one quite like it.
- How would your story change if the principal was going to read it?
- There's so much energy in your writing.
- I had no idea you were this interested in garage door openers. Now I'm interested too.
- If you had to pick one word to describe the way your writing sounds, what would it be? Fun? Serious? Lively? Thoughtful? Knowledgeable? Silly?

Teaching With the Voice Trait

Making students aware of voice couldn't be easier or more rewarding. When students are excited about an upcoming event, frustrated by a difficult task, or curious about an unfamiliar topic, point out that their voice is showing. A simple comment such as "I can tell from all the pictures you've drawn of sea animals that you are looking forward to going to the aquarium" goes a long way toward confirming that students have what it takes to write with voice. When students realize that voice is a quality they don't have to learn as much as discover and use, they enthusiastically embrace it.

For students to apply voice well in writing, they must see themselves as individuals and understand that their ideas and feelings are their own. Donald Graves (1994) is emphatic about the importance of teaching voice to our young writers: "To ignore voice is to present the [writing] process as a lifeless, mechanical act . . . Voice is the imprint of ourselves in our writing. It is that part of the self that pushes the writing ahead, the dynamo in the process" (p. 227).

You know voice is working when it jumps off the page with energy and credibility, shouting: "Look at me, I'm writing about what I know and care about." And you know it when you connect to the writer: "That piece sounds so much like Carlos. I would recognize his voice anywhere."

When teaching the lessons and activities that follow, keep in mind these general considerations:

- Validate signs of voice in students' early works: drawings with color and detail, drawings of faces with expressions, action verbs, vivid descriptions, language that is appropriate to the writer's purpose and audience, and so on.
- Demonstrate how voice makes a difference. Read aloud in a monotone and an expressive voice. Compare the readings and discuss the implications for writing.
- Ask students to describe the voices in a variety of books. Tune up their ears and eyes to the voice trait.
- Help students see how voice is present in their everyday lives. Show them examples of how voice is expressed in pictures, signs, and speech. Model how you use voice in your own speaking and writing.
- Draw heavily on the arts. You'll find great examples of distinctive voices in paintings, songs, poems, and plays.

- Encourage students to take risks when they write. Reward them generously for not writing the easy statement ("I like my dog") but reaching for the vivid ("My dog is gi-normous and slobbery"). And the same holds true for drawing: "It would've been easy to draw the house with a door and two windows, but you created something brand new. Maybe you'll be an architect someday!"
- Introduce the trait by teaching students "The Voice Song." Its tune is familiar and the lyrics easy to learn. Sing it as students draw and write. Post this song with the other trait songs students have learned. (See pages 83, 118, 188, 224, 264, and 291.) Use the songs to remind students of the key qualities of the traits.

The Voice Song

(sung to the tune of "If You're Happy and You Know It")

If you're happy and you know it, that's your voice.
If you're thoughtful and you know it, that's your voice.
If you're spunky and you know it,
then your words will surely show it.
If you're happy and you know it, that's your voice.

- Use the student-friendly guide on page 169. When students are ready, give them photocopies of the guide, discuss the descriptors at each level, and have them assess their own and their classmates' writing.
- Have students paint pictures of themselves and then draw their attention to the similarities and differences in their representations. (See samples on page 155.) Giving students chances to draw as well as write provides more opportunities for them to use voice. Indeed, successful artists often paint the same scene many, many times, always looking for the image that will connect most directly with the viewer, the one true voice. So be sure to give primary writers many outlets for expression.

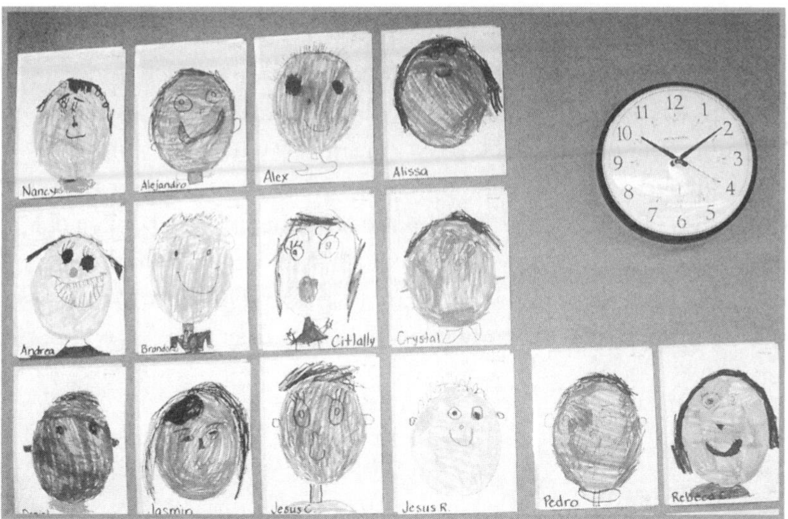

Kindergarten students draw self-portraits to express their individuality.

On the following pages, I share some of my favorite voice lessons and activities organized into the following categories:

1. Finding Voice
2. Matching Voice to Purpose
3. Discovering New Voices

Over time, you'll probably want to add your own activities as you think about what your students know and need to know, and as you discover their passions.

Finding Voice

Primary students may not have any idea how well they can express themselves until they are given opportunities to do so. Whether they are quiet or boisterous, all students have a voice that deserves to be heard. Helping students gain the confidence to be expressive on paper requires providing them with opportunities to find their voices. The following lesson and activities will help.

Tips for Students Working on Voice

- Make your writing sound like you.
- Show that you really care about your idea.
- Write with energy and enthusiasm.
- Write with your reader in mind.
- Take risks; make your writing memorable.

FOCUS LESSON

ALL-AMERICAN VOICE

There is such beautiful diversity in America. In this lesson, students listen to the book *I Am America* by Charles R. Smith, Jr. (2003), and write about the similarities and differences they share in the way they look, feel, and express themselves. *I Am America* is a stunning picture book, a collection of all things American, expressed in the voices of children: "I am diverse, soft-spoken, and loud." "I am my grandfather's dimples framing my grin." "I am a new branch sprouting in my majestic family tree." Together they paint a vivid portrait of our nation.

MATERIALS:

- a copy of *I Am America*
- paper, pencils, pens, and markers

WHAT TO DO:

1. Read *I Am America* to students and discuss how the author honors the diversity of American children by sharing what they wear, what they eat, where they live, what religions they practice, and so on.
2. Ask students to think about what makes them special as Americans or as people who live in America. Ask them to think about their hobbies, pets, favorite music, regions, birthplaces, and so on. Within these categories, ask students to list specific examples. For instance, within the category of hobbies, students may list drawing, building models, playing sports, cooking, or growing vegetables.
3. Ask students to create an "I Am" statement using one example from each of their categories, such as "I am the cook who makes dinner for my mom," or "I am the model-car builder who races against my friends."
4. For each "I Am" statement, ask students to create a colorful drawing, using the statement itself as a caption. Clip all drawings to a string and hang them across the classroom.

FOLLOW-UP:

Invite other classes to create their own "I Am America" pictures with captions. Display the pictures proudly in your school's common areas, such as the cafeteria and media center.

Ask students to listen to the audiotape or CD of *Free to Be . . . You and Me* by Marlo Thomas and friends, first released in 1972 and rereleased in 1990. The songs are lively and reinforce the importance of being yourself and finding your own voice. Buy the book by the same title for the lyrics to the songs. Have sing-alongs to help students learn about being healthy, happy individuals.

> *"The best shot writers have to attain voice begins with information that absorbs them."*
>
> —Tom Romano

Other Activities for Finding Voice

Puppet Voice

Give students a selection of simple sock puppets. Create a stage for puppet shows from cardboard, tall enough for students to hide behind. Read a favorite book with dialogue and ask students to create a puppet show based on that story or a scene from the story. My favorites for this activity are *The Web Files* by Margie Palatini (2001), *Bullfrog Pops* by Rick Walton (1999), and the all-time winner, *Walter the Farting Dog* by William Kotzwinkle (2001). Students will have a good time creating the "just right" voice for each of the characters.

Voice of the Minute

Make a list of possible "mood voices"—amused, scared, silly, angry, whiny, sad, frustrated, tired, and so on—and write each one on a big card that can be seen from anywhere in the room. Hold up the "whiny" card, for example, and ask students to talk to a neighbor using a whiny voice. Once they have it down, tell students to continue talking in that voice for the next five minutes. When time is up, ring a bell, and hold up a different voice card. Rotate through at least five cards and then discuss with students what was hard about using one voice at a time. Help them to understand that writers switch voices as their ideas for writing develop and purposes for writing change.

What Voice Is It?

Give a student a line of text to read, such as "I can't believe I won the lottery!" and a voice descriptor such as *exuberant*. Ask the student to read the line out loud in that voice. Let the other students guess the voice until they come up with it or a synonym for it such as *happy*, *thrilled*, or *excited*. Then select a different student to read a new line, such as "Every time I see the empty dog bowl and water dish, I remember my dog, Charlie," guided by a new descriptor, such as *melancholy*. Continue with new sentences, trying different voices, until everyone has had a turn.

Matching Voice to Purpose

Students need to understand that knowing the purpose for writing is a key to choosing the right voice. When students write thank-you notes to a grandparent, they use a voice that expresses their gratitude, appreciation, and love. However, if the same student writes to a toy company about a robot that broke the first time they played with it, he would most likely use a voice of frustration, disappointment, and even anger. In the lesson and activities that follow, students will have the opportunity to explore the relationship between voice and purpose in writing and discover its importance.

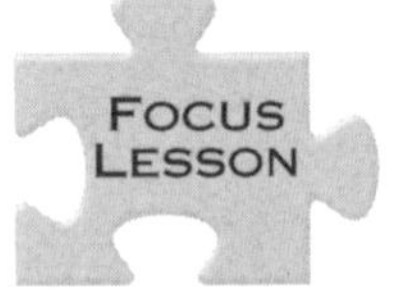

Extreme Voice Makeover

In this lesson, students redesign a residential building's floor plan to receive an important message about writing: choosing the right voice requires understanding one's purpose for writing.

Materials:

- a simple floor plan of a house, apartment, or other residential building. Contact a local architectural firm or contractor to get copies at no cost.
- paper, markers, pencils, crayons

What to Do:

1. Arrange students in groups of three to four. Give each group a copy of a floor plan. Ask each group to find the kitchen, bathroom, bedrooms, living room, laundry room, dining area, and family room.
2. Have each group select a room for an "extreme voice makeover." Tell them to radically change their room's size, shape, window locations, door locations, and so on to make the room more functional. In order to do this, it will be important for them to think about how the room was used—and could be used, given their changes.
3. Have groups draw a picture of what the room looked like before the makeover and after it. Encourage students to emphasize how much the room has changed.
4. Attach their pictures to the floor plans.

5. Ask students to describe the room before and after the makeover. They may say, "The kitchen had no counter space, so we put an island in the middle of it . . . with a built-in cotton candy maker!"

6. Have students write a description of the person they think would use the new room, matching their design decisions to the person's personality.

7. Ask students how redesigning a room to meet a specific purpose is like writing to meet a specific purpose. And how does writing to meet a specific purpose relate to the trait of voice? Record their ideas on a chart and discuss them.

Other Activities for Matching Voice to Purpose

Send Me a Letter

As a class, brainstorm a list of letters and notes that people might write and audiences for them. Make a three-column chart like the one below, listing all types of letters and notes in the first column. In the second column, list the primary audiences for each of those types. Then, write a list of voices on the board and ask students to help you match the right voice to each type of letter or note. Write the voice in the chart's third column. Discuss why some voices are only appropriate in certain circumstances.

When students finish helping you fill out this chart, ask them to think of someone they would like to write to, give them time to write a note or letter to that person, help them prepare the envelope, and mail it. Encourage students to include pictures to make their voices sing out.

Type of Letter or Note	Audience	Voice
a thank-you note	a relative	sweet, grateful
a note in class	a friend	funny, personal
a letter of excuse	a teacher	convincing, believable
a letter of application	an acceptance committee	sincere, honest
a letter of complaint	a toy company	frustrated, angry
a note of invitation	a friend	nice, welcoming
a letter to compliment	a local restaurant	kind, appreciative
a fan letter	a celebrity	adoring, flattering

What's in a Mode?

Make up cards for each of the following modes of writing with the name on the front and a short definition on the back:

- Narrative: telling a real story
- Descriptive: showing a person, place, or thing in words
- Expository: telling and explaining about something
- Persuasive: convincing someone of an idea or trying to change his or her mind
- Imaginative: telling a made-up story

Brainstorm a topic with students and ask how they would approach it according to the five modes. If the topic is sports, for instance, they may tell a realistic story about a time they played that sport (narrative), explain how to play a sport (descriptive), express what it is like to play that sport (expository), come up with a fantasy about a sport like Quidditch (imaginative), or give a speech to convince the principal to schedule more time for sports in school (persuasive). Write all their ideas on the board or overhead.

Hold up a card, read the name of the mode on the front and its definition on the back. Ask students to match it to the piece they brainstormed. For example, they would match the story about the Quidditch-like game to the imaginative mode. Discuss the voice they would likely use for such a piece: fanciful, entertaining, exciting. Determine the voice for the other pieces mode by mode. Encourage students to pick a topic and write about it, using an appropriate voice.

Write It Up!

Show students examples of signs that remind readers to do things such as turn off the lights, lock the windows, dispose of trash and recyclables, and wash their hands after using the bathroom. Then ask students to write signs for use in the classroom and around the school. Remind students to give their signs voice to capture the attention of the reader.

PLES
PUT
than K
You
BOTEL
TOP'S
IN her

A first grader uses writing to encourage others to recycle.

Discovering New Voices

Once students realize the importance of using voice and finding the right voice to match their purpose for writing, expand the range of voices for them to consider. The lesson and activities that follow get students expressing themselves by trying out voices they may not consider on their own.

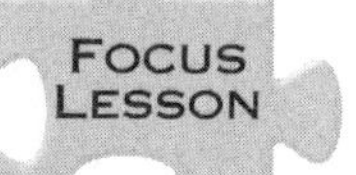

MAGNIFY YOUR VOICE

You can help students discover new voices by exploring their moods. In this fun, hands-on lesson, they assign voices to sentences by creating their own "voice magnifiers."

MATERIALS:

- a list of emotions written on a chart (See box below.)
- reproducible set of emotion faces (See next page.)
- a reproducible picture of a magnifying glass (See page 163.)
- a reproducible list of sentences expressing different emotions from the list on the chart (See page 163.)
- Scissors and tape

WHAT TO DO:

1. For each student, copy onto heavy paper the emotion faces, magnifying glass, and list of sentences.
2. Distribute the emotion faces and ask students to cut them out.
3. Tell students to mix up the order of the emotion faces and lay them out at their work space.
4. Ask students to match each emotion listed on the chart to the corresponding emotion face. For example, students would match the word *annoyed* to the face expressing that emotion.
5. Pass out copies of the magnifying glass and ask students to cut it out, making slits where indicated to hold emotion faces.
6. Give each student a copy of the list of sentences.

Emotions List

Proud
Annoyed
Determined
Excited
Unsure
Lonely
Worried
Frustrated
Tired
Concerned

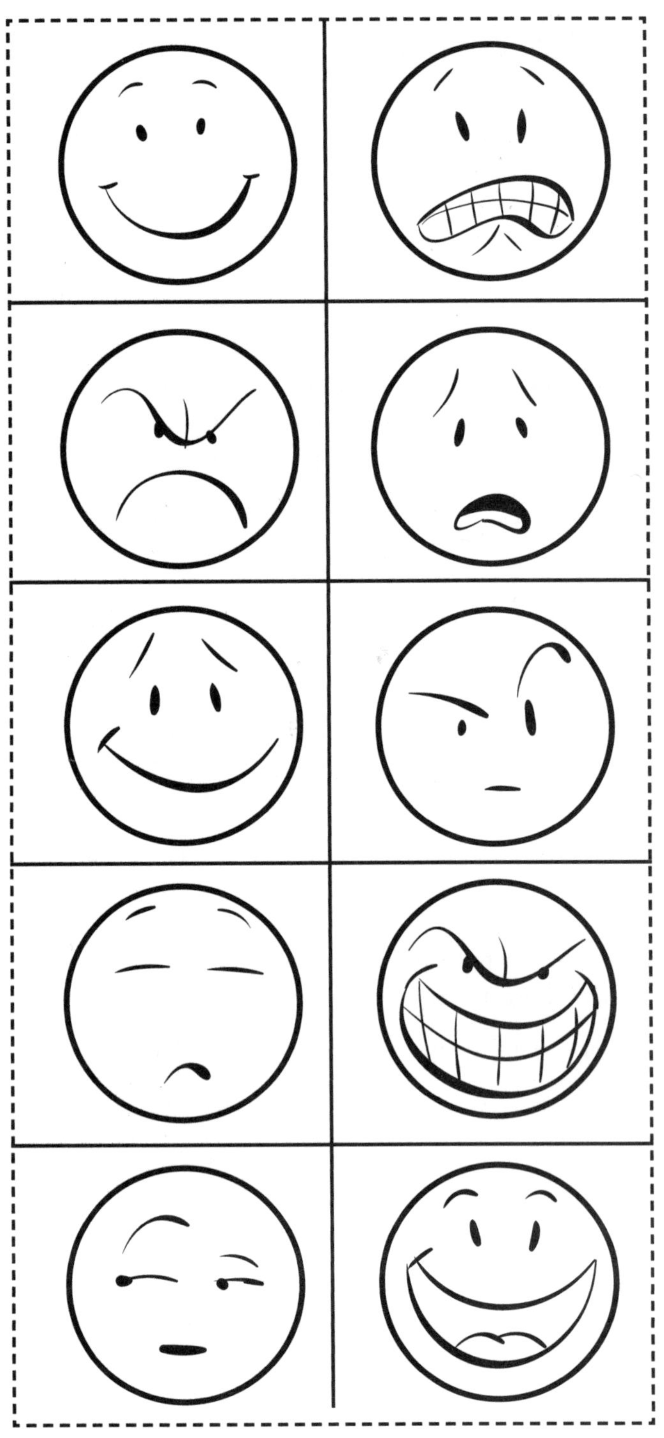

I got picked to read the morning announcements.

My brother is a pain.

I'm going to get this right no matter how long it takes.

I'm having a birthday party.

I'm not certain that's the right way to do that.

I miss my best friend since she moved away.

I really hope I finished my homework correctly.

No matter how I try, I can't draw a horse.

I've been running up and down the field for 20 minutes.

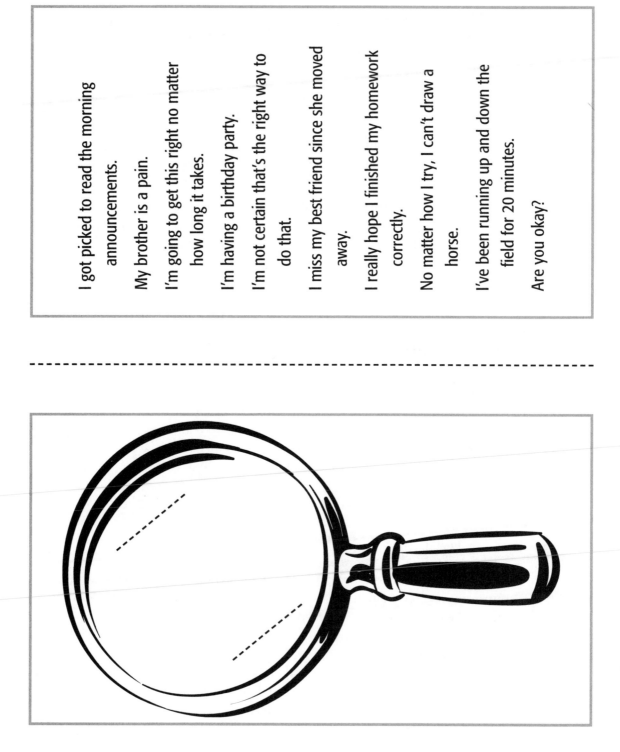

Are you okay?

7. Organize students into pairs. Ask one partner to read the first sentence and the other to select the emotion face that matches that sentence most closely. Once they've made the match, have them slip the face into the magnifying glass and pass the magnifier over the sentence.

8. Challenge pairs to write another sentence in the same voice, passing their magnifier as they read it aloud to one another.

9. Have students continue reading sentences, selecting emotion faces, and writing new sentences until they have completed the list. Discuss sentences that contained more than one emotion.

10. Talk with students about the different voices they discovered in this lesson. Ask them to use their magnifiers on their own writing to help them pinpoint and refine their voice. Ask them to draw the emotion face on their writing that shows the voice they intended readers to hear.

Other Activities for Discovering New Voices

Choices of Voices

On the board or overhead, write a simple statement, such as "Take the garbage out, Norman." As a class, brainstorm people who might use this line, such as sister, mother, or friend. Then ask for volunteers to read the line in the voice of one of those people:

- Sister: bratty
- Mother: firm
- Friend: kind

Discuss with students how voice takes on different qualities, depending on who is speaking and the relationship to the person receiving the message. Connect this idea to the importance of using the right voice in writing.

Music With Voice

Select a child-friendly piece of classical music that tells a story, such as *Peter and the Wolf* by Sergei Prokofiev. Play the piece and ask students to draw what they hear. After students have finished, discuss the story and the different "voices" that came through in the music, such as "playful" as the story begins and "scary" when the wolf enters the scene. Allow time for students to share their drawings and caption them. Other pieces that work well include *Carnival of the Animals* by Camille Saint-Saens or the *Grand Canyon Suite* by Ferde Grofe. You can use contemporary music, too.

Opposites Attract

Create two-card sets with opposite emotions written on them: happy/sad, interesting/boring, silly/serious, relaxed/tense, calm/angry, and so on. Put students into pairs and give each partner one card in the set. Be sure partners do not tell each other what their cards say. Tell students to act out the emotion using as much voice as possible until their partner guesses it. Once partners have determined their pair of emotions, tell them to turn in their cards and pick a new set of emotions to act out. Continue until students have acted out four or five pairs of emotions and then discuss how emotion may affect voice in writing.

Picture Books to Strengthen Voice

There are magnificent fiction and nonfiction pictures books that will inspire primary students to write with voice. Read your favorites to them and discuss each book's voice: its qualities, how authors create it, and how the purpose of the writing influences it. In addition to your favorites, try these favorites of mine.

Alvie Eats Soup

Ross Collins
Scholastic, 2002

Alvie eats soup. Nothing else but soup. While most babies' first words are *dada* or *mama*, Alvie's is *mulligatawny*. When Granny Fanny, a quirky yet famous chef, comes to visit, Alvie's parents are worried about what she will think of Alvie. When the family goes out to dinner, Alvie's parents order one of everything on the menu, hoping to hide Alvie's strange eating habit from Granny Fanny. But Alvie doesn't eat anything—not even soup—and neither does Granny. When the waiter asks her why, she replies, "I only eat peas." Students will delight in Alvie and Granny's shared stubborn streak and eating quirk.

Body Battles

Rita Golden Gelman
Scholastic, 1992

According to its foreword, *Body Battles* is "a blood-and-guts, true-to-life thriller about the battles that go on inside the human body." If you think science can only be written about in a dull, academic tone, read this book. The author captures how the body works in a simple yet compelling voice that leaves readers saying, "Well, I'll be!" "I had no idea," "That's amazing."

Courage

Bernard Waber
Houghton Mifflin, 2002

Courage comes in many forms, as Waber points out in this thoughtful book. In text and pictures he demonstrates simple, everyday acts of courage, such as tasting vegetables before making a face, and bigger acts such as being the first to apologize after an argument. Waber captures many voices—friendly, loving, sad, and gutsy—in this book about acts of determination and bravery.

The Dot

Peter H. Reynolds
Candlewick Press, 2003

Vashti thinks she can't draw. But when she turns in a blank paper, her teacher says she sees a polar bear in a snowstorm. When Vashti sticks a mark on the paper, her teacher accepts it and asks Vashti to sign her name since she is the artist. Slowly, as Vashti's confidence builds, she adds colors and shapes to her pictures, and experiments with design. At the end of the story, a classmate announces that he can't draw. Vashti urges him to sign his name anyway, for he is an artist, too. This book helps young students make their first courageous steps toward voice-filled writing.

Dumpy La Rue

Elizabeth Winthrop
Henry Holt, 2001

Dumpy La Rue is a pig that wants to dance. His family and the other barnyard animals are skeptical, though. But Dumpy convinces them that it's only right for him to follow his passion. In fact, he's so convincing that, by the end of the story, all the characters join in and dance right along with "Dumpy La Rue, the pig who knew what he wanted to do." Students who are a bit anxious about trying new voices in their writing will appreciate this story in which taking a risk pays off.

> *"So why does our writing matter, again? they [students] ask. Because of the spirit, I say. Because of the heart."*
>
> *—Anne Lamott*

Halloween

Jerry Seinfeld
Little, Brown, 2002

You'll laugh out loud when you read Jerry Seinfeld's little memoir about Halloween, and you'll want to share it right away. The book is loaded with voice. Seinfeld tells us that when you are little, everything is "up": "Wait up." Hold up!" "Shut up." "Mom, I'll clean up . . . " "Just let me stay up!" But when you are the parent everything is "down": "Just calm down!" "Slow down!" "Sit down." "Come down here." "Put that down!" "Keep it down in there," and "You're grounded." Seinfeld's perspective on life is one-of-a-kind. And he's made a good living expressing it in a comedic voice. Ask students to name other famous people who have distinctive voices. How might those voices translate into writing?

How Are You Peeling? Foods With Moods

Saxton Freymann and Joost Elffers
Scholastic, 1999

The colorful pages of this book feature photographs of foods with attitudes. Students see an orange that's grumpy, a cantaloupe that's shy, an angry red pepper, and an enthusiastic orange. Who knew food had so many different "voices"? Freymann and Elffers altered these fruits and vegetables so readers can really see how they are feeling. Or would that be "peeling"?

The Little Red Hen (Makes a Pizza)

Philemon Sturges
Dutton Children's Books, 1999

In this lively and fun-loving version of the classic story, the little red hen makes a pizza with no help from friends, even though those friends can't wait to eat it. Check out delightful updated versions of other much-loved stories, such as *The Boy Who Cried Wolf* by Bob Hartman (2002), *Cinder Edna* by Ellen Jackson (1994), and, of course, *The True Story of the 3 Little Pigs!* by Jon Scieszka (1989). Students will enjoy seeing how authors play with voice and may be inspired to try their own hand at updating fairy tales.

Loretta: Ace Pinky Scout

Keith Graves
Scholastic, 2002

Loretta is quite a girl—actually, she's the perfect girl. All of her ancestors were perfect as well, especially Gran. Loretta does her best to be exactly like Gran, perfectly perfect in every way. But on the day Loretta is to earn the final merit badge from the Girl Scouts, the unimaginable happens and her hopes of being perfect vanish. Feeling like a failure, Loretta seeks comfort in a photograph of Gran. From the photograph, Gran reveals that she wasn't perfect either. Loretta learns that being perfect isn't all that it's cracked up to be. It's better to be yourself.

Miss Spider's Tea Party

David Kirk
Scholastic, 1994

Miss Spider wants the neighborhood bugs to stay at her tea party, but they are apprehensive, considering that the spider is their biggest predator. Miss Spider tries to convince them that she only wants to be friends, but her guests leave nonetheless. When Miss Spider invites the bugs to another party, they all decline except for one little moth who was soaked by the rain. When Miss Spider dries him off and sends him on his way, the moth is taken aback by this unexpected act of kindness. He tells all the bugs that they may have misjudged Miss Spider and urges them to give her another chance. This is a sweet story of loneliness and friendship, two themes that students will want to give voice to in their writing.

Final Reflections on the Voice Trait

The voice we seek to develop in student writing sizzles from the get-go. It draws readers in and doesn't let go until the very end. It's honest, unique, real. Helping students realize that they have important things to say is step one. Step two is showing them how to say it so it resonates with the reader.

Encourage young students to find their voices, match voice to purpose, and discover new voices. All students have voice; drawing it out of young writers and celebrating it is one of our most sacred responsibilities.

My First Scoring Guide for *Voice*

I've Got It!

- My writing sounds like me.
- The reader will know I care about this topic.
- I have the right amount of energy in this piece.

On My Way

- My writing is safe. You only get a glimpse of me.
- I have only some interest in this topic.
- My energy level is uneven in this piece.

Just Starting

- I forgot to add what I think and feel in this piece.
- I really don't care at all about this topic.
- I'm bored and it shows.

Share this student-friendly scoring guide with students when they are ready to assess their own and their classmates' writing for voice.

CHAPTER 6

Expanding Word Choice

When my son Sam was three, he loved to go out to eat. Almost every night he'd ask, "Can we go someplace funlicious?" Sam thought restaurants were "fun" and their food "delicious," so he coined his own word. You may not find it in Webster's dictionary, but it captured exactly the message he wanted to convey.

Children use simple, fresh, original language to create meaning. They play with words and sounds to express their ideas. It's as though they are making word soup, adding new ingredients daily, and stopping to taste the result along the way. One funny word might, as it mixes with others, tickle their noses as they catch the scent of the soup. A whiff of the aroma of a sensory word can evoke powerful feelings and emotions. Or the broth may curdle because of horrid word combinations. These young writers are, after all, novices at the business of language, and as they attempt to add interesting words to their word soup, they make mistakes.

Sometimes those mistakes make us smile, as when Sam wrote a story in first grade in which all the characters went to an ice-cream store called "Basket and Robbins." On another occasion, when he was younger, he told me he had been "floored" at day care. I was puzzled until I realized he meant "grounded." Another time I heard him tell a friend, "Mind your own back garden." I think he meant "Mind your own business." This playfulness with words provoked many chuckles throughout his early years and served him well as a tool for writing throughout his life.

It's not uncommon for children to appreciate the power of words. When asked about the word-choice trait, here is what a group of primary students wrote:

- I think word choice is chosing a good word.
- Word Choice is like a menu lots of choices
- Word Choice is exciting words. It is like the sprinkles on ice cream.
- It is a word you thick. You thick ubt a word. You chose a word. Word choice is win you thick ubt word.
- Word Choice is like the movie Mary Poppins because you never know what she is going to say.
- I think that word choice means picking interesting and cool words like scolding, egads, freezing, and protected.
- Wrod choice is Have Good Wrods. Like Good iffrmashin.

Word Choice: A Definition for Primary Students

When we explore word choice in the classroom, we focus on the parts of speech that writers use to convey meaning—the nouns, verbs, adjectives, adverbs, pronouns, contractions, gerunds, and so on. These terms may conjure up chilling moments from high school English class, but word choice is not about grammar. It's about selecting words carefully to craft fluent sentences and create a lasting image in the reader's mind. We know that primary students are well on their way to making wise word choices when they

- play with letters to make words.
- attempt to write words they have heard.
- try new ways of saying things.
- express an interest in the role of different kinds of words (nouns, verbs, adjectives, and so on).
- develop a curiosity about language.
- use the perfect word in the perfect place.
- try sensory words.
- use language with precision.

> *"Artists develop a love for the feel of their tools, the smell and texture of clay, wood, or paint . . . Writers love words. And while some writers get excited over a particular pen or a more powerful word processing program, words remain the most important tool the writer has to work with."*
>
> *—Ralph Fletcher*

Word choice is a delectable trait. You can almost taste words when they are used well, like chocolate chips in ice cream. Choosing words that create a vivid picture in the reader's mind, add punch to the piece, and just plain sound right is the goal for students. This is one of the most pleasurable of traits to work on because students fall in love with language and use it to make their ideas jump off the page.

The Challenge of Teaching Word Choice

For many primary writers, getting down even the simplest words is a chore. And when they do, their sentences are often functional, serviceable, and basic: "The dog is brown." How do you lead the child who writes like that to create word pictures that are more interesting to read? In other words, how do you lead that child to write something more like "My dog looks like chocolate milk"?

There are a number of reasons students may not be able to create word pictures. Perhaps they haven't been read to at home and haven't been exposed to good models, or maybe they haven't been around adults with strong vocabularies who use language with care and precision. English may not be the most familiar language for some students, so finding the right words to express themselves in it is difficult.

Moving students from beige writing to Technicolor writing—writing with accuracy and flair—requires a lot of reading and talking. In a world where much of what students learn comes from video and computers, it's important to make sure they hear a great deal of beautifully crafted language every day. If you make it clear that words matter as you talk and read with students, you will make a difference in how they use words in writing.

Assessing Student Work for Word Choice

The Primary Scoring Guide on page 174 helps us determine the degree to which students are able to choose words wisely. Use it to assess individual pieces of writing, as follows:

STEP 1: Collect student papers you want to assess for word choice.

STEP 2: Photocopy the Primary Scoring Guide: Word Choice since you'll want to write on it and highlight key words as you go.

STEP 3: Read the scoring guide's descriptors for each of the five levels, from top—5: Established—to bottom—1: Ready to Begin. Each descriptor shows how writing typically reveals itself at that level. Also, notice that the descriptors parallel one another from level to level. For example, the first descriptor for each level deals with using everyday words and phrases.

STEP 4: Read one of the student papers carefully, paying attention to everything on the page, both pictures and text.

STEP 5: Look at the first descriptor for each level and determine the one that most closely matches the paper. Work your way through the rest of the descriptors for each level, checking off the appropriate ones. Each level has a point value; average the total to determine the piece's overall score in word choice. The process will get easier, faster, and more accurate as you practice.

Scoring Guide

Ready to move to the grades-3-and-up scoring guide!

The Primary Scoring Guide

Word Choice

Established 5	____ The writer uses everyday words and phrases with a fresh and original spin. ____ The words paint a clear picture in the reader's mind.	____ The writer uses just the right words or phrase. ____ Figurative language works reasonably well. ____ Colorful words are used correctly and with creativity.
Extending 4	____ Descriptive nouns (e.g., Raisin Bran, not cereal) are combined with generic ones. ____ The writer uses an active verb or two.	____ There is very little repetition of words. ____ The writer attempts figurative language. ____ The writer "stretches" by using different types of words.
Expanding 3	____ Some words make sense. ____ The reader begins to see what the writer is describing. ____ One or two words stand out.	____ Occasional misuse of words bogs the reader down. ____ The writer tries out new words.
Exploring 2	____ Conventional letters are present. ____ The letter strings begin to form words. ____ Letter strings can be read as words even though the spacing and spelling isn't correct.	____ Words from the board, displays, or word walls are attempted. ____ A few words can be identified.
Ready to Begin 1	____ Scribbling and random lines mark the page. ____ Imitation letters may be present. ____ There may be random strings of letters across the page.	____ Writer uses his or her name. ____ Few, if any, recognizable words are present.

Sample Papers to Assess for Word Choice

When assessing students' work for word choice, try to focus on the writer's ability to use words well, not on their ability to spell them correctly (which is part of conventions) or their ability to bring voice to them. The papers that follow represent a wide range of skill in the word choice trait. Review the scoring guide on page 174, read each student paper closely, read my descriptor-by-descriptor evaluation of the piece, and see what you think. Do you agree with my assessment of each writer's work? Do these pieces reflect the kind of work you see in your classroom? Use your own students' papers for additional practice.

If you wish, use the scoring guides in Chapter 3, 4, and 5 to score these pieces in ideas, organization, and voice. (See pages 70, 104, and 140.) And score the earlier pieces for word choice to get a sense of how writers are doing across several traits. Zeroing in on areas of strength right along with areas of need is the best way to inform yourself about writing instruction.

Paper #1
"AINMB"

Time to Assess

PAPER #1
"AINMB"

Here is a paper by a writer who is expressing herself with letters, symbols, and pictures but not conventional words. The writer would have to read this piece aloud in order for me to understand it. The descriptors at the 1: Ready to Begin level match this piece in word choice.

- Scribbling and random lines mark the page.

  Letters, lines, and symbols surround a central picture. Conventional words are not present.

- Imitation letters may be present.

  Some recognizable letters are mixed in with nonstandard ones. The reader gets a sense of what the writer intends, but has to guess a lot about the specifics.

- There may be random strings of letters across the page.

  It is impossible for the reader to understand the word or words, "AINMB," at the top of the piece.

- Writer uses his or her name.

  There is no evidence of the writer's name. The writer's distinctive drawing style may reveal who did the piece to the teacher, but it would help to have a name.

- Few, if any, recognizable words are present.

  Only "I", "is", "miss", and "you" are recognizable. The other words need interpretation by the writer to get sorted out.

PAPER #2
"ABEE"

Time to Assess

Paper #2
"ABEE"

At first glance, this piece seems to have no words, just a string of letters. However, when you read it aloud, the words appear almost magically: "A bee is in my garage." Yes! Because the writer has written these words in a string without spacing, however, I would place the piece at the 2: Exploring stage in word choice.

- Conventional letters are present.

  All letters are capitalized in standard form. The reader has no problem reading the letters.

- The letter strings begin to form words.

  No grouping of letters is present. The reader must figure out logical groupings. Reading the letters aloud and putting some together into groups helps reveal this writer's message.

- Letter strings can be read as words even though the spacing and spelling isn't correct.

  Because the letters form good approximations of words, the words shine through when read aloud.

- Words from the board, displays, or word walls are attempted.

  No evidence of words from the classroom environment, such as a name or date, is present.

- A few words can be identified.

  This piece is a series of nonstandard words that form a complete sentence. "A bee is in my garage" is clearly what the writer has written. It lacks sparkle, but it makes sense.

Paper #3
"I SLePe in the LivG room"

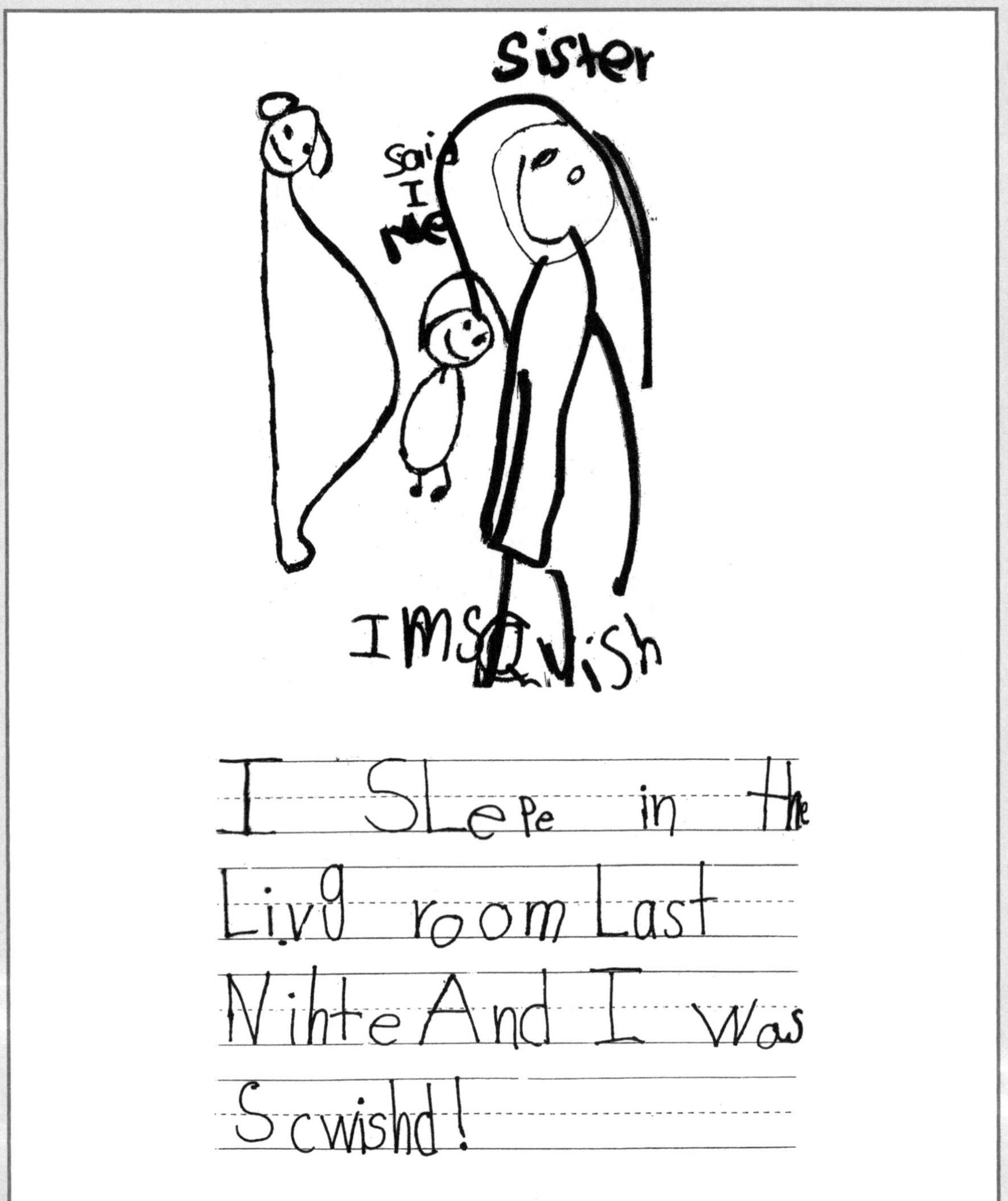

Time to Assess

PAPER #3
"I SLEPE IN THE LIVG ROOM"

The combination of two-sentence text and a supporting picture make this a stellar example of primary writing. The word "Scwishd" brings the piece to life, creating a picture in my mind of what bedtime is like for the writer. This piece scores a 3: Expanding in the word-choice trait.

- Some words make sense.

  The words in the sentences are understandable and mostly written correctly. They make this simple idea clear.

- The reader begins to see what the writer is describing.

  The writer sets the scene for the reader with specific words and phrases: "living room," "last night," "squished." In places, the letters and words overrun the picture, reinforcing the inextricable link between the drawing and writing.

- One or two words stand out.

  "Scwishd" is the perfect word to describe how the writer felt in the living room. It is onomatopoeia in action.

- Occasional misuse of words bogs the reader down.

  This point is not an issue; the words don't hinder the reading. The word choice is working just fine.

- The writer tries out new words.

  There's no way to know if "Scwishd" is a new word for the writer, but it's certainly a deliberate choice that works well.

Paper #4
"Recy-cle"

1.

recy cle

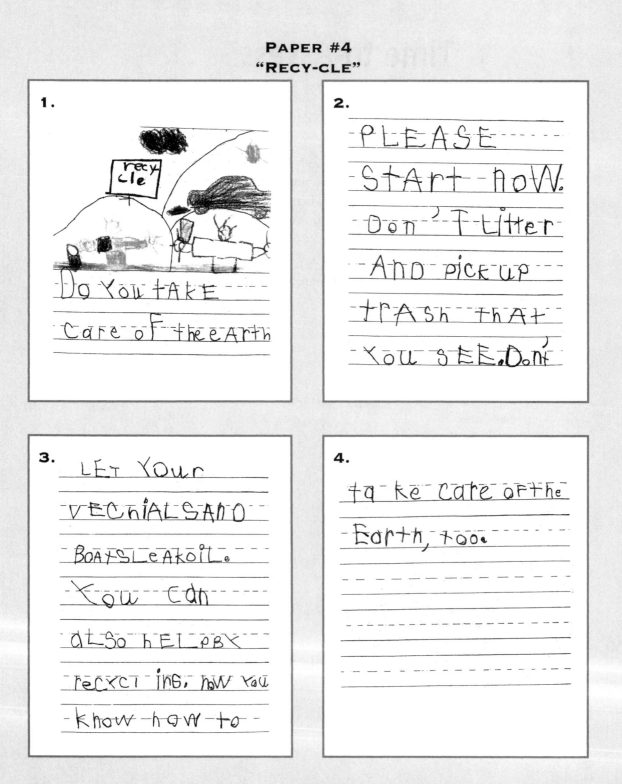

Do You tAKE care of the eArth

2.

PLEASE Start now. Don't Litter AnD pick up trASh thAt You SEE. Don't

3.

LET Your VEChiALS AnD BOAtS LEAK oiL. You can aLSo hELp BY recYcling. now You know how to

4.

ta ke care of the Earth, too.

Time to Assess

Paper #4
"Recy-cle"

In this fine essay on recycling, the writer demonstrates how to be deliberate about one's choice of words. I especially appreciate the words that are germane to the topic, such as "litter," "vEChiALS" (vehicles), and "leAkoiL" (leak oil). This piece rates a 4: Extending in word choice.

- Descriptive nouns (e.g., Raisin Bran, not cereal) are combined with generic ones.

  "Litter," "trash," "vEChiALSAnD BoAts," and "recycle," are descriptive. Generic words, such as "you" and "Earth," are present too.

- The writer uses an active verb or two.

  "Start," "pick up," "leak," and "take care" add energy to the writing. It's refreshing to see this writer using effective verbs.

- There is very little repetition of words.

  The writer does not repeat himself. Instead, he uses different words from start to finish.

- The writer attempts figurative language.

  There is no evidence of figurative language. The use of vocabulary that is specific to the topic, however, is noteworthy.

- The writer "stretches" by using different types of words.

  The deliberate use of words that fit the topic demonstrates this writer's skill. He chooses "just right" words to make the idea clear.

Paper #5
"Dear___"

Dear

your a wonderfal teacher your like
a flower bloming in spreg.
and wene its raning.
you give selter for
a btterfly.
And chiden
yor btefal.
And you are.

Time to Assess

PAPER #5

"DEAR____"

This young writer uses conventionally poetic language to describe this teacher's kind and caring qualities. It's a true tribute. Every good teacher deserves a letter like this. This piece receives a 5: Established for word choice.

- The writer uses everyday words and phrases with a fresh and original spin.

  The phrases, "you're a wonderful teacher," and "yor bteful" are tucked in with the more visual phrases such as "your like a flower bloming in spreg," and "you give selter for a btter fly. And chidren." Nice.

- The words paint a clear picture in the reader's mind.

  Teachers are people who provide shelter; they are like flowers that bloom in the spring. Both images work well to describe a teacher who makes a huge impact on students.

- The writer uses just the right words or phrase.

  This piece is poetic. Care has been taken to pick words that describe this teacher accurately. The reader gets a clear picture.

- Figurative language works reasonably well.

  "Your like a flower bloming in spreg" is not the most original simile, but it creates an image. The passage "you give selter for a btter fly. And chiden" lingers in the reader's mind.

- Colorful words are used correctly and with creativity.

  This writer has crafted the piece nicely. The reader is able to take the simple words and create a mental picture of a teacher who has had a powerful impact on the writer.

As you assess students' pieces, you may be amazed by the words they choose. Chances are, the words they like most, often sophisticated words that you may never expect of primary writers, will find their way into their pieces. Recently I listened to a second grader read her story about getting stung by many bees. When she read the line "I was terrified I'd go into anaphylactic shock," my eyes opened wide in surprise and appreciation. Her use of the verb "terrified" was excellent, but to also include the technical adjective "anaphylactic" was awesome. And when I told her so, she smiled, wisely. She knew she had nailed the words in that sentence.

It's so important to validate their choices, no matter how sophisticated or simple they are. If students don't feel comfortable expressing themselves in new ways, they are doomed to repeat the ordinary year after year. Young writers need to stretch to make their writing their own, and this stretching can and should be messy.

Conference Comments

Try comments like these on students who are using interesting words.

- That's exactly how that word sounds. Good for you.
- My favorite word in your writing is "lumpidy." What's yours?
- " . . . zipped around the corner." That's exactly how cats move. I can see it.
- Thank you for using different words to describe the rain. It makes your writing interesting to read.
- May I borrow your word "jibber-jabber"? I'm going to write it in my notebook to use in my own story.
- The verbs you use work so well in this piece. They make things happen.
- Where did you come up with that word? It's an excellent choice.
- I love how you began these three words with the same sound.
- Did you know there are several ways to say this? Let me show you a couple.
- I love how you wove in a new word with some old favorites.

Teaching With the Word-Choice Trait

When I was in first grade, I learned the longest word in the English language: *antidisestablishmentarianism* (28 letters). I remember being fascinated by it and thinking it was my ultimate word-choice weapon to fire at unsuspecting readers. I had no idea what it meant but used it in my writing anyway. I drove my parents nuts repeating it over and over again, loving how it rolled over my tongue. Recently I plugged "longest English word" into my Internet browser's search engine, and up it came, my old friend. Turns out there are longer words, scientific ones; however, *antidisestablishmentarianism* will always be my favorite. (By the way, the *Oxford English Dictionary* defines the word this way: "Properly, opposition to the dis-establishment of the Church of England, but popularly cited as an example of a long word." Catch the touch of irony here?)

It is this kind of fascination with words big and small that we seek to develop in young writers. The next section will help you do that. It contains lessons and activities organized into the following categories:

1. Falling in Love With Words
2. Choosing Precise Words
3. Selecting Words With Color, Variety, and Sparkle

Throughout the discussion of teaching students about word choice, keep in mind these general thoughts about the trait and some ideas for getting started:

- Primary writers love the sounds of words, and love repeating them over and over: "silly-slimy; silly, silly, slimy pants; slimy-blimy, silly-willy." It can go on and on. Ridiculous, I know, but encourage silly word play. From it, students begin to understand how words work and use it to reach for new ways to say important things in their writing.
- Students' speaking vocabularies are much larger than their writing vocabularies. So take time to help students jot down some of the more interesting words they say so that they can see what they look like in print.
- Your classroom should be print-rich. Make word walls and bulletin boards of interesting words and phrases for students to use in their writing.

- Choose read-aloud books that have colorful, lively, interesting words. Student will learn those words and use them, especially if you talk about them as a class.
- Primary writers need to move. Incorporate drama and dance into your language arts program by having students act out favorite words and passages from texts that invite that kind of interpretation.
- The Primary Scoring Guide on page 174 is your best resource for helping students understand word choice. Use it to help students learn the language of this trait.
- Introduce the important qualities of word choice by sharing "The Word-Choice Song" with your class. Sing it together, encouraging students to add stanzas with more word-choice tips. (See other trait songs on pages 83, 118, 154, 224, 264, and 291.)

The Word-Choice Song

(sung to the tune of "Ring Around the Rosie")

Writing with your best words–
Finding lots of new words–
Sparkle! Dazzle!
The words stand out.

- Use the student-friendly guide on page 203. When students are ready, give them photocopies of the guide, discuss the descriptors at each level, and have them assess their own and classmates' writing. Be sure to remind students of the importance of using words correctly and with style. You will know when your students are ready to use this guide.

English is a complicated language, and it is easy for students to get lost in it. Primary students need help trying new words and using familiar ones well. Reading to them, asking them questions about language, and encouraging them to develop an intellectual curiosity about words will help students understand why it's so important to find "just right" words as we write.

"For children, language stripped of meaningful context is most difficult to understand" (Fu and Townsend, 1999, p. 408). Because I believe this, you won't find vocabulary drill and practice in this section. Instead, you'll find lessons and activities meant to inspire young writers to use words creatively and effectively. This is a fun trait for you to teach and for students to learn. I hope that you find ideas here that will encourage and support your young writers.

Tips for Students Working on Word Choice

- Find descriptive words that paint a picture in your mind.
- Try unusual yet appropriate words to connect with the reader.
- Use verbs to create an active, energetic voice.
- Choose precise words rather than the first word that pops into your mind.
- Select words and phrases that are accurate.
- Use everyday words and phrases to make your writing sound real.

Falling in Love With Words

Recently, I visited a wonderful first-grade classroom, a place where every child is a writer. That day the teacher, Melissa Garner, announced to the class that she had a bad case of "logophilia." The students looked concerned.

"*Logophilia* means I'm hooked on something," she said. "Can you guess what it is, based on these clues? First, I can't stop reading them. I stop and write them in my notebook. My eyes are tired from scanning signs and posters for interesting ones all the time. I make lists and lists of them. I hear them in my mind. My heart starts to race when I find a new one. Boys and girls, I have a bad case of logophilia. What is my problem?"

The students jumped right in. "You're hooked on words," one of them said, gleefully.

At this, Melissa smiled and asked, "Do you think it's serious, doctors? Will I ever recover?"

By now the students were laughing out loud and having a gay old time.

"No," another one said. "You won't ever get over it."

Melissa wrote "logophilia" on the board and asked the kids to pronounce it with her. She told them that *logo* was from the Greek for "word," and *philia* was Greek for "love of a particular person or subject." With her help, the students figured out that *logophilia* means "the love of words," and wrote the definition under the word.

Then Melissa told the students that other words, such as *abacus*, *habitat*, and *memento* come from ancient Greek and Latin, languages that don't change. But English is a language that *does* change. New words, such as *muggle*, *24/7*, and *blog*, are added frequently. Then Melissa asked the students if any languages other than English were used in their homes and made a list: Russian, Spanish, Japanese, Korean, and Vietnamese. Like English, all of these languages change, Melissa told them. They grow with use, an important word-choice lesson for young writers.

Melissa is an amazing teacher. In ten minutes, these first-grade students learned a new, technical word and a thing or two about different languages. Because of her genuine love of words, Melissa opened the door for her students to become logophiles right along with her. It was a good day for word choice.

FOCUS LESSON

WHAT'S IN A WORD

New words are added to the English language regularly. Browse the latest edition of an unabridged dictionary in your school library. You'll find words and phrases that are part of today's American culture, such as *9/11* and *hanging out*. Little ones enjoy looking through this voluminous text to find words and phrases like these. This lesson shows you how to excite students to create their own words and phrases to add to the dictionary.

MATERIALS:

- writing paper and pencils
- drawing paper and pens

What to Do:

1. Encourage students to explore the dictionary and make lists on the board of words they find interesting.
2. Brainstorm a list of words students can't find in the dictionary but think should be added. These words might include references to popular TV shows, commercials, movies, favorite foods, or music they enjoy, such as *Big Mac* or *fantabulous*.
3. Ask each student to select one word from the list and write it down.
4. Tell students to illustrate the word, putting it in an appropriate context to help a reader understand its meaning. For example, if the word is *Spider Man*, the student might draw a picture of the superhero scaling the Empire State Building and casting a web.
5. Ask students to write one interesting thing about the word on the same page. They may write, for example, "Spiderman is a brave hero who saves people."
6. Post the work in a place for everyone to read and enjoy. Encourage students to use the words in their writing.

Follow-Up:

Students may enjoy hearing *Frindle* by Andrew Clements (1998), in which the main character creates a new word, *frindle*, to stand for "pen" and tries to get everyone to use it so it will find its way into the dictionary. Although this book is intended for older, more independent readers, I've found that students at all ages enjoy it.

Other Activities for Falling in Love With Words

Top Ten Words

Ask students to brainstorm a list of their top ten favorite words and post them on a bulletin board so everyone can use them in their writing. When students discover a new favorite in their reading or conversations, ask them to consider adding it to the list and removing one of the others. Keep the list posted all year, adding and deleting words regularly.

> *"I love words: choosing them, manipulating them, considering them, arranging them. I love words so much that I cut them whenever I can."*
>
> *—Tom Romano*

Word Fun

Ask students to make a list of favorite words in their notebooks, organized into these categories:

- Splendid Words
- Worst Words
- Misused Words
- Funny Words
- Strange Words
- Tasty Words

As students discover new and interesting words in their reading or class discussions, encourage them to add them to their lists. A good book to read to students is *Becoming Naomi Leon* by Pam Muñoz Ryan (2004). The main character keeps a list of Splendid Words in English and, toward the end of the book, begins one in Spanish.

And the Winner Is . . .

Ask students to choose a Word of the Year. It can be any word they like, perhaps from a list of favorites or from everyday life. Ask them to write an acceptance speech for the word, including who the word would thank (other words in its "family"), how much the award means to it, and why it is worthy of this great honor. Give students art supplies to create a picture of the trophy and a stylized drawing of the word. Hold an awards ceremony at which students give their acceptance speeches for their words and receive their trophies.

Choosing Precise Words

Broccoli books. This is a term I coined for books that you read because they are good for you, like *War and Peace*. There is so much meaning in that one simple word *broccoli*. It says it all. It's precise.

The primary student's world is chock-full of opportunities to learn meaningful, potent words—from an overheard conversation between a parent and a neighbor, a news article explaining why a local sports hero got traded, and so on. They learn them from road signs, menus, and stories. New words are everywhere. As students try them in writing, though, they don't always use them correctly, and that's okay. Learning to write using words with precision is a little like learning to talk. You don't do it well at first, but competence builds, one word at a time. The following lesson and activities will help you build that competence in your students.

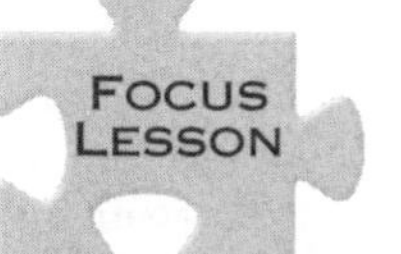

SUITCASE MYSTERY

Picture this: On the airport baggage carousel, you spot an old and battered suitcase that hasn't been claimed. As you reach for it, the lock disengages, the lid opens, and the contents spill all over the floor. You examine the pile of clothing and toiletries, and draw some conclusions about its owner. In this fun lesson, students describe items in a suitcase and the person to whom they think it belongs, using the most precise words they can find.

MATERIALS:

- an old, well-used suitcase
- 10 pieces of colorful clothing such as a shirt, a skirt, shoes, pants, socks, a coat, a hat, pajamas, and so on
- 5 toiletry items such as hairbrush, shampoo, toothpaste, aspirin bottle, and bandages
- writing paper and pencils
- drawing paper, pens, and paint

WHAT TO DO:

1. Fill the suitcase with the clothing and toiletries, and bring it to the classroom. Put it on a table and ask students what they notice about it. Encourage them to use precise words to describe the suitcase.

2. Tell students to imagine that the suitcase was left by someone at the airport in the baggage claim area. In order to help the baggage handlers return the suitcase to its owner, they are going to describe the items inside as clearly as possible and match them to the type of person who would use them.

3. Open the suitcase and show students its contents item by item. Then pair students and give each set of partners one item.

4. Have partners describe the item in writing in as much detail as possible. For instance, if students have a pair of jeans, they may write, "They're light-colored jeans. They look really old and worn. They have a tear on the back pocket. The pants have ragged edges on the bottoms."

5. Ask students to draw a picture of their item next to their description. Students who can't write much on their own should concentrate on adding details to the picture and labeling it to the best of their ability.

6. One by one, ask partners to show their item to the class, read their description, and explain who the owner might be. If they described the jeans, students may say, "We think these belong to a young man who doesn't have much money." Ask them to write a summary of the person who might own the item beneath the picture: "Man in his twenties, poor."

7. Put the descriptions and pictures in the suitcase with the clothing and toiletries, and thank students for their help writing with such precision and detail. Tell them that if the story were real, you would return the suitcase to the airport so baggage handlers could track down the rightful owner.

Other Activities for Choosing Precise Words

Stretching With Phonemes

As students gain awareness of the individual sounds, or phonemes, in words, such as the *-er* in *better*, the *st-* in *street*, and the *-oy* in *boy*, stretch their vocabulary by encouraging them to come up with different, more sophisticated words that contain the same phonemes. For example, if students are working with the *oy* sound and can identify it in *boy*, show them a longer, more interesting word that contains the same phoneme, such as *flamboyant*. Write the sound and the words that go with it on the board so students can add more words as they think of them or find them in their reading.

Delightful Descriptions

Primary students tend to stick with the safe words because they are the first words that spring to mind, and many are easy to spell. So they need to know that even one word or one interesting turn of phrase can transform an ordinary paper into a treat for readers. Write the following list of nouns on the board or overhead:

- boy
- dog
- ball
- apple
- house
- woman
- car

In small groups, ask students to pick one of the nouns, list words to describe it, and then, using a chart similar to the one below, organize the list into categories related to sight, sound, taste, touch, and smell. Ask them to write a summary made up of their descriptors. If students select *car*, they may write, "Ford, white, 2004 model, smooth paint, black leather interior, mag wheels, engine that sounds fast, floor mats, smells new, power steering."

Name ______________ Date 9 27

Topic: Apples

Looks	Feels	Tastes	Smells	Sounds
Spherical Shinny Lumpy botton Smoth sides Diffrent colors savory tasty	Firm | hard smooth Squshey wet	delcious sweet sour/bitter Jucy	Fruity delcious sweet savory tasty flavor-ful fresh terific fragrant	Crunchy quit (inaudible) drippy still thud

When you smell an apple it smels fresh and terificly fragrant.

When I sink my teeth in the wonderful apple it taste delcious. The apple looks spherical and shinny on smooth sides.

Students chart sensory words to describe apples.

My Experience

I was walking along with a graahdpa this korean kind of grandpa and we went t ot t back of the house to see the dog. The coler of the dog was I thik brown. I was going to pet it but it sudinly bit me. Th dog was a wach dog and wach dog bit people.

A first grader chooses words carefully to write this memorable piece about his grandfather.

Finally, have students search a piece of their own writing for a noun that needs a precise descriptor to bring it to life. In the example to the left, notice how the addition of "a Korean kind of" creates a clearer picture.

Vivid Verbs

Explain to students that a verb is an important kind of word because it adds life and action. Give pairs of students a well-written picture book and ask them to go on a hunt for verbs. (See pages 199–202 for a list of books to consider.) Model this activity by selecting a book, reading a sentence, and pointing out which word is the verb. In *Moon Rope* by Lois Ehlert (1999), for example, you could read, "Fox twirled the rope high over his head." Write *twirled* on the board. Ask students to read the sentences in their book, calling out the verbs as they read. Write them down and have students use the list for inspiration. If your students can't read the text, read it to them, one sentence at a time, pausing to let them try to identify the verb.

Selecting Words With Color, Variety, and Sparkle

"Ca-ching." That's what you hear in Ursula White's classroom when students use an interesting word. She stops everything and says, "Ca-ching," letting kids know that a classmate has used a "money word," a word that has great value to writers because it taps into one of the senses or expresses a familiar idea in an unusual way. Her students call out "ca-ching," too, at appropriate moments. Ursula and her class focus on words with color, variety, and sparkle, and they celebrate their use. You can do that, too, by carrying out the following lesson and activities.

FOCUS LESSON

WORDS WITH COLOR

The picture book *Yesterday I Had the Blues* by Jeron Ashford Frame (2003) contains words that are literally colorful, making it perfect for showing students how to apply word choice. The book tells the story of a young boy with many emotions about his family. From the blues that convey sadness, greens that convey optimism, and yellows that make the characters sing out loud, Frame shows how to write words with color to paint a vivid picture in the reader's mind. In this lesson, students write their own colorful, emotional pieces.

MATERIALS:

- a copy of *Yesterday I Had the Blues*
- writing paper, pencils, and pens
- drawing paper, markers, paint, and brushes

WHAT TO DO:

1. Read aloud *Yesterday I Had the Blues*, showing students the pictures as you go.
2. On the board, list the colors Frame describes: blue, green, gray, pink, indigo, yellow, red, silver, and gold.
3. Ask students to name their favorite color; accept any color, whether it's in the book or not, and be sure to add one of your own. Be creative to encourage students to think beyond the common ones. Try magenta, periwinkle, goldenrod, and so on.
4. Tell students to think of an interesting time or place from their own life that they associate with their color. Read an example from the book, such as "The runnin' my hand along the hedges greens," and ask them to write their own sentence like it. Model by doing this for your color of choice: "I've got the stand-out-in-a-crowd and never-going-to-miss-it goldenrods."
5. Read the book's opening line replacing Frame's color, blue, with yours followed by the sentence you wrote in Step 4. Then ask students to take turns reading their colorful sentences aloud.
6. Give students paper and drawing materials to make pictures that go with their sentences. Hang them on the bulletin board or create a class book for everyone to enjoy.

Other Activities for Selecting Words With Color, Variety, and Sparkle

Interjections!

Interjections, short exclamations such as "Oh!" "Yes!" and "Ouch!" spice up the dialogue in any piece of writing. And, because they usually end with an exclamation mark, they are good for teaching conventions, too. Ask students to point out interjections they notice in books and magazines and then ask them to use them in sentences. Encourage students to use interjections in their stories with dialogue to add interest and energy.

Idiom of the Week

"Push the envelope." "Throw in the towel." "Make no bones about it." English is filled with idioms, which is part of the reason it's such a hard language for many non-native English speakers to learn. Idioms are confusing to all students who have not heard them often enough to understand their underlying meaning. To help them, give students a list of idioms and talk about how each one represents a big idea. Following are some favorites:

- apple of my eye
- cold turkey
- Don't look a gift horse in the mouth.
- driving me up the wall
- Elvis has left the building.
- pie in the sky
- raining cats and dogs
- shake a leg
- under the weather
- Your name is mud.

Each week, post one idiom and focus on it during writing lessons. Have students act out the idiom and talk about their interpretations. Ask them to illustrate it by showing the literal and figurative meaning. If you're looking for a picture book to help students visualize idioms, try Rick Walton's *Why the Banana Split* (1998).

Onomatopoeia: More Than Just a Funny Name

Teaching students about onomatopoeia, words that imitate the sound they represent, is a fun way to build skill in word choice. Ask students to cut out pictures from magazines that show people, things, or animals in action. Tell them to paste the picture on paper and describe the action in writing. Ask them to brainstorm words that describe the action. For example, a snake could *hiss* a warning sound, a contented cat *purrs*, a cannon *booms*, and breaking glass *crashes*. Teach students to notice examples of onomatopoeia as they read and encourage them to try it in their writing.

Picture Books to Strengthen Word Choice

Picture books can help students fall in love with words and use precise, colorful words in their own writing. As you read favorite picture books to the class, stop and savor the language. Read them many times, allowing students to marinate in the sounds of the words and their relationships to the pictures. Here are some of my favorite books for modeling word choice for primary students. Each one shows students how to use language well in a different way.

Alphabet Adventure

Audrey Wood
Scholastic, 2003

Every night at bedtime, the letters in Charley's alphabet set come to life and shout out their names in roll call. One night, they discover that little x is missing. After searching high and low, the other letters spot x at a creepy castle made in the shape of a gigantic capital M, the mean master of the castle. Little x is quite happy there because he has been given the job of playing the xylophone. M threatens to make soup of the alphabet letters if they don't leave him and little x alone. The letters convince x to leave the castle, promising him a new job at home—making x's on a birthday cake for Charley's mom. After hearing this story, students will enjoy figuring out jobs for other alphabet letters.

Cassie's Word Quilt

Faith Ringgold
Alfred A. Knopf, 2002

Cassie shows readers objects and places from her neighborhood, such as plants, table and chairs, and a clothesline. Then she represents them on squares of a quilt, each highlighting the first letter of the special object. Cassie's world comes to life in this colorful book. Primary students can use this book as an inspiration for their own word quilts, for which they can name and draw things in the classroom and from their lives.

Dinosailors

Deb Lund
Harcourt Children's Books, 2003

In this imaginative story, a group of adventurous dinosaurs set sail for the high seas. Unfortunately, sailing turns out to be hard on their stomachs: "Their dinotummies slosh and churn. They groan with every twist and turn." After spending one miserable night on the ocean, they finally dock, happy to be back on stable ground. They sell their boat and " . . . go home to those they miss, to cuddle, hug, and dinokiss." Told in rhyme, this story illustrates how to take a core word, in this case *dinosaur*, and turn it into verbs, adjectives, and other nouns. Lund's language play is bound to make her book a read-aloud favorite.

Hello Ocean

Pam Muñoz Ryan
Scholastic, 2001

Pam Muñoz Ryan is one of my favorite authors. Whether she's writing a picture book or chapter book, she takes great care, using words with skill and imagination. In this simple text, she draws on all five senses to describe the ocean. Ryan re-creates all the marvelous feelings of being at the beach in language such as this: "Amber seaweed, speckled sand, bubbly waves that kiss the land" and "foggy songs from distant boats, gentle clangs from bobbing floats." Use her book as a model for sensory images in writing.

My Chair

Betsy James
Scholastic, 2004

You can build a poignant book around a simple idea, as James proves here. Her book takes place in a park, where neighbors gather to enjoy a fun-filled afternoon in their favorite chairs, which they bring from home. The reader learns about each character through reflections about their special chairs: "I wear my chair to zoom like a roller skater, dance like a bear." "My chair smells good . . . because it used to be a tree." Use this book to show students how to write and draw with flair about other everyday objects.

My Light

Molly Bang
Scholastic, 2004

Energy is all around us, in many, many forms. Molly Bang uses simple, colorful language to describe how energy from the sun is transformed into electricity. She takes this traditionally dry subject and draws readers in with descriptions such as "Whoosh! The water spins the turbines round and round. It spins my energy to generators, which make electricity." Imagery like this makes electricity, a sophisticated subject, interesting and accessible to students of all ages.

Moon Rope

Lois Ehlert
Harcourt Children's Books, 1999

In English and Spanish, Ehlert updates a classic Peruvian tale called "The Fox and the Mole" for a new generation of readers. Fox is tired of watching Mole eat worms, so he decides to go to the moon for an adventure. He makes a strong rope from grass and talks the birds into carrying one end to the moon so that he can climb his way there. Verbs such as *digging, running, tickled, hitch, blinked,* and *growled* create an active voice. The adventures of Fox and Mole are cleverly told. Read and enjoy them for excellent word choice.

The Old Woman Who Named Things

Cynthia Rylant
Harcourt Children's Books, 1996

This is the story of an old woman who outlives all her friends and family and is tired of saying good-bye. She decides to name objects that she knows will be around long after she dies. She names her car Betsy, her chair Fred, and her house Franklin. One day, a shy, brown puppy comes to her gate. The old woman gives the puppy some food and sends it away, afraid to name it for fear that it, too, will die before her. The puppy visits every day for a year but suddenly stops. Where could he be? With great relief, the old woman finds the dog at an animal shelter and brings it home. She names it Lucky, realizing that it is more important to embrace love than to fear it.

A Place to Grow

Soyung Pak
Scholastic, 2002

Seeds travel to find a good place to grow and so do people. That is the lesson we learn in this book, which was inspired by the hopes of immigrants to the United States. Pak tells us that some immigrants are born where it is inhospitable. They, like seeds, travel to places where they can be nurtured. "Even if I fly across the tallest mountains, the longest roads, and the widest seas, there will always be a garden in [my father's] heart for me." The language in this book is as lovely as its message. Students can pick favorite words and phrases from *A Place to Grow* and use them in their own writing.

Where Is the Green Sheep?

Mem Fox
Harcourt Children's Books, 2004

"Here is the moon sheep. And here is the star sheep. But where is the green sheep?" In this book, Mem Fox uses a variety of adjectives to describe unconventional sheep and will inspire primary writers to use their imaginations when coming up with their own adjectives. Simple words and short sentences make this a natural read-aloud book for even the youngest students.

Final Reflections on the Word-Choice Trait

The words students use can be ordinary or they can ignite the reader's imagination. In classrooms that are print-rich and emphasize the trait of word choice, students learn to use language to become powerful writers.

Teach students to be inquisitive about words so they can fall in love with them, choose them wisely, and combine them to create colorful, powerful writing. Make words matter, for they are the building blocks of well-constructed sentences, the focus of the next chapter.

My First Scoring Guide for *Word Choice*

I've Got It!

- I've picked exactly the right words.
- My words are colorful, fresh, and snappy.
- The words help my reader see my ideas.

On My Way

- Some of my words work well, but others don't.
- I've used too many ordinary words.
- My words paint a general picture of the idea.

Just Starting

- I'm confused about how to use words well.
- I've left out key words.
- Many of my words are the same or just wrong.

Share this student-friendly scoring guide with students when they are ready to assess their own and their classmates' writing for word choice.

◆ CHAPTER 7 ◆

Developing Sentence Fluency

Words are to writers as notes are to musicians. Whether it's jazz, country, classical, or rock and roll, music begins one sound at a time, adding up to a combination of sounds that creates the melody, harmony, and rhythm. Writing is created much the same way. Once students have the right words, they put them into a phrase, turn the phrase into a simple sentence, and add a clause, replace a word or two, insert a punctuation mark for emphasis, and they have it—a sentence that sounds good to the ear.

Primary students are capable of creating fluent sentences. Take the following two samples, for example. Both sentences are constructed correctly. In the first, the writer has simply and graciously said thank you to a teacher. It contains the key elements of a sentence, a subject and a verb, and therefore gets right to the point. Read aloud, it sounds fine.

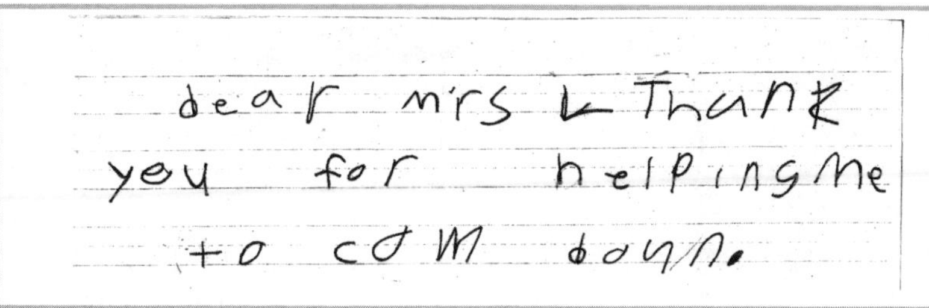

dear mrs L Thank
you for helping me
to com down.

The writer of the second sample not only includes a subject and a verb, but also creates a tempo with elegant positioning of the words.

THE BUTrFLIY

Early one day a
Big BLOU And pek
ButrFLI Was FLI
ing IN THE Forist.

The writer of "Thank you" understands the basics of a sentence. The writer of "Butterfly" seems to understand more. However, I'd need to see longer pieces to know if these writers are truly skilled in sentence fluency because this trait is about much more than well-written single sentences. It is about how well-written sentences work together to convey ideas as smoothly and clearly as possible.

Here are two more examples of sentences from first graders. The first one, "Sarah," contains six sentences, which use the same subject and verb along with a few adjectives and prepositional phrases for good measure. It's typical of first graders to create simple and grammatically correct sentences that aren't particularly fluent.

Sarah.

She is nice.
She is vary nise.
She is Supr nise.
She is good at Math.
She is good at kalindr.
She is good at Swing.

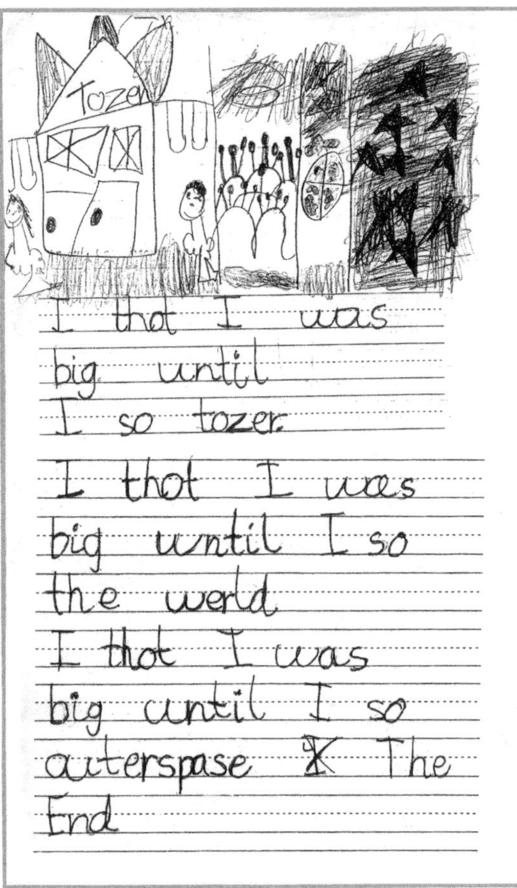

Tozer
I thot I was
big until
I so tozer.
I thot I was
big until I so
the werld
I thot I was
big until I so
outerspase The
End

Now consider the second sample. It's constructed in a similar manner, but it reads more smoothly. In fact, it's almost poetic. There is a sense of flow as the writer builds from "tozer" to "mountains" to "the werld" and finally to "outerspase." Using words with different numbers of syllables helps, too. Although in both pieces the subject and verb are repeated, the technique works in the second piece. It's more fluent. The writer draws upon oral language to make the piece sound natural, whereas the writer of "Sarah" doesn't, and the result is stilted.

Have you ever been around young children who are learning to talk? As they crawl into your lap for a bedtime story, they beg for the familiar, a book that you have read so many times you think you'll go insane if you have to read it again. "No, no," they cry as you reach for a new book. "This one." So you read *Green Eggs and Ham* by Dr. Seuss (1960), *Goodnight Moon* by Margaret Wise Brown (1947), *Time for Bed* by Mem Fox (1997), or *Charlie Parker Played Be Bop* by Chris Raschka (1998) yet again. They eat it up, then beg to hear it one more time, absorbing a little more about how language works from each reading.

Because of such experience, children understand, long before they are proficient in writing, that sentences are important. Here are examples of what a group of students wrote when asked to define sentence fluency:

- I think Sentene fluency is that you write sentences and read it quit.
- Sentence Fluency is like a flowing river.
- Sentence Fluency means not repeting words.

The Challenge of Teaching Sentence Fluency

Get this. In some states, legislators expect children as young as six to be able to craft letter-perfect sentences, and they make sure those children do so by imposing benchmarks and standardized tests. Parents and principals put pressure on teachers to turn out young "writers" who score well on the tests. Canned curricula are adopted, bringing a one-size-fits-all perspective to the writing program, and guess who suffers the most? The students. Lost is their desire to learn to write well. Our goal should be loftier than getting high test scores; it should be to create writers for life.

Let's be honest here. Writing is a highly complex task that requires time, practice, and hard work to master. Pounding skills into young students instead of supporting them with developmentally appropriate instruction isn't the answer. I believe it's far more important to help students write one beautiful sentence than to allow them to write many sentences badly. And bad writing is what we get when we emphasize volume over quality.

However, it's all too common to walk into any primary classroom and see students completing sentence starters on worksheets. As we've discussed, that is no way to learn to write. "I love the rain because . . . " Who cares about finishing the sentence of someone you don't even know? Maybe the student doesn't love the rain. Maybe she loves something else entirely, but her willingness to find a way to express it is squashed by mindless writing activities. Sentence starters and activities like them deprive the emerging writer of the joy of transforming their wiggly lines into words and sentences.

Sentence Fluency: A Definition for Primary Students

The sentence fluency trait has two important dimensions: the grammar that makes a group of words a sentence and the way sentences sound to the ear. Indeed, this is the auditory trait, where we learn to read with our ears right along with our eyes. Signs that writers are working well with the sentence fluency trait include:

- working with several words in a row, with attention to phrasing.
- being more concerned about sentence quality than sentence correctness.
- experimenting with different sentence beginnings.
- crafting sentences of varying lengths.
- weaving questions and statements into the text.
- using transitional words to connect one sentence to the next.
- repeating sounds, words, and phrases to create a pattern.
- writing passages that can be read aloud with ease.

Assessing Student Work for Sentence Fluency

The Primary Scoring Guide on page 209 helps us determine the degree to which students are able to write with sentence fluency. Use it to assess individual pieces of writing, as follows:

STEP 1: Collect student papers you want to assess for sentence fluency.

STEP 2: Photocopy the Primary Scoring Guide: Sentence Fluency since you'll want to write on it and highlight key words as you go.

STEP 3: Read the scoring guide's descriptors for each of the five levels, from top—5: Established—to bottom—1: Ready to Begin. Each descriptor shows how writing typically reveals itself at that level. Also, notice that the descriptors parallel one another from level to level. For example, the first descriptor for each level deals with length of sentences.

STEP 4: Read one of the student papers carefully, paying attention to everything on the page, both pictures and text.

STEP 5: Look at the first descriptor for each level and determine the one that most closely matches the paper. Work your way through the rest of the descriptors for each level, checking off the appropriate ones. Each level has a point value; average the total to determine the piece's overall score in sentence fluency. The process will get easier, faster, and more accurate as you practice.

Sample Papers to Assess for Sentence Fluency

The papers that follow represent a wide range of skill in the sentence-fluency trait. Review the scoring guide on page 209, read each student paper closely, read my descriptor-by-descriptor evaluation of the piece, and see what you think. Do you agree with my assessment of each writer's work? Do these pieces resemble your students'?

If you wish, use the guides on pages 70, 104, 140, and 174 to score these pieces in ideas, organization, voice, and word choice. Analyze the five scores for each paper to determine the trait or traits for which the student needs the most help.

Ready to move to the grades-3-and-up scoring guide!

The Primary Scoring Guide

Sentence Fluency

Established 5	____ Different sentence lengths give the writing a nice sound. There is playfulness and experimentation. ____ Varied sentence beginnings create a pleasing rhythm.	____ Different kinds of sentences (statements, commands, questions, and exclamations) are present. ____ The flow from one sentence to the next is smooth. ____ The piece is a breeze to read aloud.
Extending 4	____ Sentences are of different lengths. ____ Sentences start differently. ____ Some sentences read smoothly while others still need work.	____ Connectives are correctly used in long and short sentences. ____ Aside from a couple of awkward moments, the piece can be read aloud easily.
Expanding 3	____ Basic subject-verb agreement occurs in simple sentences–e.g., "I jumped." ____ Sentence beginnings are identical, making all sentences sound alike. ____ Longer sentences go on and on.	____ Simple conjunctions such as *and* and *but* are used to make compound sentences. ____ The piece is easy to read aloud, although it may contain repetitive or awkward sentence patterns.
Exploring 2	____ Written elements work together in units. ____ Words are combined to make short, repetitive phrases. ____ Awkward word patterns break the flow of the piece.	____ The reader gets only one or two clues about how the pictures and text are connected. ____ The writer stumbles when reading the text aloud and may have to back up and reread.
Ready to Begin 1	____ It's hard to figure out how the elements go together. ____ Words, if present, stand alone. ____ Imitation words and letters are used across the page.	____ There is no overall sense of flow to the piece. ____ Only the writer can read the piece aloud.

PAPER #1
"CHICKENPOX"

Time to Assess

PAPER #1
"CHICKENPOX"

This story appears to be about having chicken pox, although we rely completely on the picture to get that information. The text, which isn't written in any discernable language, traverses the page, which suggests an awareness of sentences. Still, the paper scores at the 1: Ready to Begin level in sentence fluency.

- It's hard to figure out how the elements go together.

  Without any text, the reader turns to the picture to figure out the writer's message. That picture, however, reveals a lot.

- Words, if present, stand alone.

  In this case, the picture stands alone. No words are present, not even a name, although there is a scribble where the name would likely be found.

- Imitation words and letters are used across the page.

  This descriptor applies perfectly to this paper. The loopy lines show the writer has a visual sense of how words flow across a page.

- There is no overall sense of flow to the piece.

  Without letters, words, or sentences, it's difficult for the reader to tell what the writer is trying to say and, therefore, check for fluency. However, the scribbles across the page show some understanding of how text looks when it flows across the page.

- Only the writer can read the piece aloud.

  Without a doubt, this piece needs writer interpretation. The picture gives the reader a sense of topic, but the writer would need to explain it.

PAPER #2
"MY FAVORITE SHOES ARE"

My favorite shoes are.

Run shoes.

Red.

My mom. I night.

My brotherAnthony.

Time to Assess

Paper #2
"My Favorite Shoes Are"

This writer is just beginning to put words together into groups and will develop the skill necessary to transform those groups into complete sentences. He is already using punctuation to separate one thought from the next, which is a sign of sentence awareness. This piece receives a 2: Exploring score for sentence fluency.

- Written elements work together in units.

  "My favorite shoes are," "My mom," and "My brother Anthony" are examples of how this writer has grouped words into phrases. No sentences are present, though.

- Words are combined to make short, repetitive phrases.

  This piece is made up entirely of short phrases. They don't repeat, however. This writer uses new words in each line.

- Awkward word patterns break the flow of the piece.

  "I night." is an incomplete thought that is not understandable.

- The reader gets only one or two clues about how the pictures and text are connected.

  The writer draws a character moving, which matches the detail about running shoes in the text.

- The writer stumbles when reading the text aloud and may have to back up and reread.

  Most likely the writer would have a hard time reading this piece fluently. Words would have to be added and sentences created.

PAPER #3
"A CHEETAH"

a cheetahrun's fast.
a cheetah has a tail.
a cheetah has eyes.
a cheetah is yellow.
a cheetah has spot's.

Time to Assess

Paper #3
"A Cheetah"

This is a typical example of fluency, or lack thereof, at the primary level. Though these sentences are grammatically correct, they are of the cookie-cutter variety: each one is virtually the same. "A cheetah" receives a 3: Expanding in this trait.

- Basic subject-verb agreement occurs in simple sentences—e.g., "I jumped."

  Every sentence in this piece contains the same subject, "a cheetah," and a simple verb with an object, making them very repetitive.

- Sentence beginnings are identical, making all sentences sound alike.

  Every sentence begins with "a cheetah," making the piece repetitious and predictable.

- Longer sentences go on and on.

  The sentences are the same length; none of them is longer than five words. The writer should stretch some out to create more rhythm.

- Simple conjunctions such as *and* and *but* are used to make compound sentences.

  The writer attempts compound sentences. The reader wishes for more complexity, however.

- The piece is easy to read aloud, although it may contain repetitive or awkward sentence patterns.

  The repetition is monotonous when the piece is read aloud. The reader has problems engaging with the topic.

Paper #4
"My Special Time"

My Special time

My Special time was when I went
to my cousin's house I had Fun and
Play alot and play NFl and I
throw it far and my cousin kicked the
ball good and we went biciciling and
I Played Game boy color and I sleep
two days and then I went home and
play nintendo all day.

Time to Assess

Paper #4
"MY SPecial time"

In "MY SPecial time," the writer tries to take basic sentences, like those in "A cheetah," and combine them, which is admirable. The result, however, is one long, run-on sentence. This piece also scores a 3: Expanding in sentence fluency.

- Basic subject-verb agreement occurs in simple sentences—e.g., "I jumped."

  Buried in this text are simple sentences: "I went to my cousin's house," "We went biciciling," and "I played Game boy color."

- Sentence beginnings are identical, making all sentences sound alike.

  This piece is a run-on sentence, so there is only one sentence beginning to examine.

- Longer sentences go on and on.

  Oh yes. This is one long, mixed-up sentence. The reader has to gulp for air as he or she reads this aloud.

- Simple conjunctions such as *and* and *but* are used to make compound sentences.

  The word "and" is used nine times, creating a series of thoughts that doesn't read smoothly. As readers, we appreciate the writer trying for longer, more complex sentences, though.

- The piece is easy to read aloud, although it may contain repetitive or awkward sentence patterns.

  Although the reader could read this piece aloud, he or she would need to mentally edit it, putting words in, taking words out, and pausing to create flow.

Paper #5
"Money"

Money

I like money is cool
money is rad cash is money.
I Love cash and money makes the
world go round and round.
I Wish I have money, money I
Think money is fun to have and
spenned it on vidoe games I have
a bank full money now I have
money. NOW I will be happy for
to day; to day, to day I wish I get
money allawlwsy.

The End

Time to Assess

PAPER #5
"MONEY"

Is there any doubt that this student is into money? The repetition of the word gives the piece a rhythm. The writer would only have to add a few words here and there to create a piece that is easy and entertaining to read aloud. "Money" scores a 4: Extending in sentence fluency.

- Sentences are of different lengths.

  "I like money." "Money makes the world go round and round." "Now I will be happy for today; to day, to, day I wish I get money allawlwsy." Nice, varied sentences create tempo and flow.

- Sentences start differently.

  Some sentences begin with "I" and others with "Money." Toward the end of the piece the reader finds "Now I have . . . " and "Now I will . . . "

- Some sentences read smoothly while others still need work.

  Missing words here and there keep this piece from being completely fluent, but it's a strong effort overall.

- Connectives are correctly used in long and short sentences.

  The word "money" serves to connect the ideas throughout the piece.

- Aside from a couple of awkward moments, the piece can be read aloud easily.

  A few sentences need end punctuation and capitals to show where they begin and end. It's easy to read aloud and add what is missing, however.

Paper #6
"The Anchunt Desert"

The Anchunt Desert

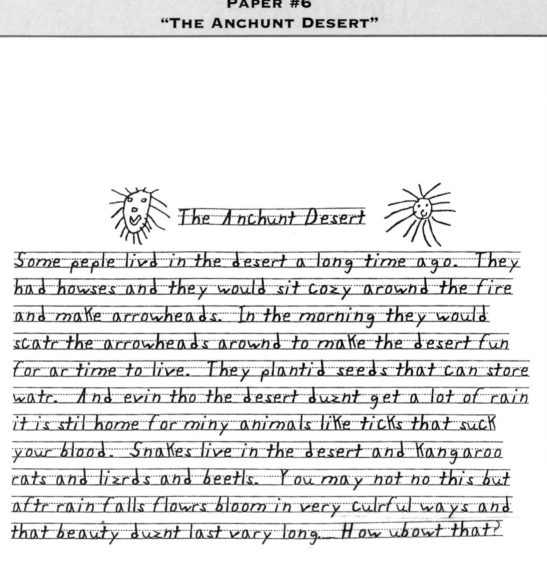

Some peple livd in the desert a long time ago. They had howses and they would sit cozy arownd the fire and make arrowheads. In the morning they would scatr the arrowheads arownd to make the desert fun for ar time to live. They plantid seeds that can store watr. And evin tho the desert duznt get a lot of rain it is stil home for miny animals like ticks that suck your blood. Snakes live in the desert and Kangaroo cats and lizrds and beetls. You may not no this but aftr rain falls flowrs bloom in very culrful ways and that beauty duznt last vary long. How ubowt that?

Time to Assess

Paper #6
"The Anchunt Desert"

"The Anchunt Desert" is an example of a first grader writing beautiful, descriptive sentences. This piece flows from beginning to end. It receives the highest score, 5: Established, for sentence fluency. Try scoring this piece for other traits as well. It's a wonderful piece of writing.

- Different sentence lengths give the writing a nice sound. There is playfulness and experimentation.

  From the opening line of ten words to the closing line of three, this piece contains different sentence lengths and constructions throughout.

- Varied sentence beginnings create a pleasing rhythm.

  "Some people lived . . . They had howses . . . In the morning . . . They planted seeds . . . And evin . . ." all the way to the last line, a question, "How ubowt that?" are examples of how skilled this writer is.

- Different kinds of sentences (statements, commands, questions, and exclamations) are present.

  There are two kinds of sentences in this piece: statement and question.

- The flow from one sentence to the next is smooth.

  A prepositional phrase, a conjunction, nouns, and pronouns are used to link sentences. This writer shows a lot of strength in sentence fluency at a young age.

- The piece is a breeze to read aloud.

  A reader most likely would be able to read this piece aloud without stumbling, a sure sign of fluency.

It's important to assess primary writing for "sentence sense." In other words, listen for how the piece sounds as you examine it for how the sentences read. We want sentence to sound as good as they read. Encourage writers to read their work aloud as they write so they can hear its fluency for themselves. This will develop their ability to self-assess.

> *"[I] wonder whether we, as teachers of writers, focus too much on the mind: have we forgotten, or did we ever know, the explosive power, the necessity of focusing also on the ear?"*
>
> *—Mem Fox*

Conference Comments

Share comments like these with students as their sentences begin to take shape.

- I love how this part of your piece sounds. Let's read it together.
- Look at how you're grouping your words.
- It's good that you started your sentences differently.
- I felt like tapping my toe to the beat when I read your piece. It has rhythm.
- I love how you've added dialogue. Now I can hear the character's voice.
- Your letters flow across the page. That is a great start toward sentences.
- Every sentence has a subject and verb. Way to go.
- Your pictures and words work together like hand and glove.
- As you read, I can see the sentences with my eyes closed.
- Thanks for adding punctuation to help me figure out where to stop and where to pause.
- Ending your piece with a question really works.

Teaching With the Sentence-Fluency Trait

> *"Unlike medicine or the other sciences, writing has no new discoveries to spring on us. We're in no danger of reading in our morning newspaper that a breakthrough has been made in how to write a clear, English sentence— that information has been around since the King James Bible."*
>
> —*William Zinsser*

Taking a cue from Zinsser, we're not going to boldly go where no writing teacher has gone before. Instead let's look to the masters for guidance on how to write sentences. We may discover strategies to teach young writers. Thomas Jefferson, for example, can show us a thing or two about rhythm and cadence. Read this passage from the Declaration of Independence:

> *We hold these truths to be self-evident; that all men are created equal;*
> *that they are endowed by their Creator with inherent inalienable Rights;*
> *that among these are Life, Liberty, and the pursuit of Happiness.*

I suspect Jefferson listened as he wrote. He created a tempo to underscore the most important ideas, and smoothed them out by using parallel construction. There are no wasted words in this passage. Jefferson's tight, well-constructed sentences are honed to perfection.

Now read the final words of one of the finest children's books ever written, *Charlotte's Web* by E. B. White:

> *"Wilbur never forgot Charlotte. Although he loved her children and grandchildren dearly, none of the new spiders ever quite took her place in his heart. She was in a class by herself. It's not often that someone comes along who is a true friend and a good writer. Charlotte was both."*

Text this good changes us as writers. The first time I read this passage, I wondered, "Is this as well written as I think it is?" The second time confirmed it—

"Yes!" The syntax, or the sentence structure, is masterful. Using short sentences followed by longer ones and ending on a simple, three-word sentence gives the piece a satisfying sound and keeps its meaning crystal clear.

I sometimes ask students to memorize pieces like these and practice reciting them so that they absorb how they sound. I find students often learn the rhythms long before they understand the message fully and use those rhythms as they write.

There are a variety of ways to teach students to write well-constructed, easy-on-the-ear sentences. Before we consider them, however, here are some general ideas for getting started.

- Teach poetry lessons. Poetry helps primary writers learn how to make rhythms in language.
- Play music as students write. Try different types to see which they respond to best. I've always found that classical creates a peaceful tone and calms students. But, upbeat music—country, rock and roll, and jazz—can be energizing. For many students, writing goes more smoothly with the beat of the music playing in the background.
- Read, read, read to students. Then read some more. There's no better way to learn how to write well than by hearing fluent texts read aloud.
- Nudge students to try dialogue, even if they can't punctuate it correctly. They will break out of standard sentence patterns when they start introducing spoken words.
- Encourage talk in your classroom. Look for different dialects, study them, celebrate them, and discuss how they might play out in writing.
- Use the Primary Scoring Guide on page 209 to support your teaching of sentence fluency and help students understand your goals.
- Sing "The Sentence Fluency Song" with your students to

The Sentence Fluency Song

(sung to the tune of "Frère Jacques")

Sentence fluency,
Sentence fluency.
The writing flows.
The writing flows.
Sentences are longer.
Sentences are tighter.
It sounds smooth; it sounds right.

help them understand the importance of creating writing that flows.

Post the lyrics to "The Sentence Fluency Song" along with other trait songs so students can refer to them as they write. (See pages 83, 118, 154, 188, 264, and 291.)

- Introduce sentence fluency with the student-friendly guide on page 239. When students are ready, give them photocopies of the guide, discuss the descriptors at each level, and have them use it to assess their own and their classmates' writing.

Tips for Students Working on Sentence Fluency

- Listen for rhythm as you read passages aloud.
- Use poetry to focus on the sound of the language.
- Find favorite sentences and talk about what makes them strong.
- Try beginning sentences with words and phrases you've never used before.
- Vary the lengths of sentences to make ideas shine.
- Play with phrases until they sound right to the ear.

Because many primary students are not using words in writing yet, creating sentences may be out of their reach. Most babies crawl before they walk, after all. There are things we can do, however, to get them ready for sentences. The lessons and activities that follow address the range of sentence fluency skills at play in every primary classroom, from scribbles across the page to artfully crafted paragraphs. I've organized them into three areas:

1. Beginning Sentences in Different Ways
2. Creating Sentences of Different Lengths
3. Reading Sentences Aloud to Check How They Sound

I've always said that we don't teach the traits. We teach children to write using the traits as a guide. This is an important distinction. If we teach sentence composing in isolation, students won't develop an ear for language.

It's prudent to recall Mem Fox's wise words about sentence fluency: "If writers (or speakers) *don't* have an ear for rhythm they'll place their words in any old order without realizing the danger inherent in such carelessness" (1993, pp. 109–110). One of our most important jobs, then, is to help primary students understand how to write not only correct sentences but fluent sentences. And on this important note, we begin.

Beginning Sentences in Different Ways

This section shows you how to teach students to start sentences with variety and punch. It's better for students to write one sentence with a strong, original beginning than a whole page of sentences with weak, tired ones. After all, we want them to develop options for when they are ready to craft whole paragraphs.

FIND A NEW WAY TO BEGIN

Share this fun lesson with students to help them think of fresh ways to begin their sentences. To start, you come up with a topic for a story or informational piece together. Then you build the piece by coming up with sentences in a variety of lengths with a variety of beginnings, determined by the roll of a die.

MATERIALS:

- a large, foam, six-sided die, available at most discount stores
- an overhead projector and pens

WHAT TO DO:

1. Ask students to help you decide on a topic for writing, such as "the day we lost the power at school." Write this topic on the overhead so students can refer to it as they help you compose a story.
2. Roll the die and tell students to call out the number it lands on. Ask them to help you write an opening sentence of as many words.
3. If necessary, show students how to compose a sentence on the overhead. If you roll a four, you might write, "I couldn't see anything."
4. Ask students to roll the die again, call out the number, and give you a second sentence of as many words, *without using the same first word they used to start the first sentence.* If you roll a five, students may suggest, "The lights suddenly went out."
5. Write their second sentence on the overhead. Continue rolling the die and writing new sentences with different beginnings until the class feels the piece is finished. About eight to ten sentences should be enough.
6. Read the whole story back to the class, revise as you and your students see fit, and discuss the importance of using sentences with different beginnings.

Other Activities for Beginning Sentences in Different Ways

Lots of Color

Using a favorite chapter book or another well-written text, select a paragraph and write it on the computer. Highlight the first word of every sentence in a different color. If any sentences begin with the same word, highlight them in the same color. Ask students to look at the model and tell you how many colors they see and how many different ways the author begins sentences. Ask them to use crayons or markers to highlight the first word of each sentence in a piece of their writing. If students use the same color for every sentence, ask them to consider revising a couple of sentences. Using color this way helps students pinpoint problem areas.

Box It Up

In this activity students learn two important sentence-building skills: 1) creating interesting beginnings and 2) using end punctuation. Start by displaying a sentence and drawing a box around the first word. Then write a second sentence that begins with a different word and ask a student to draw a box around its first word. Draw an arrow from the box to the punctuation at the end of the previous sentence. Write a third sentence that begins with a different word and ask another student to draw the box and arrow.

> Example:
>
> [Madeline] was a funny little girl. ←—[She] played outside all day, driving toy trucks up and down roads made out of dirt piles. ←—[Most] of all she loved being grubby.

Now ask students to do this in a piece of their own writing, drawing boxes around the first words and arrows back to the punctuation at the end of the previous sentence. Help them notice which word begins the sentence and which punctuation mark ends the sentence before it, and also help them add punctuation at the end if it was forgotten.

Mix It Up

Make a list of possible ways to start sentences and post it where students can see it easily. Examples may be

1. An interjection (Wow! Yes! No!)
2. A sound (zoom, screech, plunk)
3. Location phrases (Over the hill, Around the block, Under the stairs)
4. Dialogue ("Oh, no!" "Come over here." "Wait a minute.")

Make a second list of sentence starters you'd prefer students to avoid:

1. "Hello. My name is . . . "
2. "I . . . " (more than three times per paper)
3. "Well . . . "
4. "And . . . "

Expand both lists as new ideas come up in your discussions about writing.

Creating Sentences of Different Lengths

Remember how Goldilocks declared, "This bed is too hard. This one is too soft. But this one is just right." Sentences can be the same—too long, too short, or just right. It's this sense of how much is enough that we seek to develop in student writers.

One of the first things you can do is require students to write complete sentences when answering content-area questions. For instance, in math, if the answer to a problem is 5, ask students to write, "The answer is 5." Or better yet: "The answer is 5 chocolate chip cookies." If the answer to a science question is "magnets," students should write, "The answer is magnets" or "The answer is magnets marked North and South." Once students have a clear sense of the length of a typical complete sentence, they will be in a better position to reduce and expand sentences in their writing.

You may be wondering, What about fragments? Should students be allowed to use them? Students will see fragments used effectively in magazines, newspapers, and books, so it's only natural for them to want to try them in their own writing. But giving them free reign is risky because students may not know that they are using a fragment and why. One teacher I know issues a "license to frag." She assesses readiness by asking students to explain why they used a fragment. If the student replies, "Because it sounds right," they are licensed to frag and given a certificate. However, until students can articulate in some way that fragments are a stylistic choice to create fluency, she insists they use complete sentences.

Primary students also struggle with sentence variety—combining long, short, and medium-length sentences to create an engaging flow. Some students write such short sentences they don't develop fluency, while others don't know when to stop. But combining sentences of different lengths is a key to creating fluent text. Here are a lesson and three activities to help students develop skill in writing sentences of different lengths.

FOCUS LESSON

STANDING SENTENCES

What better way to help primary students learn about sentences than by acting them out? In this engaging lesson, students make sentences in a variety of lengths, using word cards, their bodies, and their imaginations.

MATERIALS:

- $8^1/_2$-by-11-inch cards and markers

WHAT TO DO:

1. Come up with a basic sentence, such as "My dog is brown," and write each word on a separate card. Give the cards to four students and ask them to create the sentence by lining up in the right order with their cards facing out. Ask the students to read their sentence aloud one card at a time.
2. Create more cards with words for expanding the basic sentence. You could write *fuzzy* or *snuggly* to modify *dog*. Give the cards to other students and ask them to figure out how to weave them into the basic sentence in a way that makes sense, then to stand where they think their word would go.
3. Add as many words as you like and allow students time to make the best sentence they can. Each time students incorporate a new word, have them read the sentence aloud in its entirety one card at a time.
4. Repeat this activity often, using new, interesting words to help students learn how to write sentences of different lengths.

Other Activities for Creating Sentences of Different Lengths

Draw-Along

Proclaim a Draw-Along Day. Ask students to select a topic that suggests a progression of thoughts, events, or stages, preferably related to your curriculum, such as "the life cycle of a frog," "the history of Native Americans of (your state)," or "the water cycle." Using a white board, chalkboard, or long pieces of butcher paper, have students write and draw major steps in the progression from left to right. When they are finished, ask them to write sentences of different lengths as captions for different parts of their work. Students can also do draw-alongs based on events from favorite books.

Kindergarten students create a Draw-Along picture to demonstrate how their ideas flow.

Grandma Is . . .

Display a sentence such as "Grandma is the most fun-loving person in my family." Ask students to reconfigure the sentence by moving the first two words to the end: "The most fun-loving person in my family is Grandma." Challenge students to create a third sentence by placing that word in yet another location, omitting and adding words as necessary to make sense: "Of all the people in my family, Grandma is the most fun-loving." Continue coming up with ways to say the same thing in sentences of different lengths until you have exhausted the possibilities. Then try another topic.

Finding Sentences That Work

On the computer, type a passage of at least six sentences from a favorite read-aloud book. (I've used *The War With Grandpa* by Robert Kimmel Smith [1984] with great success.) Highlight each sentence a different color so that their varying lengths are clearly visible. Ask students to count how many words are in each sentence and write the results on the board. Read the passage aloud, asking students to listen for how sentence variety affects the sound of a piece.

Select a piece by an anonymous primary writer that has sentences of the same length, type it on the computer, count the words in each sentence, and read it aloud. Ask students which piece they prefer—the one containing sentences of about the same length or the one containing sentences that are more varied? Discuss how they might use this information in their writing to create fluency.

Reading Sentences Aloud to Check How They Sound

By reading aloud, writers learn a lot about the rhythm, cadence, and flow of language. So share passages from favorite books to give students ideas of what to work toward in their writing. As primary students luxuriate in the language of beautifully written books, they internalize the syntax and will begin to replicate it.

Writers of all ages should read their own work aloud, too, to determine what is working and what needs smoothing. I read my writing to my assistant, Mary Sue, all the time, much to her dismay. Saying the words aloud helps me to pinpoint problems that I would probably miss if I read the piece silently.

You can help students read their work aloud independently by giving them

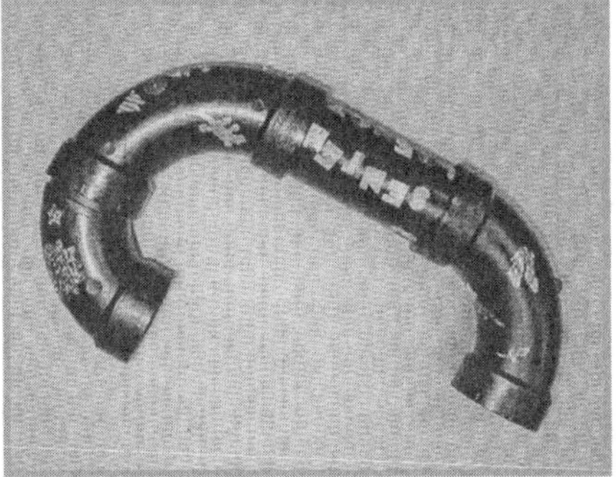

Students read their writing into the "fluency phone" and listen to the flow of their sentences.

"Fluency Phones." Fluency Phones are simple sound-amplifying devices made out of PVC pipe, which is available at home-improvement stores. Students read their writing into one end of the phone and listen to it from the other. Even the quietest student can hear how his or her writing sounds, and revise it accordingly, using these ingenious little devices.

> *"The writer's ear tells the writer how to modulate the language . . . The ear plays up the subject or plays it down. Beginning writers should read aloud, not just after they have written a draft to test it, but while they are writing or editing to produce writing that the reader can hear."*
>
> —*Donald Murray*

The following lesson and three activities will help students read writing aloud to check how it sounds. Have fun trying them out with your students.

FOCUS LESSON

RESOUNDING REFRAINS

Good writing has rhythm, and a good way to teach this to students is by using favorite songs with repeating verses and refrains, such as "Old McDonald," "Bingo," and "Row, Row, Row Your Boat."

Picture books also have rhythm. Take Mem Fox's *Tough Boris* (1994), for example, in which rhythm is created by the use of the recurring phrase "All pirates. . . ." Read *Tough Boris* to students and allow them to chime in with the details to complete that phrase. In the process, they get to hear Fox's beautiful sentences and create their own.

MATERIALS:

- a copy of *Tough Boris*
- large index cards
- drawing paper, pencils, and pens

WHAT TO DO:

1. Read *Tough Boris* to students, encouraging them to repeat the pirate descriptors in the refrain, such as "All pirates are massive" or "All pirates are scruffy" until the end, "All pirates cry, and so do I."
2. Ask students to tell you what the author does to create sentences that are enjoyable to hear. Students will most likely identify the repetition.
3. Give students the index cards and ask them to write down their favorite "All pirates . . . " line as you read the book again. When you're finished, collect the cards and read the lines back to the class.
4. Ask students to tell you why the last line, "All pirates cry, and so do I," is a little different from the others. (It contains a rhyme, which gives the story a sense of closure.)
5. Challenge pairs of students to come up with a new ending line that begins with "All pirates . . . " and contains a rhyme, then write it on the back of their card. Read their examples to the class.
6. Allow pairs time to copy their new line onto drawing paper and illustrate it.

Other Activities for Reading Sentences Aloud to Check How They Sound

Sentence Sense

Find a well-written paragraph, transcribe it, removing all punctuation marks and changing all uppercase letters to lowercase. Photocopy it onto an overhead transparency and ask the class to read it aloud. You should expect them to have trouble.

Ask students to help you punctuate the sentences and add capital letters where needed to create sentences that are smooth and easy to read aloud. Then share the picture book *Punctuation Takes a Vacation* by Robin Pulver (2003), which illustrates the connection between sentence fluency and conventions.

Bubble Talk

Dialogue can add interest to stories and provides an authentic reason for students to create different types of sentences, such as questions and statements. This activity helps students learn the value of dialogue, without getting bogged down by capitalization and punctuation. Cut out a cartoon from the newspaper that features characters students enjoy, such as "Peanuts" or "Hi and Lois." White out the dialogue copy and cut the frames apart. Organize students into groups of three to four. Give each group a set of dialogue-free frames and ask students to put the cartoon back in order and add dialogue that fits the pictures. When they're finished, ask groups to read their dialogue to the class and act out their cartoons.

Sentence Scavengers

Send students to look through books in your classroom library for a sentence they love and have them write it on a large strip of paper. Then hang the strips in a prominent place, adding the title of the book at the bottom in case students want to read more. Have students read them aloud to their classmates and explain why they chose them. Be sure to include a sentence from one of your favorites. Mine is from Truman Capote's *A Christmas Memory* (1956): "That is why, walking across a school campus on this particular December morning, I keep searching the sky. As if I expected to see, rather like hearts, a lost pair of kites hurrying toward the sky." Okay, it's one sentence and a fragment, but you get the idea. Recorded books, such as *Mem Fox Reads* (1992), are another good source for sentences. There's nothing like hearing the words read the way the author intended them to be heard.

Picture Books to Strengthen Sentence Fluency

When we read aloud well-written picture books, students hear how authors combine individual sentences to create extended text that is easy on the ear. But don't assume students will understand an author's techniques intuitively. They may need some help. So as you read, don't be afraid to stop and reread strong passages and point out what makes them that way. To get you started, here are some of my favorite picture books for sentence fluency.

> "*It's the books read and reread, savored and shared, that will affect us as writers..*"
>
> —Lucy Calkins

Agent A to Agent Z

Andy Rash
Scholastic, 2004

In this clever alphabet mystery, Agent A, a super spy on assignment, must find out which of the other agents, B to Z, is the fake. Each spy's identity and mission are revealed as the reader tries to guess the imposter. Through a series of rhyming couplets, the plot takes interesting twists and turns until, finally, the answer is clear. The ending came as an amusing surprise to me.

The Alphabet Tree

Leo Lionni
Alfred A. Knopf, 1968

An ant tells a magical story about how letters make words and words make sentences. The story opens with letters settled in on their favorite leaves of a tree. But in a strong wind, the letters are blown together in a pile. Then a word bug comes along and teaches the letters how to make themselves into words so they can be stronger against the wind. A little caterpillar then tells the words that he finds them confusing and suggests they make themselves into a sentence to "*mean* something." And so the words happily go about forming simple sentences until the caterpillar challenges them to make a really important sentence, which they do: "Peace on earth and goodwill toward all men." Bruno Bettelheim says, "*The Alphabet Tree* shows rather than tells what literacy is all about." I couldn't agree more.

Cloud Dance

Thomas Locker
Harcourt Children's Books, 2000

In this simple, descriptive text, Locker paints a picture of the ways clouds look in different seasons, times of the day, and weather. With lines like "Nighttime clouds with silver edges shimmer in the moonlight," this book is poetic and a good choice for choral reading. Locker's other books, such as *Mountain Dance* and *Water Dance*, make excellent additions to your sentence-fluency collection too.

Dream Weaver

Jonathan London
Harcourt Children's Books, 1998

"Nestled in the soft earth beside the path, you see a little yellow spider," begins this book filled with lyrical sentences. It's a good choice for reader's theater because so many of the passages, such as " . . . trees hum, the branches creak" and " . . . around a bend—crash, thrash, crash. A hiker. 'Watch out! The spider!'" lend themselves to sounds and actions. This is one of my all-time favorite books for sentence fluency. The language is beautiful.

Fireflies

Julie Brinckloe
Simon & Schuster, 1985

This story takes place at twilight, when fireflies appear. Dialogue, long descriptions, and one-word exclamations come together to provide a model of sentence variety. The book contains a variety of voices, too, ranging from sad to ecstatic as the protagonist catches the fireflies and sets them free. This book is a joy to read.

In the Space of the Sky

Richard Lewis
Harcourt Children's Books, 2002

The wonders of nature are captured in this simple yet poignant text. Magnificent sentences describe the world's beauty, such as "There—in the space of the sky are paths of birds, rivers of air, gardens of light . . . " and "There—in the space of the earth are hills bending, waters gathering, seeds opening." Do you feel the beat? Lewis elegantly captures the feel of the sky, the earth, and his home.

Joyful Noise: Poems for Two Voices

Paul Fleischman
HarperCollins, 1988

The various ways that insects look, sound, and behave are the central concerns behind this volume of short poems meant to be read aloud by more than one person. When students read together, they become aware of phrasing—when to pause, when to accelerate, when to raise and lower their voices. Fleischman's *I Am*

Phoenix: Poems for Two Voices and *Big Talk: Poems for Four Voices* are also sure to get your primary students reading and writing.

The Magic Hat

Mem Fox
Harcourt Children's Books, 2002

"Oh, the magic hat, the magic hat! It moved like this, it moved like that! It spun through the air like a bouncing balloon and sat on the head of a hairy baboon!" No one writes more rhythmically than Mem Fox. She is masterful at creating text that just sounds right. No syllable is out of place, no word too short or too long. Students will enjoy reading this book for the same reasons they like all of her books—it is well written and about things that kids enjoy. You might also want to read Dr. Seuss's *The 500 Hats of Bartholomew Cubbins* (1996) and compare the two authors' ideas and writing styles.

Saturdays and Teacakes

Lester L. Laminack
Peachtree, 2004

"Pedal, pedal, pedal . . . " In his trademark Southern lilt, Laminack gives us a glimpse into the life of a young boy who rides his bike through town every Saturday to "Mammaw's" place. Using gorgeous, sensory sentences, he draws the reader into the kitchen, and interspersing authentic dialogue throughout, creates a read-aloud story that is as delicious as Mammaw's teacakes. It's a celebration of the unconditional love between grandmother and grandson.

Tanka Tanka Skunk!

Steve Webb
Scholastic, 2003

This offbeat piece is perfect for teaching students to listen for rhythm in text. Resembling drum beats, the words burst off the page. "Say their names together, and hear the beat like this . . . Sunka Tanka Sunka Tanka, Tanka Tanka Skunk!" Young writers will want to shout the words, delighting in the way Webb puts them together.

Final Reflections on the Sentence-Fluency Trait

"See you later, alligator? In a while, crocodile." We still smile at catch phrases like those. Why? Because we're readers and writers at heart, and readers and writers love the sound of language. Teachers who regularly share words, phrases, and sentences aloud open the door to fluency. Their students write words, phrases, and sentences that are beautiful, not just correct. In my travels, I've seen this happen time and time again.

Celebrating language should be standard practice in the writing classroom. Primary students can learn how to begin sentences, vary their length, and check for how they sound right from the beginning. To craft sentences beautifully, however, students must also have knowledge and application of conventions, which are covered in the next chapter.

My First Scoring Guide for *Sentence Fluency*

Strong

I've Got It!

- My sentences are well built.
- It is easy to read my sentences aloud.
- The way my sentences begin makes them interesting.
- I've varied my sentence lengths.

Developing

On My Way

- I've got sentences!
- There are some places to make smoother when I read aloud.
- I've tried a couple of different ways to begin my sentences.
- I might put some sentences together or I could cut a few in two.

Beginning

Just Beginning

- My sentences aren't working well.
- I'm having trouble reading my piece aloud.
- The beginnings all sound the same.
- I've used "and" too many times.

Share this student-friendly scoring guide with students when they are ready to assess their own and their classmates' writing for sentence fluency.

CHAPTER 8

Strengthening Conventions

Reading specialist Janet Malek was working in a first-grade classroom recently. When she stopped by a group of students to find out how things were going, Terrence asked, "How do you spell *violence?*"

Janet replied, "What are you writing that you need to use the word *violence?*"

"You know, Mrs. Malek, 'Roses are red, violence are blue . . . "

There is no place like a beginning writing class. Young students listen to the language and write what they hear. Sometimes the spelling is off and, as in Terrence's case, it gives us a chuckle. Sometimes it's just wonderful, as is this second grader's assessment of her peer: "She coulden't even spell 'culdn't' Her spelling was abyzmall." Spelling is only part of the conventions trait; the trait also covers punctuation, capitalization, paragraphing, grammar, and usage. Students usually consider conventions at the editing point in the writing process, although conventions can also be used to shape meaning (Angelillo, 2002).

More than a rigid set of rules, conventions invite choices. They can clarify or confuse the meaning of text. They can make an otherwise dull passage come alive (as dashes, capital letters, or ellipses can). But a sentence with no end punctuation, no capital letters, or incorrect spelling only befuddles a reader. And we all know that a written work is clearer and easier to read when it's well edited. As a sous-chef coordinates the elements of a meal for the diner, students must put the finishing touches on their writing in preparation for the reader. Donald Graves (1994) says, "[conventions], like sign posts, help you, the reader, enter familiar ground so you can concentrate on the information without distraction" (p. 191). The primary purpose of conventions is to help the reader.

Here is what kindergarten and first-grade students wrote about conventions:

- Conventions means punctuation. And Capitols.
- Conventions are help foll because they help us. Rite.
- Conventions means whriting periodsand question marks and explanation marks. Also using proper engish and spelling write. Now that's good!
- Conventions means use punctuation and be shore to proofread and edit.
- You hal to uas capdoso sic in you rading. (You have to use capitals in your writing.)
- I think conventions are like choies.

Conventions: A Definition for Primary Students

Primary writers are too young and inexperienced to show control over sophisticated conventions, but there are certain ones they can follow to make their writing correct and understandable, including using

- imitation and real letters.
- upper- and lowercase letters.
- phonetic spelling.
- the conventional spelling of simple words.
- end punctuation.
- capital letters at the beginning of sentences, on proper nouns, and in titles.
- "s" for plurals or possessives.
- contractions.
- indenting.

Students learn editing skills in a somewhat linear fashion, moving from simple skills such as shaping letters to more complex ones such as spelling correctly. Reading helps them along. As students look at text in published materials, they notice letter shapes. They see that there is space between letters and words. They figure out that words go in sentences and that sentences start with capitals and end with punctuation marks. Students who interact with texts learn a great deal about how conventions work, setting the stage for the use of conventions in their own pieces. As Janet Angelillo (2002) puts it, "Children who engage with text regularly are used to seeing punctuation . . . As they sit listening, children pick up more than just plot and character" (pp. 24–25).

I firmly believe that the person who edits is the person who has been taught how to edit. So, this chapter helps you coach students in editing their own work one skill at a time. You'll find activities later that show how to help primary students take charge.

Addressing Parent Concerns About Conventions

Sometimes it seems the only thing parents care about is good use of conventions, right? That's probably because when they were in school they were led to believe that conventions were the be-all and end-all of writing. It's important, therefore, to inform parents that conventions are only part of writing and that students learn how to use them correctly over time, as they revise and edit their own work.

- At back-to-school nights or curriculum fairs, explain the basics of the writing process, the traits, and the role of conventions. Show how you will teach students to revise and edit.
- Send home notices and newsletters with details about how you're helping students edit their work one convention at a time. Include copies of that work so that parents can see how much their child is learning.
- Invite parents in during writing workshop to listen and respond positively to students' work, and answer questions about conventions. Have them use the "Tips for Students Working on Conventions" on page 265 as a handy reference.
- Send home examples of student work that have been edited by their child. If students have only worked on one convention (for instance, spelling) and therefore have not addressed other errors, write a note explaining that fact.
- Keep samples of students' work in folders so you can show parents the improvement their child has made since the beginning of the year.
- Make sure parents have a copy of The Primary Scoring Guide on page 245 so they know the criteria upon which you're measuring students. You can give them the student-friendly version on page 273 if you feel it is more appropriate.

The Challenge of Teaching Conventions

> *"From experience, we have come to see again and again that children learn about the craft and process of writing at the same time as they are learning about the conventions of the language. It's not a chicken-and-egg question."*
>
> *—Katie Wood Ray and Lisa B. Cleaveland*

Worksheets. Daily drills. Meaningless activities. These are the weapons of mass instruction. And they don't work. Students do not become skilled at using conventions from inauthentic practices. As with all other aspects of writing, students learn conventions by practicing on their own writing. Look for opportunities to help students learn new skills as the need arises. As you teach students conventions and they apply them to their work, their text will become more readable and interesting. And each time students make sound editing decisions, they become more confident about using conventions. Using them correctly becomes a way of life.

To move primary writers in that direction, pose questions as they edit such as "Why did you add a quotation mark here?" "Have you considered a different way to spell this word?" "Why have you capitalized this word but not that one?" When students learn to edit for a reason, and not just to complete a worksheet assignment, conventions become a means to an end, not an end in itself.

Assessing Student Work for Conventions

The Primary Scoring Guide on page 245 helps us determine the extent to which students are using conventions correctly and stylistically in writing. Use it to assess individual pieces of writing, as follows:

STEP 1: Collect student papers you want to assess for conventions.

STEP 2: Photocopy the Primary Scoring Guide: Conventions since you'll want to write on it and highlight key words as you go.

STEP 3: Read the scoring guide's descriptors for each of the five levels, from top—5: Established—to bottom—1: Ready to Begin. Each descriptor shows how writing typically reveals itself at that level. Also, notice that the descriptors parallel one another from level to level. For example, the first descriptor for each level deals with the piece's spelling.

STEP 4: Read one of the student papers carefully, paying attention to everything on the page, both pictures and text.

STEP 5: Look at the first descriptor for each level and determine the one that most closely matches the paper. Work your way through the rest of the descriptors for each level, checking off the appropriate ones. Each level has a point value; average the total to determine the piece's overall score in conventions. The process will get easier, faster, and more accurate as you practice.

Sample Papers to Assess for Conventions

The student papers that follow represent a wide range of skill in the conventions trait. To practice scoring conventions, read each paper closely and assess it against the scoring guide on page 245. Then read my descriptor-by-descriptor assessment of the piece and see if my score matches yours.

Remember, the skills identified at each level are typical. Don't be surprised if you find your students experimenting with conventions they haven't even come close to mastering, placing periods at the end of each line, for example, even though the sentence is not complete.

If you wish, score these pieces in ideas, organization, voice, word choice, and sentence fluency, using the scoring guides in Chapters 3 through 7. (See pages 70, 104, 140, 174, and 209.) Remember that your assessment may be higher in one trait than another. It's quite possible for a student to write with interesting words, for example, but have trouble with conventions. Or vice versa. When you assess for all the traits, you build a profile of student performance that allows you to target your instruction to the areas where students need the most help.

Ready to move to the grades-3-and-up scoring guide!

The Primary Scoring Guide

Conventions

Established 5	____ High-use words are spelled correctly and others are easy to read. ____ The writer applies basic capitalization rules with consistency. ____ Punctuation marks are used effectively to guide the reader.	____ One or more paragraphs with indenting are present. ____ Standard English grammar is used. ____ Conventions are applied consistently and accurately.
Extending 4	____ Spelling is correct or close on high-use words (*kiten, saed, want*). ____ Sentence beginnings and proper nouns are usually capitalized. ____ The writer uses end punctuation and series commas correctly.	____ The writer may try more advanced punctuation (dashes, ellipses, quotation marks) but not always with success. ____ Only minor editing is required to show thoughtful use of conventions.
Expanding 3	____ Spelling is inconsistent (phonetic spelling–e.g., *kitn, sed, wtn*) but readable. ____ Upper- and lowercase letters are used correctly.	____ Capitals mark the beginning of sentences. ____ End punctuation marks are generally used correctly. ____ The writing correctly follows simple conventions.
Exploring 2	____ The words are unreadable to the untrained eye (quasi-phonetic spelling–e.g., *KN, sD, Wt*). ____ There is little discrimination between upper- and lowercase letters.	____ Spacing between letters and words is present. ____ The writer experiments with punctuation. ____ The use of conventions is not consistent.
Ready to Begin 1	____ Letters are written in strings (prephonetic spelling–e.g., *gGmkrRt*). ____ Letters are formed irregularly; there is no intentional use of upper- and lowercase letters. ____ Spacing is uneven between letters and words.	____ Punctuation is not present. ____ The piece does not employ standard conventions.

PAPER #1
"HIPPO-EYU-"

hiPPo—EYU-
ikmO-EKUO
iVWTqUEiuuuu
VABYPbGCV
YBVQGVWi
iTVOi-vahiLY

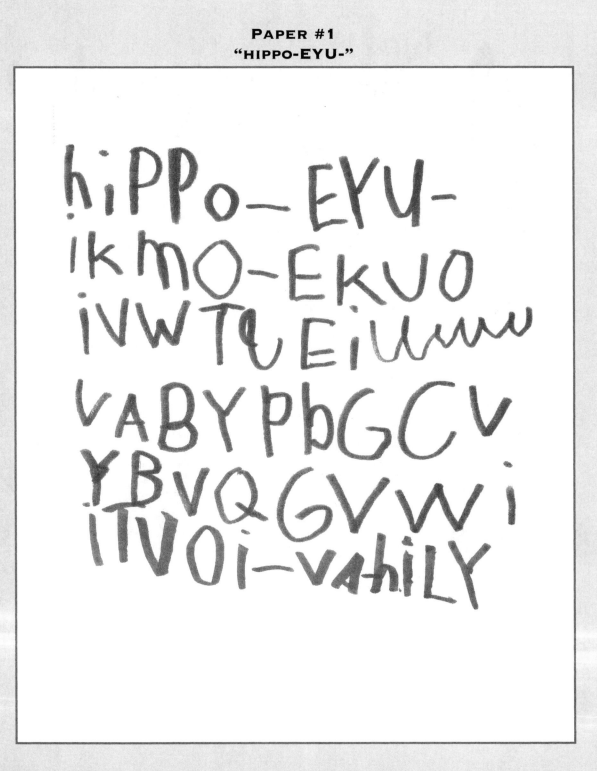

Time to Assess

PAPER #1
"HIPPO-EYU-"

Clearly, this student has worked hard on this piece. In fact, she's written a whole story, which I'm sure would make perfect sense if she read it aloud. However, as it stands, she uses only imitation words, makes no distinction between upper- and lowercase letters, and for some reason, punctuates only to link letters. Therefore, this piece receives a 1: Ready to Begin score in conventions.

- Letters are written in strings (prephonetic spelling—e.g., *gGmkrRt*).

  Some of the letters are grouped into word-like units and set off with a dash, but otherwise the letters are written in strings.

- Letters are formed irregularly; there is no intentional use of upper- and lowercase letters.

  This piece is a real mishmash of upper- and lowercase letters. The writer does not show control over either form.

- Spacing is uneven between letters and words.

  Spacing is consistent between letters but uneven between letter groups. A dash separates some "letter words" from others. This is a good start at using spacing to help the reader identify separate words.

- Punctuation is not present.

  The only punctuation mark is the dash, which appears to work as a spacer. It would be very interesting to ask the writer to explain the use of the dash here—to shed some light on the intent.

- The piece does not employ standard conventions.

  Standard conventions of spelling, punctuation, and capitalization are not evident.

Paper #2
"CArN. I."

CArN. I. HAV
SUM. DZnt

Time to Assess

PAPER #2
"CARN. I."

This charmer of a piece was written by a girl to her mother after she was sent to her room for misbehaving at the dinner table. It reads, "Can I have some dessert?" What a great moment to celebrate—the child is using writing for real communication. Notice the phonetic spelling and the interesting use of periods between words. It gets a score of 2: Exploring for conventions.

- The words are unreadable to the untrained eye (quasi-phonetic spelling—e.g., *KN, sD, Wt*).

  Primary teachers can read this piece, but others might have problems. The words "hav" for "have" and "sum" for "some" are the closest approximations.

- There is little discrimination between upper- and lowercase letters.

  There does not appear to be any pattern to upper- or lowercase letters. They are mixed together.

- Spacing between letters and words is present.

  The words are "punctuated" with a period between each one. The student knows that words require room around them.

- The writer experiments with punctuation.

  The student knows just a little about using periods and applies that knowledge here. Ironically, she doesn't put punctuation at the end.

- The use of conventions is not consistent.

  Playing with punctuation, phonetic spelling, spacing, and upper- and lowercase letters shows that this student is on her way to using conventions correctly, even though she has virtually no control yet.

Paper #3
"On Satterday"

On Satterday I got
my tree. I4 was
mediem sized.
We all liked it.
So we got it. Then we
talked to Santa.
I could tell he was fake.

Time to Assess

Paper #3
"On Satterday"

This funny little piece is an excellent example of conventions at the halfway point. There are as many strengths in conventions here as weaknesses. Capital letters at the beginning of sentences, simple words spelled correctly, and end punctuation used correctly are why I gave this a 3: Expanding for conventions.

- Spelling is inconsistent (phonetic spelling—e.g., *kitn, sed, wtn*) but readable.

  The spelling on this piece works well. "Satterday" and "mediem" are wrong but close. The spelling in the rest of the piece is correct.

- Upper- and lowercase letters are used correctly.

  This writer has upper- and lowercase letters figured out and uses each with consistency. When writers begin showing control over upper- and lowercase letters, individual words begin to pop out.

- Capitals mark the beginning of sentences.

  Capitals not only mark the beginning of sentences but also a proper noun, "Santa." The writer is using capitals effectively here.

- End punctuation marks are generally used correctly.

  Five sentences, five periods. It works. There is an interesting apostrophe placed in the middle of the word "It," but the end marks are all correct.

- The writing correctly follows simple conventions.

  Easy to read, the writing contains the basics to guide the reader.

Paper #4

"Hi, my nickname is____."

Hi, my nick name is [illegible].
My grandpa was a workaholic.
He worked as a barber and also
worked at the ESKIMO PIE
factory. I realy never met my
grandpa because I was little.
But anyway I do remember
my famliy reunion wich my
grandpa was at but now my
grandpa has past away but every
time I watch the family reunion
video I can always remember
my grandpa.

Time to Assess

Paper #4

"Hi, my nickname is____."

Like "On Satterday," this piece contains correct spelling and use of capital letters, but here the vocabulary is more sophisticated. There is even an accurately placed comma after the greeting: "Hi, my nickname is ________." Because of these strengths, I give this piece a 4: Extending in conventions.

- Spelling is correct or close on high-use words (*kiten, saed, want*).

  Tricky words are handled well ("workaholic," "Eskimo Pie," and "reunion") with only a few misses: "wich" for "which," "realy" for "really," "nick name" for "nickname," and "past" for "passed." Credit should be given for trying harder words and for getting many right. So I say, "Way to go!"

- Sentence beginnings and proper nouns are usually capitalized.

  Each sentence begins with a capital. "Eskimo Pie" is not only capitalized, it is outlined to make it stand out, a noteworthy moment of presentation.

- The writer uses end punctuation and series commas correctly.

  Periods are in place. The run-on sentence that begins "But anyway" is a bit confusing. However, to fix it would take rewording, not just adding capitals and punctuation, so it should be assessed as a sentence-fluency issue.

- The writer may try more advanced punctuation (dashes, ellipses, quotation marks) but not always with success.

  The comma after the greeting is the only evidence of more advanced use of conventions.

- Only minor editing is required to show thoughtful use of conventions.

  A bit of editing and some revision is needed to make this a really strong piece in conventions and sentence fluency. This writer is well on the way.

Paper #5
"Stranger Snowman"

Stranger Snowman

First, the blue jays said, "Stranger in the woods!" Then, the animals went to See the Stranger. Next, the animals ate the food off the stranger. Last, the children put more food on the Stranger. The stranger was a Snowman!

Time to Assess

Paper #5
"Stranger Snowman"

You don't see many primary writers with this amount of control in conventions. This is a standout piece. The spelling, the capitalization, and the punctuation are astounding. I'm not wild about the organizational structure—very formulaic—but the conventions are terrific. Without a doubt, this piece scores a 5: Established in conventions.

- High-use words are spelled correctly and others are easy to read.

  All the words in this piece, from the simple to the more challenging, are spelled correctly. This writer has great skill and control.

- The writer applies basic capitalization rules with consistency.

  Basics, plus! I love how the writer capitalized "Stranger" and "Snowman" for emphasis. Outstanding.

- Punctuation marks are used effectively to guide the reader.

  Quotation marks, commas, and an exclamation mark are all placed where they belong. The punctuation in this piece is shining brightly.

- One or more paragraphs with indenting are present.

  There's no indenting here, but most likely it won't be a struggle for the writer when the time is right.

- Standard English grammar is used.

  Tenses and subject/verb agreement are consistent and correct throughout.

- Conventions are applied consistently and accurately.

  This piece is ready for a public appearance.

> *"The secret in assessing (and teaching) conventions is to notice what the student does know and to build on that. Remember that nothing is automatic—even writing from left to right. All must be learned."*
> *—Vicki Spandel*

It's easy to see mistakes first as students write, but try to look for what they do well, point it out, praise them, and then discuss what needs improvement. Writers need to know what they're doing successfully so that they can repeat it. Writers who stumble need encouragement to try again. No one should fail at writing. We should use our assessments to tell us what comes next in writing instruction. When we keep this in mind, the link between assessment and instruction is strong.

Recently, my friend Bridey's young son A. J. begged her to let him play football. Although Bridey was nervous about his getting hurt, she relented and signed him up for a novice league. After several weeks of nightly practices, I went to the first scrimmage. There was A. J., standing on the sideline, suited-up and waiting to be put in, but the coach didn't call his name. I watched as he stood, nervously shifting from one foot to the other, anticipating his big moment. Toward the end of the scrimmage, A. J. pulled on the coach's shirt.

"Coach, Coach, put me in."

The coach replied, "A. J., you're a little behind. Watch the plays and the other kids, then you'll learn."

A. J. answered, "But Coach—you said we're all beginning, right? How can I be behind if I'm beginning?"

How, indeed, could he be behind at the beginning? How can any of us? Keep A. J.'s question close in mind when you think about how much, how fast, and how well primary students can learn to write. They are, indeed, at the beginning. They should be put in the game and allowed to play.

Teaching With the Conventions Trait

As we've discussed, when it comes to teaching conventions, it's important to start simply and put students in control as quickly as possible. You can edit for students or you can teach them how to do it themselves. It's not a hard decision when put that way, is it? A word of warning, though: young writers won't edit as well, work as quickly, or be as thorough as mature writers. But if students learn new skills gradually, perhaps one each week, and practice it until it becomes second

Conference Comments

You can build and reinforce students' correct use of conventions with comments such as these.

- Look at how you've added spaces between your words. That's new for you.
- I like how you've started every sentence with a capital.
- Tell me why you added a comma here.
- Read this to me with a period at the end. Now read it with the exclamation mark. What a difference!
- Why don't you add this word to your personal spelling list? I notice you use it quite a bit.
- This sounds just like the word you are trying to spell. Let me show you how it looks in writing.
- You've begun using more vowels as you write. It's helping your words sound like they spell.
- When you wrote "I," you capitalized it. Good for you.
- You wrote this word with all capital letters. I can tell it's important.
- Thanks for putting a period at the end of this line. It makes me stop for a minute.
- I notice that you've added a question mark. Do you hear this in your head differently than your other sentences?

nature, they will learn quickly. Have faith in them and in your teaching.

To get to the point where students are truly in charge of their own editing, we have to abandon time-honored methods of correcting with a red pencil, giving students worksheets as practice for editing, and only publishing work that is perfect. The purpose of this section is to provide some activities to help you do that.

As we begin the conversation about teaching conventions, I want to make an important belief clear: the vast majority of primary students are not ready for serious instruction in grammar. However, you can build a sensitivity to written language structures by examining texts with your students and reading aloud every day from books and other resources that are models of excellent grammar usage. Carol Avery (2002) points out that "the language-rich environment of the classroom—

lots of talk and lots of reading aloud—gives children experience with standard English" (p. 206).

Paragraphing is another convention that should not be taught formally until students are ready—specifically, when they are able to write multiple sentences on the same topic and therefore should begin thinking about paragraphing. It is not a hard skill to learn once the student is able to produce enough text to warrant it.

Before we look at specific methods and activities, let's examine the principles behind teaching conventions.

Core Principles for Teaching Conventions

Help Students Understand the Why and How of Conventions

Draw upon what students notice about language. Maybe an apostrophe in a book catches a student's eye and you see it sprinkled all over her next paper like pepper. Have a discussion about how to use apostrophes with a little restraint, if you wish. But be satisfied that she was perceptive and brave enough to try them.

Look at examples from excited first-grade students learning to use punctuation marks. Their willingness to play and experiment with conventions is evident. Over time, this play and experimentation builds to understanding and skill as we nudge students to consider how to use conventions to make meaning clear as they write.

As I mentioned earlier, this journey toward meaning happens more quickly if students practice skills in the context of writing, rather than through isolated skill-and-drill worksheets. Isolated practice deadens students' minds to the connections between what they want to say and how to say it clearly. Danling Fu and Jane Townsend (1999) found that primary students in classrooms where there was extensive use of worksheets put forth little effort to get the best grade, wrote nonsense, and used words carelessly. When one student, Keith, was asked if he understood what he was doing, he replied, "No. I just do it" (p. 408).

When we shift the emphasis in conventions from being right to being clear, it makes all the difference. When students use conventions in new ways, it is a sign that conventions matter to them. The energy to master conventions will bubble up and spill out onto the page. If students don't apply them perfectly every time, it's okay. That's how they learn.

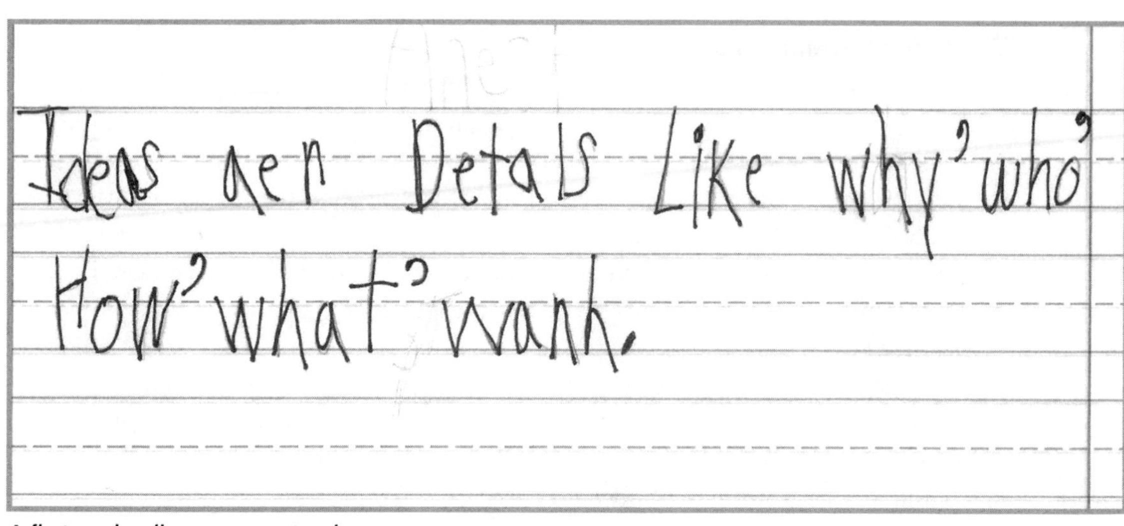

Ideas aer Detals Like why'who'
How'what'wanh.

A first grader discovers apostrophes.

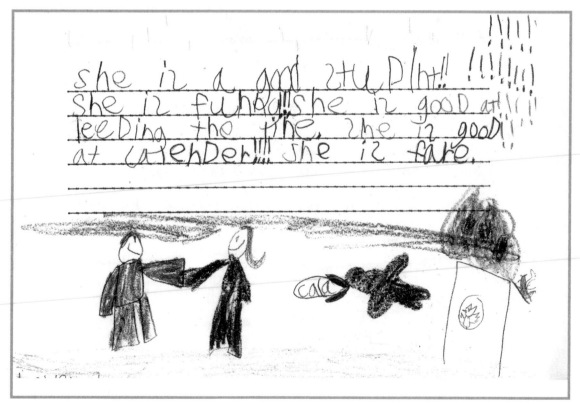

she iz a good stuDlnt!! !!!!!
She iz fuhny!!She iz gooD at!
leeDing the line. She iz gooD
at calenDer!!!! she iz fare.

The many exclamation marks in this piece suggest that this student is excited about the topic.

Build Conventions Skills Over Time

What skills should students have by the time they leave kindergarten? What about first grade? Or second? These are important questions to ask and talk about with your colleagues. Most states have benchmarks you can check, and districts and schools often have them, too. But just because benchmarks have been established does not change the fact that every child learns in a different way and at a different rate. They're kids—complicated, frustrating, maddening, lovely, ingenious, fabulous kids.

Students come to your class "as is." Although you don't control what they've learned before they arrive, you have a great deal to do with what they learn before they move on to the next grade. Students who start out scribbling in kindergarten write whole sentences by the time they go to first grade. How does this happen? One day at a time, one skill at a time. Oh, sure, there are a few steps backward. But mostly it's a steady push forward every day.

Use the Primary Scoring Guide on page 245 to discuss grade-level expectations for conventions with your colleagues. And create your own grade-level list of conventions based on the abilities and needs of students in your school, keeping in mind that some students will do more, some will do less, and that's just fine. All children will improve if you teach conventions steadily and slowly. And isn't that what's most important?

Create a Conventions-Ready Classroom

To help students with editing, have resources for them that are easy to find and use. Here are some suggestions to get you started.

1. Post large, easy-to-read posters and charts that illustrate basic conventions such as spacing between words, capital letters, and end punctuation. It could look like this:

   I[_]am[_]using[_]spacing.

   I can correctly spell [gargantuan].

   [W]riters should capitalize the first word in sentences.

   Look at my end punctuation[!]

2. Create a developmentally appropriate list of the editing symbols that you want students to use. Photocopy the list for students and make a chart to hang in the writing center. Be sure all teachers in your building are using this list if possible so students only need to learn them once and can apply them from year to year.

Editing Symbols for Beginning Writers

Symbol	Meaning	Example
^	Add a word.	I'm a ^ friend. (great)
# (under ^)	Add a space.	I'm agreat friend.
⊙	Add a period.	I'm a great friend ⊙
≡	Change to a capital letter.	i'm a great friend.
/	Change to a lowercase letter or a different punctuation mark.	I'm a great Friend? ⊙
SP (circle)	Correct spelling.	I'm a great (frnd) SP

3. Make a list of the editing skills you have taught and expect students to use. Teach students to refer to this list before they turn in papers. Add more to the list as students learn new skills. It could look like this:

Editor Alert: Does my paper have . . .

- my name?
- space between words?
- capital on the first word and *I*?
- my best spelling?
- punctuation at the end?

Getting Started With Conventions

After you assess your students to see what skills they have, you will have a clearer idea about where to begin. Here are some general ideas for teaching conventions that your students will enjoy and that will boost their editing skills.

- Set up four stations around the room for spelling, capitalization, punctuation, and expert help. At each station, post a few tips about the convention. Tell students to rotate from station to station, check their work, and write "S" for spelling, "C" for capitalization, or "P" for punctuation in the bottom right corner of their page as they edit for each convention. If they want expert help from you or another student, have them write "E" on their papers.
- Encourage students to wear an "editor's hat" when they are checking papers for conventions. Wearing the hat encourages them to take the job seriously because they have a physical reminder to help them focus on the editing tasks. Keep the hats at the writing station or wherever writing tools are kept.

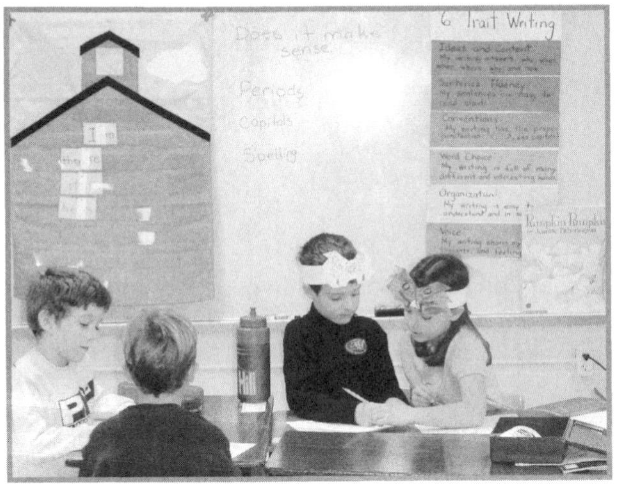

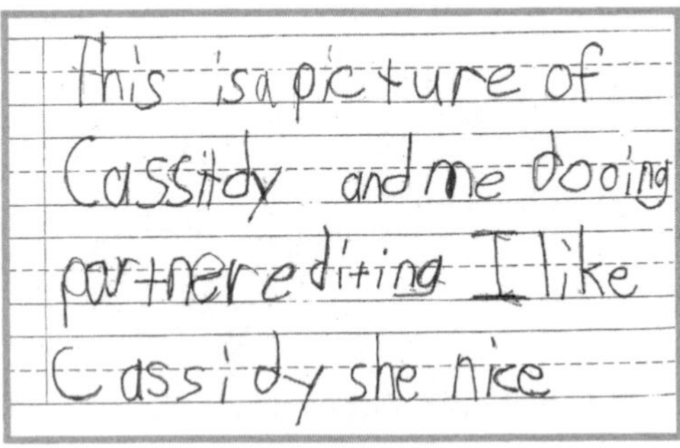

Laura Sadler's first graders wear hats as reminders to edit their writing.

- Create a box in which students turn in edited work. Label the box with the conventions that you've taught and expect students to check on their own before turning in their work. Add new conventions to the box as students learn them. Don't accept papers that are not edited for conventions you know students can check independently. When you find such papers in the box, hand them back, and ask students to edit them and turn them in again.
- Teach students to use a different colored pencil or pen to mark examples of incorrectly used conventions—for example, blue for words they feel they may have misspelled, green for punctuation, red for capitalization, and so on. Color coding allows writers to see the different conventions and where to focus their energy. It can also be used to mark examples of correctly used conventions. This emphasizes how much students know rather than how much they don't know.
- It's typical for students to begin writing by creating letter strings that often run together with little or no spacing. Breaking up the letter strings is the first step toward writing words. A simple way to help students create wordlike units from letter strings is to put a finger down at the point where the child says a word ends. Tell the child to end a word on one side of the finger and start a new one on the other. You can use a frozen-dessert stick instead of your finger to ensure that spacing is always consistent.
- Metal cookie sheets make excellent practice pads. Using magnetic upper- and lowercase alphabet letters and different punctuation marks, students can write words out on the cookie sheets. Let them practice capitalizing their name and the first word in a sentence, then they can add and exchange end punctuation. Give them fun words to spell. You can also buy magnetic sheets, write the letters and punctuation marks using a permanent marker, and cut them apart in strips.
- Post "The Conventions Song" on page 264 with the other trait songs. (See pages 83, 118, 154, 188, 224, and 291.) Sing it *to* students, sing it *with* students, and encourage students to sing it on their own. They may enjoy adding another verse or two over time as their knowledge about conventions increases.
- Use the student-friendly guide on page 273 to introduce the conventions trait and a range of editing skills. Photocopy it and give it to students to refer to as you work on the trait. They can use it to assess their own and classmates' writing.

The Conventions Song

(sung to the tune of "The Hokey Pokey")

You put your periods in,
You pull some spelling out.
You put your capitals in,
And you shake them all about.
You make your paper better
When you edit it just right.
That's what it's all about.

The collection of activities that follow are not meant to be a recipe for teaching conventions. Quite the opposite. It's meant to be more like a menu. Select activities as the need arises based on quantifiable evidence that students require help in spelling, capitalizing, or punctuating to make meaning clear. And whenever possible, teach them in the context of real writing. I've organized these activities into three categories:

1. Learning How to Spell Words That Matter
2. Practicing Accurate Capitalization
3. Using Punctuation to Enhance Meaning

Learning How to Spell Words That Matter

Learning to spell is a challenge for many students. Richard Gentry (1982), building on the work of Charles Read (1975), explains that there are five stages of spelling development: precommunicative, semiphonetic, phonetic, transitional, and correct. Typically, primary students first string random letters together, then they write first and last consonant sounds ("DD" for "David"). Finally, they add vowels. They tend to spell environmental text conventionally first—their name, the date, and so on—and then use sight words, such as *me*, *the*, and *dog*. Temporary spelling comes as writers learn to encode the sounds that make up words. From there, conventional spelling begins to emerge on first simple and then more complex words as students discover them. (Calkins, 1994; Graves, 1994; Ray and Cleaveland, 2004).

To move students toward using conventional spelling consistently and automatically, we must encourage them to do more than rely on memory. We must teach them to embrace and analyze everyday written language and explore the interrelationship of words and their sounds (Reed, 1975). In my experience, the best approach to learning to spell is three-pronged: 1) memorize the words needed most often, 2) learn basic spelling patterns for new words, and 3) use resources (people, dictionaries, and computerized spell checkers).

Students should use specific and accurate words, not just words they know how to spell. So encourage them to attempt words they are thinking and tell them it's okay to get them wrong. If students don't give it a go, we'll never know what they can spell or where to begin spelling instruction. They must feel safe enough to try and comfortable enough to ask for assistance. The activities that follow help students spell words that matter to them.

Tips for Students Working on Conventions

- Make spaces between letters and words.
- Add punctuation marks to show where to stop or pause.
- Try a new punctuation mark to change how the writing sounds.
- Use capitals on the first word of the sentence.
- Always capitalize *I* as a pronoun.
- Use capitals on important names and places.
- Spell words the way you hear them.
- Check spelling to be as "dictionary-like" as possible.

Kid Spell

Ask students to look at their writing and give you examples of words that are in "kid spell"—words that aren't right but are good approximations because they contain correct phonetic elements. List the words for all students to see. Ask for help to spell them correctly, writing the new words next to the old until you arrive at the conventional spelling. Have students identify one or two words that are challenging for them and find an example of them in their writing. Circle each misspelled word and write the correct spelling above it. Ask students to write these words on a personal spelling list or in their own spelling dictionary or pictionary (see activity in this section) for quick reference when they want to use them again.

Here is an example of "kid spell" that will make you and your students giggle:

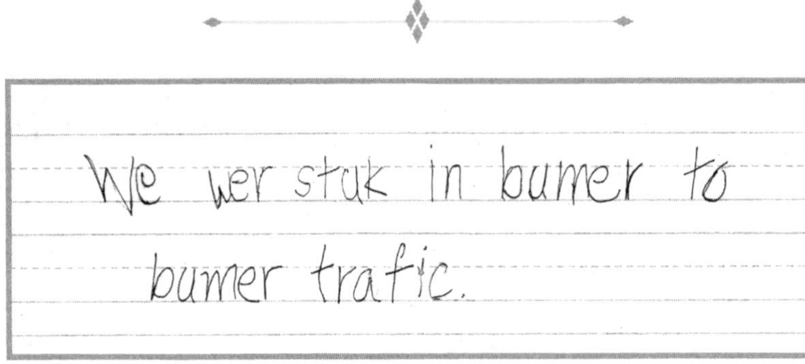

We wer stak in bumer to
bumer trafic.

Spelling With Shaving Cream

Give students a handful of shaving cream to spread out evenly on their desks. It might be a bit messy, so have them wear work shirts over their clothes if possible. Ask them to call out words that they find challenging, then guide them through spelling them correctly, one at a time, in the shaving cream with their fingers. After they spell each word, have them wipe the desktop smooth again and try another word. Students can practice writing capitals and using punctuation marks with shaving cream, too.

Spelling Pictionaries

Primary students are not too young to learn about writing resources such as dictionaries and thesauruses. Give each student a 12-page booklet made from folded sheets of $8\frac{1}{2}$-by-11-inch paper. Put two letters on each page, one at the top and one at the bottom, and group W, X, Y, and Z on one page. As students learn to spell a new word, encourage them to write and illustrate it in their booklet. Young writers can use their personal pictionaries to look up words as they write.

Reading Backward

This is an old trick my teachers taught me. When you are checking for spelling, read your text from ending to beginning. That way you won't read what you thought you wrote; you read what you really wrote, one word at a time, out of context. Backward reading allows students to see the word without getting swept up in the meaning. It works!

> *"My spelling is wobbly. It's good spelling, but it wobbles and the letters get in the wrong places."*
>
> *—Winnie the Pooh*

Practicing Accurate Capitalization

When students learn the alphabet, they learn upper- and lowercase letters. Distinguishing between them is a first step toward using capitalization in writing. I've noticed that writers typically first learn to put a capital at the beginning of their name, and then at the beginning of sentences, and finally at the beginning of proper nouns. It's a logical progression. Here are some ideas for helping students learn how and where to capitalize.

> *"Almost as soon as children begin to write, they will begin to spell certain words automatically, from memory, and this is necessary if they are to become fluent spellers. . . . They need to know that their image of a word is an important resource to draw on when they spell."*
>
> —Lucy Calkins

Clap for Caps

Read aloud a favorite book without showing the text to students and ask them to clap at points where they think there is a capital letter. To keep it simple, pause at the end of each sentence to emphasize the beginning of a new one. Model how to do this by selecting one student to read the text while you clap for capitals. After students clap for the beginning of sentences, ask them to clap for *I*. If students know to capitalize names, have them clap for those, too. Ask students to read their own pieces aloud and have a classmate clap where the capitals should go.

Stop-and-Go Capitalization

Give students small, round, green stickers or green highlighters. Ask them to sticker or highlight letters that should be capitalized in a piece of their writing. Give students red stickers or highlighters for end punctuation. Red for stop, green for go. As they look through their writing, they should see the ending and beginning of sentences marked appropriately.

This Is Why

As you talk with students individually or in small groups, ask them to tell you why they used capitals in a piece of writing. Students should be able to say, "It's the first word of the sentence," "*I* is always capitalized," or even "It's my name. It starts with a capital." By asking them to articulate how they use capitals as a convention, you reinforce what they know and are doing correctly.

Capitalization Bee

Create individual cards that each contain three words: a lowercased proper noun, a common noun, and a pronoun without capitalization, such as *ramon*, *boy*, and *he* or *portland, city*, and *my*. Put students in two lines. Hold up a card and ask the students at the head of the lines to call out the word that should be capitalized and why. ("'Ramon' should be capitalized because it's a person's name.") The first person to call out the right word and the reason goes to the back of the line. The other person sits down. Continue holding up cards until only one student is left standing. As students become more skilled, make the words more challenging.

Using Punctuation to Enhance Meaning

There are rules for punctuation just as there are for the other conventions. But punctuation is about much more than following rules, it's about creating writing that works. With an eye toward correctness and an ear toward fluency, writers use punctuation to guide the reader smoothly through the text. The lovely rhythms and cadences that were discussed in the chapter on sentence fluency are the result of the choice of punctuation as much as the choice of words. Punctuation completes sentences; without it sentences can't be fluent.

Using punctuation well is a skill that comes over time, like the other conventions. Students need to hear beautifully written language read aloud to develop an ear for how sentences should sound, and, therefore, how they should be punctuated. It's pretty easy to teach students to add a period at the end of a sentence; the work gets harder when we fold in the other punctuation marks. Here are some fun and effective ideas for teaching the basics and more sophisticated forms of punctuation.

Handmade Editing Charts

Put students into small groups and ask them to write out simple guidelines for using punctuation, such as "End a sentence with a period," "Put spaces between words," and so on. Tell them to include an example with each guideline. Give students time to create a final copy on poster-sized butcher paper, decorate it with markers and crayons, and hang it up as a reminder of what to do when they write. Student-made charts are more effective than commercial ones because of the thinking that students must do to create them.

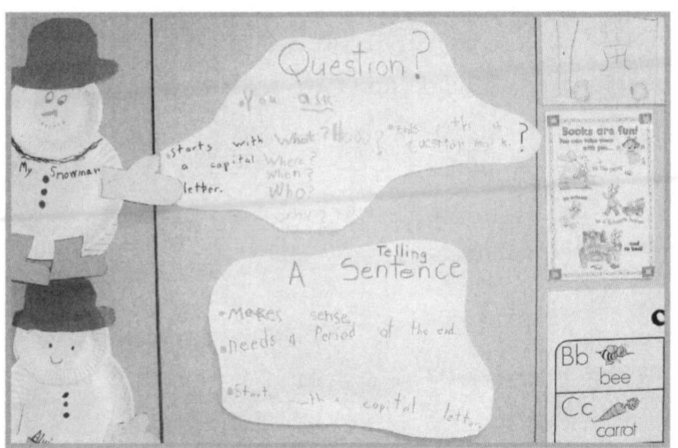

Handmade editing charts provide a reference for students as they write.

Splat!

Many years ago, pianist-comedian Victor Borge performed a hilarious routine that featured sounds for punctuation marks. Primary students can make up their own punctuation comedy routines. On a chart, list the punctuation marks the class knows and have students suggest sounds for each. For instance, a period could sound like *splat*, a comma, *zoo-ip*. Practice them together. Then give students several lines of text that contain different kinds of punctuation marks (periods, exclamation marks, quotation marks, apostrophes, and so on) and let them read it aloud, using sounds where the marks fall. Have them practice until their readings are smooth, then invite another class to enjoy the performances. Encourage students to use the sounds as they write to check their punctuation.

Everywhere You Look

Collect examples of various kinds of texts and explore them as a class, looking specifically at how the writers used punctuation. Make a list of what students notice and discuss how punctuation is used.

- fiction and nonfiction books
- comic strips
- board-game directions
- menus
- road signs
- junk mail
- receipts
- daily announcements
- advertisements
- personal notes
- lists
- letters
- e-mail
- greeting cards
- poems and song lyrics
- newspaper and magazine articles

The Royal Court

Create a royal title for each of the punctuation marks and have students design banners:

- The Earl of Exclamation Marks
- The Lord of Apostrophes
- The Countess of Question Marks
- The Prince of Periods
- The Duke of Dashes
- The Queen of Quotation Marks
- The Sovereign of Spaces
- The Count of Commas

Hang the banners on string that goes across the room. This whimsical touch makes working with punctuation fun for students and reminds them of the different kinds of marks available to them as they write.

Working With Dialogue

Young writers like to include dialogue in their writing, but often they don't know how to punctuate and capitalize it correctly. Ask students who have included dialogue in one of their pieces to highlight spoken lines in different colors to show which character is speaking. If there are three characters speaking in the story, one might be in yellow, another blue, and a third in orange. Introduce quotation marks to students to show the traditional way dialogue is indicated. When they are ready, show them how to capitalize and indent for dialogue, too.

Picture Books to Strengthen Conventions

The books listed in Chapters 3 through 7 are excellent resources for teaching students about conventions. Many contain sophisticated use of quotation marks, dashes, ellipses, and capitals, and words that are tricky to spell. Have students hunt through these books for good examples of the accurate and creative use of punctuation. Then return to these books regularly as questions about conventions arise in classroom discussions.

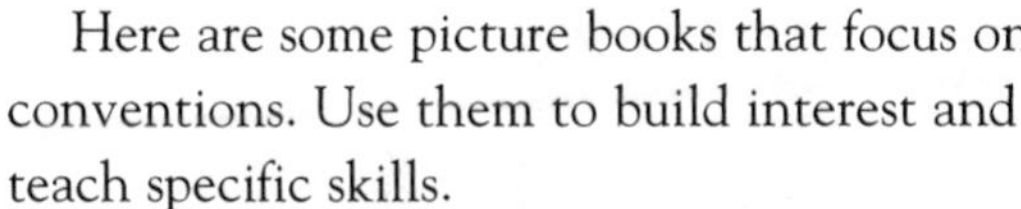

> "Punctuation cannot save poor writing. But it will bring luster and personality, as well as clarity, to good writing. It is a powerful tool in the writer's hand and the reader's eye."
>
> —Janet Angelillo

Here are some picture books that focus on conventions. Use them to build interest and teach specific skills.

A Picture Book on Punctuation

Punctuation Takes a Vacation

Robin Pulver, Holiday House, 2003

This is one of my favorite picture books in recent years. Mr. Wright, a frustrated teacher, gives the punctuation marks a day off from school because the students are not using them correctly. At first students are excited, but they quickly realize they can't write clearly without punctuation and find that they miss the marks more than they thought they would. After your students read this book, discuss the marks in the story. Maybe your students would enjoy writing their own stories about the day punctuation takes a vacation. Or perhaps they could write new stories about other conventions: "Spelling Takes a Vacation," "Capitalization Takes a Vacation," and so on.

A Picture Book Series on Conventions

Grammar Tales

Scholastic, 2004

Each title in Scholastic's *Grammar Tales* series is written with a clever spin on a conventions skill that is bound to make kids smile. From *Francine Fribble, Proofreading Policewoman* to Steve Scoop, the reporter for the *Hoopletown Evening Herald* in *The Mystery of the Missing Socks*, every character is on the case to make an exciting, exacting adventure. The books can stand alone, but I advise making the whole series available for students.

The Bug Book (adjectives)

Maria Fleming

Chicken in the City (nouns)

Maria Fleming

Francine Fribble, Proofreading Policewoman (proofreading)
Justin McCory Martin

The Mega-Deluxe Capitalization Machine (capitalization)
Justin McCory Martin

The Mystery of the Missing Socks (quotation marks)
Justin McCory Martin

The No Good, Rotten Run-on Sentence
Liza Charlesworth

The Planet Without Pronouns (pronouns)
Justin McCory Martin

Tillie's Tuba (adverbs)
Maria Fleming

A Verb for Herb (verbs)
Maria Fleming

When Comma Came to Town (commas)
Liza Charlesworth

Final Reflections on the Conventions Trait

> "*No passion in the world is equal to the passion to alter someone else's draft.*"
> —*H. G. Wells*

There aren't any secrets to creating good student editors, just a lot of hard work. We know, though, that the work is worth it. Primary students learn faster and more deeply if they do their own editing on their own writing, concentrating on one convention at a time. When they spell, capitalize, and punctuate correctly, students create writing that is clear and easy to navigate.

We have many years to teach students what they need to know about editing. If we start by teaching and modeling the basics, the rest will follow.

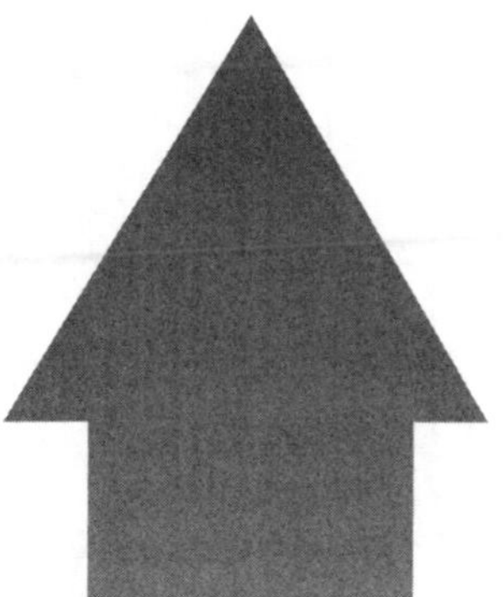

My First Scoring Guide for *Conventions*

I've Got It!

- My spelling is magnificent.
- All my capitals are in the right places.
- I used punctuation correctly to make my writing easy to read.
- I used correct grammar and added paragraphs where needed.
- I did a great job proofreading.

On My Way

- Only my simpler words are spelled correctly.
- I used capitals in easy spots.
- I have correct punctuation in some places but not in others.
- I proofread quickly and missed some things.

Just Starting

- My words are hard to read because of the spelling.
- My capitals don't follow the rules.
- I haven't used punctuation well at all.
- I forgot to proofread.

Share this student-friendly scoring guide with students when they are ready to assess their own and their classmates' writing for conventions.

◆ CHAPTER 9 ◆

Spotlighting Presentation

Creating text with visual appeal is challenging for young writers. It's hard for them to make everything fit together in a clean, polished way. Often letters run into the pictures, letters and words extend above and below lines, pictures are sketchy at best, or cross-outs and smudges abound. These are not problems, however. This is primary writing in all its glory.

The presentation trait, the "+1" of the 6+1 TRAIT model, relates to the appearance of writing. When it's handled well, presentation can make reading a breeze.

When we assess and teach for presentation, we think about margins, white space, letters on lines, separation of pictures and text, neatly formed and printed letters, and an overall pleasing look. We do not think about content or even the correct use of conventions. Presentation is the visual polish writers give text to make it easy to read. "Your paper is a princess in rags. Let's dress her up for the ball," commented one first-grade teacher to a student. This is it exactly.

Presentation is sometimes overrated, of course. When people ask what I do for a living, I tell them I help teachers and schools develop strong writing programs. The typical response is "Good for you. My child's handwriting is terrible." If the poor soul is sitting next to me on the airplane, he or she is then subjected to a two-hour treatise on the other, more important traits of writing. It's a common misconception, since many of our report-card grades for writing were actually based on handwriting. Of course, good handwriting is an important skill to learn, which is why it is central to the presentation trait. But it's not writing, even at the primary level.

The presentation trait is strongly connected to the final step of the writing process, publication. After students have gotten what they want to say on paper, they are ready to publish. Publishing is an important step because it solidifies and provides evidence of the students' position as writer. Work is put on bulletin boards, made into books, shared with other classes or audiences, or sent home as "finished." So presentation is key.

Students tend to buckle down and create their best work when they know that an "outsider" will read it. A real audience is a great motivator for them to make a clean copy with "curb appeal." It also brings them great pride.

Presentation: A Definition for Primary Students

Presentation relates to how the writing appears on the paper. It's often a measure of how much care students have put into the work. If they have spent a lot of time drafting, revising, and editing, they usually want the final product to look good. They want to publish and share it. You and they may both check for

- margins that frame the writing and pictures.
- carefully formed letters.
- neat, legible printing.
- letters and words that stay on the lines.
- clearly laid out pictures and text.
- carefully drawn pictures.
- cross-outs or smudges kept to a minimum on final copies.
- appropriate and simple use of fonts (if word processed).
- a finished, polished piece of writing.

The Challenge of Teaching Presentation

The physical challenges that young writers face when they create text and pictures cannot be underestimated. We don't want kids equating writing with pain, the inevitable outcome of overemphasizing neatness. Understanding that fine-motor skills and eye-hand coordination are still developing in primary students helps us to keep the presentation trait in check. Donald Graves (1994) notes, "Like gunners shooting at a moving target, children undershoot and then overshoot the lines" (pp. 243–44). Therefore, although neatness is important, we should only expect it to the best of children's abilities.

> *"Handwriting is the vehicle carrying information on its way to a destination. If it is illegible the journey may not be completed."*
>
> —Donald Graves

The cross-outs, eraser marks, and often an overall unpolished look are actually good things. The fact that the writer is making changes is a sign of growth. It's evidence that he sees writing as a process. We want students to feel comfortable with the process, not obsess over creating the final product. If some "sloppy copy" emerges at the beginning, fine. And if some children make a clean copy without much effort very early on, that's fine, too. But don't expect it of all your students.

Model for students how to make neat margins, form letters, and draw pictures that work well with text. Try doing a few projects in large or small groups and then publish them. But don't go overboard. Little ones need lots of time to practice writing to gain confidence and skill in presentation.

Assessing Student Work for Presentation

The Primary Scoring Guide on page 278 helps us determine how well students are handling presentation. Use it to assess individual pieces of writing, as follows:

STEP 1: Collect student papers you want to assess for presentation.

STEP 2: Photocopy the Primary Scoring Guide: Presentation since you'll want to write on it and highlight key words as you go.

STEP 3: Read the scoring guide's descriptors for each of the five levels, from top—5: Established—to bottom—1: Ready to Begin. Each descriptor shows how writing typically reveals itself at that level. Also, notice that the descriptors parallel one another from level to level. For example, the first descriptor for each level deals with margins.

STEP 4: Read one of the student papers carefully, paying attention to everything on the page, both pictures and text.

STEP 5: Look at the first descriptor for each level and determine the one that most closely matches the paper. Work your way through the rest of the descriptors for each level, checking off the appropriate ones. Each level has a point value; average the total to determine the piece's overall score in presentation. The process will get easier, faster, and more accurate as you practice.

Scoring Guide

Ready to move to the grades-3-and-up scoring guide!

The Primary Scoring Guide

Presentation

Established 5	___ The margins frame the text for easy reading. ___ Pictures and text look planned and work where they are placed. ___ The handwriting is legible and consistent in form.	___ There are no stray marks, cross-outs, or tears on the paper. ___ The overall appearance is neat and pleasing to the eye.
Extending 4	___ Margins are present but not consistent. ___ White space is used effectively, but words or pictures are often jammed at the end of lines.	___ Most letters are formed correctly and legibly. ___ A few cross-outs and smudges mar an otherwise pleasing appearance. ___ The overall presentation is organized with only minor distractions.
Expanding 3	___ Margins show awareness of left-to-right/top-to-bottom directionality, though they are not evenly spaced. ___ White space is present but inconsistent in size.	___ The handwriting is more legible at the beginning than at the end. ___ There are cross-outs and stray marks but only a few small smudges or tears from erasing. ___ The piece looks rushed.
Exploring 2	___ Attempts at margins are inconsistent. ___ The writing contains irregular chunks of white space. ___ Letters slant in different directions and form different shapes and sizes.	___ Many cross-outs, marks, and tears divert attention. ___ Only a last-minute attempt was made to create a readable piece.
Ready to Begin 1	___ No margins are present. ___ The use of white space is random and ineffective. ___ The handwriting is messy and illegible.	___ There are many cross-outs, stray marks, or tears from erasing. ___ Little care went into this piece to make it readable or understandable.

Sample Papers to Assess for Presentation

The following five pieces were written by the same student from kindergarten through second grade. His work shows remarkable progress in every trait, but for the sake of discussion, let's look at it through the lens of presentation.

PAPER #1
"MYEENEW . . ."

Time to Assess

PAPER #1
"MYEENEW . . ."

There's energy here, but because the text runs together and only confuses the reader, this little piece is just a start toward strong presentation. I've seen even messier papers, but I give this one a 1: Ready to Begin for presentation.

- No margins are present.

  A line defines the margins, but the text dribbles past on the right. The writing is difficult to read.

- The use of white space is random and ineffective.

  The picture overruns the text, which also makes the piece very difficult to read.

- The handwriting is messy and illegible.

  Clearly, making these letters was a struggle for this young writer. The letters are wobbly and uneven in size and shape.

- There are many cross-outs, stray marks, or tears from erasing.

  There are no erasures or other stray marks. Neatness counts in the presentation trait, so this piece scores high on this front.

- Little care went into this piece to make it readable or understandable.

  The incomplete pictures are made with quick, bold strokes, indicating that the writer didn't spend much time on this piece.

PAPER #2
"I TICK IT"

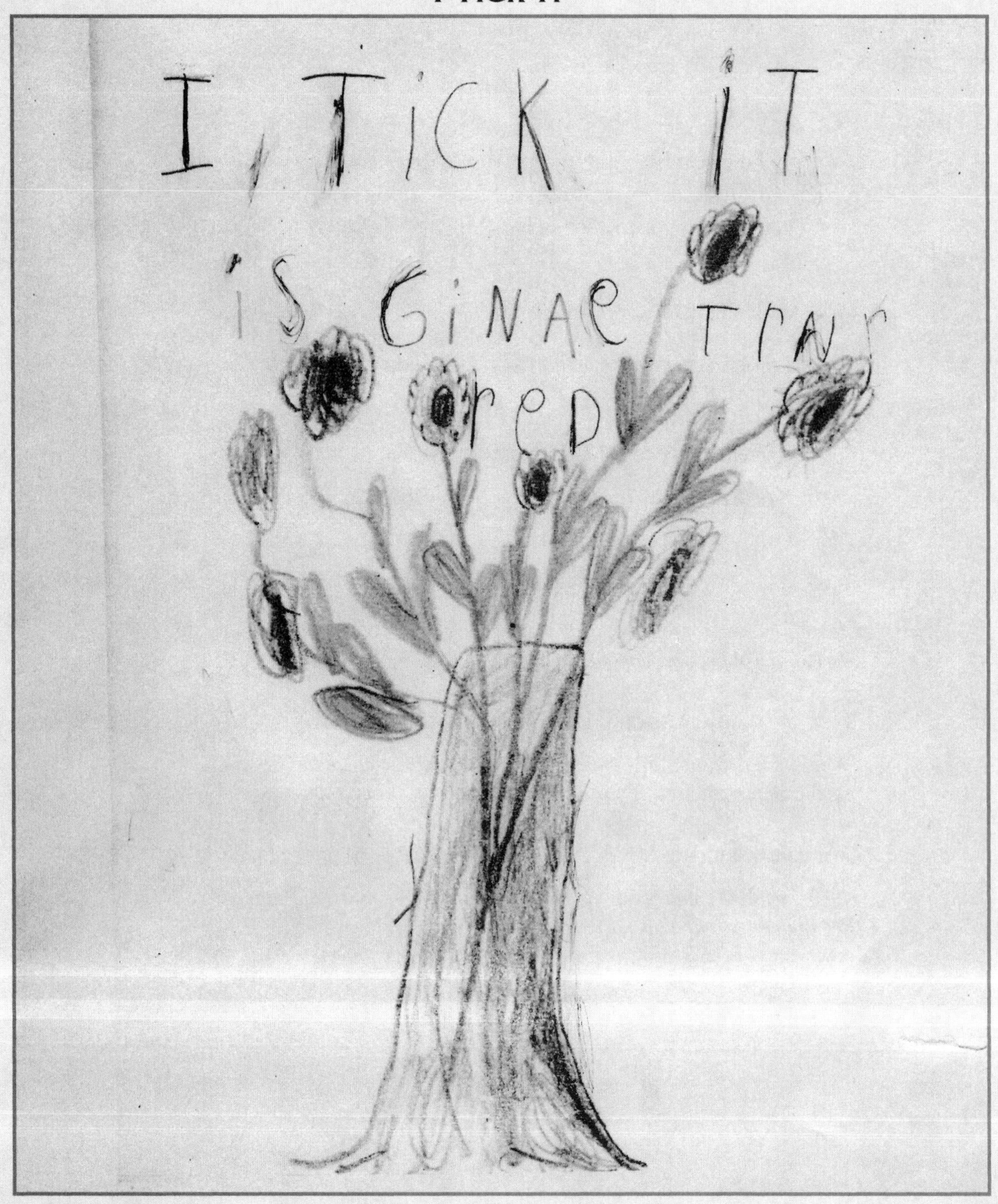

Time to Assess

Paper #2
"I Tick it"

The writer's prediction that the flower will turn red is so sweet. But the smudges and erasures, along with the letters that drop into the picture's space, make the piece hard to read. For presentation, I score it a 2: Exploring.

- Attempts at margins are inconsistent.

  White space frames the piece nicely, but after the first line, the letters and picture become jumbled.

- The writing contains irregular chunks of white space.

  There is white space to the right and left of the flower vase, drawing the eye up to the petals, blossoms, and words.

- Letters slant in different directions and form different shapes and sizes.

  The letters are different sizes, starting with a large one at the top and getting smaller as the writer runs out of room.

- Many cross-outs, marks, and tears divert attention.

  A few letters have been smudged and written over. The small tear at the bottom is hardly noticeable.

- Only a last-minute attempt was made to create a readable piece.

  The drawing has visual appeal, but the text feels rushed. The reader's eye is drawn to the picture which is nicely done. The text, however, could be more visually appealing.

Paper #3
"Now I am going to . . ."

now I am going to tell you
family about my famiy
in my family I have a
mom she is a great
mom, my Dad is nice
to.

Time to Assess

PAPER #3
"NOW I AM GOING TO . . ."

The letters here are so much more clearly formed and readable than they were in this student's earlier work, but I have trouble reading the piece because some of the writing isn't on the lines and is bunched together in the top margin. I give it a 3: Expanding for presentation.

- Margins show awareness of left-to-right/top-to-bottom directionality, though they are not evenly spaced.

  The writing in the top margin makes this piece confusing to read. When the writer begins using the lines, the text becomes much easier to follow.

- White space is present but inconsistent in size.

  There is an inconsistent amount of space between words. Toward the end, the space is as big as the word it follows. The space in the top margin is not used well either; the words slant down to the right until they reach the lines.

- The handwriting is more legible at the beginning than at the end.

  Just the opposite is true here. The text at the top is harder to read, although most letters and words are legible throughout.

- There are cross-outs and stray marks but only a few small smudges or tears from erasing.

  A few letters have been written over. Other than that, the piece is clean. Readers appreciate a piece that is neat.

- The piece looks rushed.

  Some letters are not well formed, which makes the piece feel like it was created in somewhat of a hurry.

PAPER #4
"ON HALOWEN"

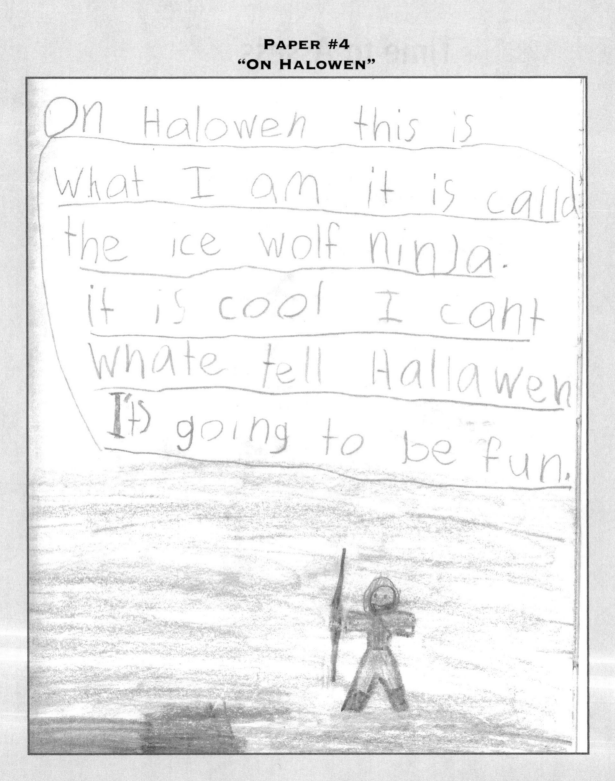

On Halowen this is
What I am it is calld
the ice wolf ninJa.
it is cool I cant
whate tell Hallawen
It's going to be fun.

Time to Assess

PAPER #4
"ON HALOWEN"

Remember, all the pieces in this section were written by one child over three years. So look back at paper #1 and notice how much he has improved. This student now knows a great deal about presentation and proves it with this piece. I score this one a 4: Extending for presentation.

- Margins are present but not consistent.

  The left margin is attempted, but the text slants inward a little more with every new line. The right side feels tight. There is a small top margin, and the picture beneath the text fits well.

- White space is used effectively, but words or pictures are often jammed at the end of lines.

  The writer uses the page well. He has added his own lines to keep his text reasonably straight. The words at the right are condensed a bit to fit.

- Most letters are formed correctly and legibly.

  The letters are consistently formed for the most part and straight up and down.

- A few cross-outs and smudges mar an otherwise pleasing appearance.

  This text is clean. What a gift to the reader!

- The overall presentation is organized with only minor distractions.

  The lines are distracting but the picture is a nice touch and, in general, the piece is easy to read.

Paper #5
"My Secret Jurrnl"

My Secret Jurrnl

Once upon a time this
boy named AJ had a
Secret Jurnul. The next day
AJ's friends told AJ to go
to the park. AJ had
nowida where the park was.
So he looked in his
secret Jurrnul and it
told him were the park
was he had nowida it
wood tell him where
the park was.
So the mistery was
solved. So he went to
the park and played
with his friends all
because of his secret
Jurrnul!

Time to Assess

Paper #5
"My Secret Jurrnl"

This student's three-year journey toward strong presentation ends on a positive note. This piece is easy on the eye and a pleasure to read. What an accomplishment. He started with poorly formed letters and pictures that overlapped and ended with a piece that certainly deserves a 5: Established in presentation.

- The margins frame the text for easy reading.

  Left, right, and bottom margins are working beautifully. The title in the top margin is a little distracting. However, the writer made it stand out by using big capitalized and underlined letters. Nice!

- Pictures and text look planned and work where they are placed.

  The text reads easily from first word to last. There is nothing last-minute about it.

- The handwriting is legible and consistent in form.

  Each word is clearly a unit and separated by just the right amount of space. The form is consistent, which makes the piece easy to read.

- There are no stray marks, cross-outs, or tears on the paper.

  No edits are evident; this is a polished piece. When writing has this kind of visual appeal, it's a treat to read.

- The overall appearance is neat and pleasing to the eye.

  The even margins, the good handwriting, the consistent letter, word, and line spacing, and the eye-catching title add up to a piece that is strong in presentation.

Teaching With the Presentation Trait

All young writers deserve a payoff for the hard work of writing, and encouraging them to take work public is one way to provide it. Having a real audience is sure to give them a rush.

I never felt that rush as a student because I wrote only to please the teacher, caring little about the quality of the writing or how it looked. I didn't consider myself a writer with ideas and voice of my own. It wasn't until I was an adult that I began to make my papers look as good as possible. I began spending time choosing fonts, checking spacing, and evaluating point size before printing out one last clean copy. Now I do that regularly. In fact, last year I let Uncle Sam know a gratifying discovery about myself. On the "occupation" line of my tax form, I boldly wrote, "Writer." I haven't been audited yet.

"I am a writer." We must help all primary students say that with confidence. Paying attention to how writing looks on the page moves them in that direction. When writers publish, they announce to the world, "I am a writer."

Conference Comments

As you help students bring visual appeal to their writing, you may want to make comments like these.

- My eyes are so happy when they read papers this neat. Thank you.
- Double spacing is a good idea when you write. It gives you extra room.
- Your margins make a beautiful frame around your writing.
- Thanks for erasing and rewriting so clearly.
- Each of your letters is perfectly shaped. Nice work.
- Isn't it amazing what difference a little extra space at the top can make?
- Your choice of font makes this easy to read.
- The drawing and the writing take up just the right amount of space.
- I like how you styled the most important word. It really stands out.
- Your writing is a pleasure to read.

The Presentation Song

(sung to the tune of "Yankee Doodle")

Take a look at what you wrote.
Does it look nice and neat?
Have you done the best you could
So reading is a treat?
Have you written carefully?
Is your writing clear?
Not a cross-out or a smudge
Will you or I find there.

Tips for Students Working on Presentation

- Picture how it should look when you are finished.
- Make your work easy on the eyes.
- If you cross out or erase, do it as neatly as you can.
- Frame the words and pictures with margins.
- Take your time and work carefully as you write and draw.

As with all the traits, you can introduce presentation with a song. Post "The Presentation Song" in your classroom along with the other trait songs (see pages 83, 118, 154, 188, 224, and 264) and sing them as the spirit moves you.

Another way to introduce the presentation trait is with the student-friendly guide on page 296. Photocopy it and give it to students to refer to as you discuss the trait.

Students who are familiar with all the traits may want to make student-friendly posters to remind classmates of each trait's important qualities, thereby putting the trait of presentation into action. At right, see one of three posters created by Ben, a second grader.

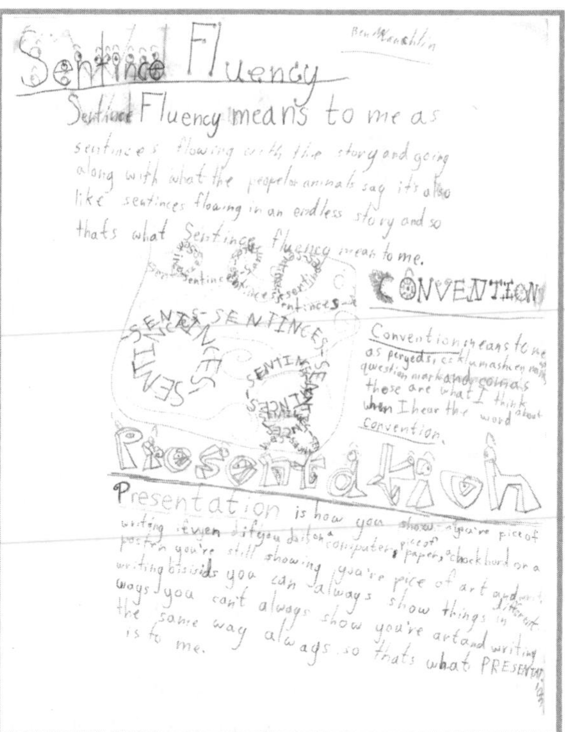

By composing and illustrating definitions of the traits, Ben learns an important lesson about presentation in particular and writing in general.

Some Ideas for Getting Started and Keeping the Momentum Going

These ideas are guaranteed to bring excitement and joy to your students as they prepare to share their work.

- Keep plenty of writing supplies available: pens, pencils, markers, scissors, tape, glue, stickers, and paper of different types and colors.
- Take time to show students how to make books by folding paper and, if your students are ready, cutting and stapling it. Keep models available for students to follow.
- Encourage students to practice making neat letters in their own writing, not on worksheets. Ask students to select a sentence or passage to rewrite in their best handwriting.
- Ask students to leave plenty of space between lines in drafts to allow room for revisions and edits.
- Show students interesting text layouts as you discover them. One of my favorites is the *Geronimo Stilton* chapter-book series from Scholastic. Key words and phrases throughout the texts are presented in color and creative shapes for emphasis. Encourage students to try writing this way.
- Hang students' work in the room, in the hallway, and all around the school.
- Attach a photo of the student to his or her work to make a powerful connection between the writing and the writer. If possible add a photo of a parent or guardian with the child to reinforce the fact that writing should extend beyond school walls.

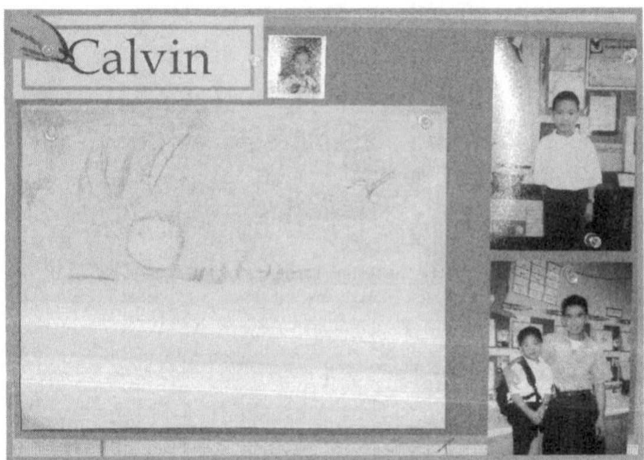

Calvin's finished writing is proudly displayed with photographs.

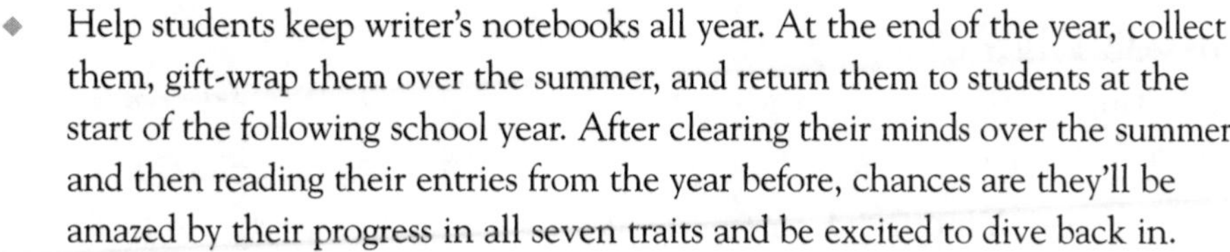

- Help students keep writer's notebooks all year. At the end of the year, collect them, gift-wrap them over the summer, and return them to students at the start of the following school year. After clearing their minds over the summer and then reading their entries from the year before, chances are they'll be amazed by their progress in all seven traits and be excited to dive back in.

Picture Books to Strengthen Presentation

There is no better way to reinforce the importance of writing's visual appeal than with picture books. The authors and illustrators of the books listed below use techniques simple enough for students to replicate. Many of the books in this list were mentioned as models for other traits, too, which make them perfect for covering more than one trait simultaneously. Most important, they are sure to inspire students to write creatively, beautifully, and purposefully.

Alphabet Adventure

Audrey Wood
Scholastic, 2001

Alphabet letters are the characters in this cute story. Have students write a sequel using Wood's technique.

Alphabet City

Stephen T. Johnson
Viking Press, 1995

Johnson depicts alphabet letters that he finds in everyday objects around the city. Ask students to do the same by looking around the classroom and the school.

Amelia's Easy-as-Pie Drawing Guide

Marissa Moss
Pleasant Company Publications, 2000

Any of the books in the Amelia series will give students ideas for spicing up their writing with colors, illustrations, and type techniques.

Cassie's Word Quilt

Faith Ringgold
Alfred A. Knopf, 2002

Make a paper quilt of words that students know, using this book as inspiration.

Charlie's Checklist

Rory S. Lerman
Orchard Books, 1997

This book features childlike illustrations and notes and letters in different handwriting-like fonts, which makes it a natural for young students to emulate.

Hello Ocean

Pam Muñoz Ryan
Scholastic, 2001

Within the text of this lovely book about a trip to the seashore, sensory words are boldfaced which makes it easy for students to see them and try them in their own writing.

How Are You Peeling? Foods With Moods

Saxton Freymann and Joost Elffers
Scholastic, 1999

Expressive photographs of fruits and vegetables will inspire students to create their own "foods with moods."

I Am America

Charles R. Smith, Jr.
Scholastic, 2003

Photos bring America and Americans to life. Students may wish to create a volume that celebrates their lives as Americans, using photos that they bring from home.

The Night I Followed the Dog

Nina Laden
Chronicle Books, 1994

This hilarious story contains illustrated words—a technique that students may want to use in their own writing.

Where Is the Green Sheep?

Mem Fox
Harcourt Children's Books, 2004

Each page of this book shows a sheep doing something fun, such as skiing down a slide and juggling. Your class can choose a different animal, and each student can create a page showing that animal doing something equally fun.

Final Reflections on the Presentation Trait

Students need to understand that how their writing looks matters less than what it says. After all, flat, uninspired writing is flat, uninspired writing, no matter how it is presented. That said, students should make their pieces as attractive and inviting as possible—readers will appreciate that. Presentation helps students go public with pride.

> *"The key to believing in our students' ability to do really big work in our writing workshops is to remember they will do it like five- and six- and seven-year-olds. It will look and sound like five- and six- and seven-year-olds wrote it."*
>
> —*Katie Wood Ray with Lisa B. Cleaveland*

My First Scoring Guide for *Presentation*

I've Got It!

- My paper is neat—no smudges or cross-outs.
- My letters are printed and written clearly.
- I have margins that make a frame.

On My Way

- My paper can be read, but it's not my best.
- Some of my letters are well done, but some are not.
- My margins work better in some places but not others.

Just Starting

- My paper is very hard to read.
- My letters are a mess.
- I forgot to use margins.

Share this student-friendly scoring guide with students when they are ready to assess their own and their classmates' writing for presentation.

Conclusion

Over the years teachers have asked me time and again, "Is it too early to start using the traits with primary writers?" The answer is an emphatic No. It's not too early; it's never too early. Your students need these traits to become the writers that they want to be. The truth is, the traits have always been a part of effective primary writing classrooms. Sure, they may have been called something different, but they've been there forever.

Plain and simple, the traits help students become better writers. They support assessing and teaching writing, but they aren't an end in themselves. Teaching students about the traits means embracing the writing process and learning how to weave the traits into that process. The trait model empowers young students to think like writers, talk like writers, and write like writers because it gives them the language to do so. The stunning simplicity of the traits, the shared vocabulary of writers, will add energy—an "I can do it" spirit—to your writing program.

It has been a joy to create this new resource book. I hope it serves you and your students well. And to that end, I have one last piece of advice: Be fearless. The energy you bring to your work, your faith that young writers have no limitations, and your willingness to try new things right along with them will make all the difference. Commit to leaving no stone unturned in your quest to inspire young writers. Stretch the bounds of your imagination to believe that anything is possible. The writing lives of your young students are at stake.

Professional References Cited

Anderson, R. C., Hiebert, E. H., Scott, J. A., & Wilkinson, I. A. G. (1985). *Becoming a nation of readers: The report of the Commission on Reading*. Washington, D.C.: National Academy of Education, Champaign, IL: University of Illinois, Center for the Study of Reading. (ERIC Document Reproduction Service No. ED253865)

Angelillo, J. (2002). *A fresh approach to teaching punctuation*. New York: Scholastic.

Angelillo, J. (2005). *Making revision matter: Strategies for guiding students to focus, organize, and strengthen their writing independently*. New York: Scholastic.

Applebee, A. (1986). Problems in process approaches: Toward a reconceptualization of process instruction. In A. Petrosky & D. Bartholomae (Eds.), *The teaching of writing: Eighty-fifth yearbook of the Nation Society of the Study of Education* (pp. 95–113). Chicago: University of Chicago Press.

Arter, J. A., Spandel, V., Culham, R., & Pollard, J. (1994). *The impact of training students to be self-assessors of writing*. Paper presented at the American Educational Research Association, New Orleans, LA.

Avery, C. (2002). *. . . And with a light touch* (2nd ed.). Portsmouth, NH: Heinemann.

Braddock, R., Lloyd-Jones, R., & Schoer, L. (1963). *Research in written composition*. Urbana, IL: National Council of Teachers of English.

Calkins, L. M. (1980). When children want to punctuate: Basic skills belong in context. *Language Arts*, 57(5), 567–573.

Calkins, L. M. (1986). *The art of teaching writing*. Portsmouth, NH: Heinemann.

Calkins, L. M. (1994). *The art of teaching writing* (New ed.). Portsmouth, NH: Heinemann.

Calkins, L. M. (2003). The nuts and bolts of teaching writing. *Units of study for primary writing: A yearlong curriculum*. Portsmouth, NH: Heinemann.

Calkins, L. M. & Mermelstein, L. (2003). Launching the writing workshop. *Units of study for primary writing: A yearlong curriculum*. Portsmouth, NH: Heinemann.

Diederich, P. (1974). *Measuring growth in English*. Urbana, IL: National Council of Teachers of English.

Dyson, A. H. & Freedman S. W. (2002). Writing. In J. Flood, D. Lapp, J. Squire, & J. Jensen (Eds.), *Handbook of research on teaching English language arts* (2nd ed.) (pp. 754–774). Mahwah, NJ: Lea Publishers.

Fletcher, R. (1993). *What a writer needs*. Portsmouth, NH: Heinemann.

Fletcher, R. (1996). *A writer's notebook: Unlocking the writer within you*. New York: HarperCollins.

Fox, M. (1993). *Radical reflections: Passionate opinions and teaching, learning, and living*. San Diego, CA: Harcourt Brace.

Fu, D. & Townsend, J. (1999). "Serious" learning: Language lost. *Language Arts*, 76, 404–408.

Fulghum, R. (1991). *Uh-oh: Some observations from both sides of the refrigerator door*. New York: Villard Books.

Gentry, J. R. (1982). An analysis of developmental spelling in GYNS AT WRK. *The Reading Teacher*, 36, 1992–2000.

Graves, D. H. (1982). A case study observing the development of primary children's composing, spelling, and motor behaviors during the writing process. Final report, September 1, 1978–August 31, 1981. Washington, D.C.: National Institute of Education. (ERIC Document Reproduction Service No. ED218653)

Graves, D. H. (1983). *Writing: Teachers and children at work*. Portsmouth, NH: Heinemann.

Graves, D. H. (1994). *A fresh look at writing*. Portsmouth, NH: Heinemann.

Graves, R. L. (1999). *Writing, teaching, learning: A sourcebook*. Portsmouth, NH: Heinemann.

Hairston, M. (1999). The winds of change: Thomas Kuhn and the revolution in the teaching of writing. In R. L. Graves (Ed.), *Writing, teaching, learning: A sourcebook*. Portsmouth, NH: Boynton/Cook. (Reprint of *College Composition and Communication*, 33 (1982), pp. 76–88 by NCTE. Urbana, IL: NCTE.)

Hillocks, Jr., G. (1986). *Research on written composition: New directions for teachers*. Urbana, IL: National Conference on Research in English.

International Reading Association (IRA) & National Council of Teachers of English (NCTE). (1996). *Standards for the English Language Arts*. Urbana, IL and Newark, DE: IRA and NCTE.

Jefferson, T. (1776). *The Declaration of Independence*. The Library of Congress: Washington, D.C.

Johnson, B. (1999). *Never too early to write*. Gainesville, FL: Maupin House Publishing.

Johnson, S. (1905). The life of Pope. In G. B. Hill (Ed.), *The lives of poets*. Oxford: Clarendon Press.

Lamott, Anne. (1994). *Bird by bird*. New York: Anchor House.

Le Guin, U. K. (1997). Openings and endings. In D. Brodie (Ed.), *Writing changes everything*. New York: St. Martin Press.

Lutz, E. (1986). *Invented spelling and spelling development*. Urbana, IL: ERIC Clearinghouse on Reading and Communication Skills. (ERIC Document Reproduction Service No. ED272922)

Murray, D. (1985). *A writer teaches writing*. Boston: Houghton Mifflin.

Murray, D. (1996). *Crafting a life in essay, story, poem*. Portsmouth, NH: Boynton/Cook.

National Writing Project & Nagin, C. (2003). *Because writing matters: Improving student writing in our schools*. San Francisco: Jossey-Bass.

Noden, H. R. (1999). *Image grammar*. Portsmouth, NH: Boynton/Cook.

Parker, T. (1997). Openings and endings. In D. Brodie (Ed.), *Writing changes everything*. New York: St. Martin Press.

Popham, W. J. (1995). *Classroom assessment: What teachers need to know*. Needham Heights, MA: Allyn and Bacon.

Purves, A. C. (1992). Reflections on research and assessment in written composition. *Research in the Teaching of English*, 26, 108–122.

Ray, K. W. with Cleaveland, L. B. (2004). *About the authors: Writing workshop with our youngest writers*. Portsmouth, NH: Heinemann.

Read, C. (1975). *Children's categorization of speech in English*. Urbana, IL: ERIC Clearinghouse on Reading and Communication Skills. (ERIC Document Reproduction Service No. ED112426)

Robb, L. (2004). Insights and connections: Discussing, journaling and writing about books (speech). International Reading Association. Reno, NV.

Romano, T. (2004). *Crafting authentic voice*. Portsmouth, NH: Heinemann.

Routman, R. (2001). *Conversations*. Portsmouth, NH: Heinemann.

Simpson, J. A. & Weiner, E. (Eds.), (1989). *The Oxford English dictionary* (2nd Ed.). Oxford: Oxford University Press.

Spandel, V. (2004). *Creating young writers: Using the six traits to enrich writing process in primary classrooms*. Boston: Allyn & Bacon.

Stiggins, R. J. (1994). *Student-centered classroom assessment*. New York: Macmillan College Publishing.

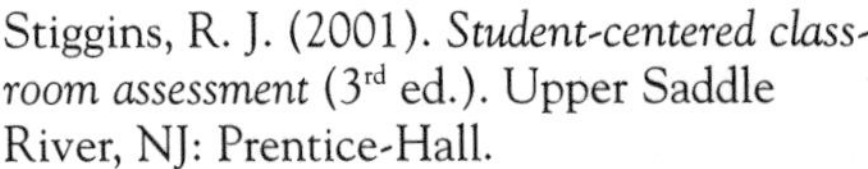

Stiggins, R. J. (2001). *Student-centered classroom assessment* (3rd ed.). Upper Saddle River, NJ: Prentice-Hall.

Strunk, Jr., W. & White, E. B. (2000). *The elements of style* (4th ed.). Needham Heights, MA: Allyn & Bacon.

Thomason, T. & York, C. (2000). *Write on target: Preparing young writers to succeed on start writing achievement tests*. Norwood, MA: Christopher-Gordon Publishers.

Truss, L. (2004). *Eats shoots and leaves*. New York: Gotham Books.

Weaver, C. (1979). *Grammar for teachers: Perspectives and definitions*. Urbana, IL: National Council of Teachers of English.

Weaver, C. (1996). *Teaching grammar in context*. Portsmouth, NH: Boynton/Cook.

Wiggins, G. (1998). *Educative assessment: Designing assessments to inform and improve student performance*. San Francisco: Jossey-Bass.

Zinsser, W. (1998). *On writing well* (6th ed.). New York: HarperCollins.

Children's Books and Media Cited

Abercrombie, B. (1995). *Charlie Anderson*. New York: Simon & Schuster.

Baker, K. (1990). *Who is the beast?* San Diego, CA: Harcourt Children's Books.

Bang, M. (1999). *When Sophie gets angry—really, really angry . . .* New York: Scholastic.

Bang, M. (2004). *My light*. New York: Scholastic.

Baylor, B. (1986). *I'm in charge of celebrations*. New York: Simon & Schuster.

Blos, J. W. (1987). *Old Henry*. Clarksville, IN: Mulberry Books.

Briggs, R. (1978). *The snowman*. New York: Random House.

Brinckloe, J. (1985). *Fireflies*. New York: Simon & Schuster.

Brown, M. W. (1947). *Goodnight moon*. New York: Random House.

Burleigh, R. (2000). *I love going through this book*. New York: Joanna Cotler Books.

Capote, T. (1956). *A Christmas memory*. New York: Alfred A. Knopf.

Charlesworth, L. (2004). *Grammar tales: The no good, rotten, run-on sentence*. New York: Scholastic.

Charlesworth, L. (2004). *Grammar tales: When comma came to town*. New York: Scholastic.

Clements, A. (1997). *Double trouble in Walla Walla*. Broomfield, CO: The Millbrook Press.

Clements, A. (1998). *Frindle*. New York: Simon & Schuster.

Collins, R. (2002). *Alvie eats soup*. New York: Scholastic.

Ehlert, L. (1999). *Moon rope*. San Diego, CA: Harcourt Children's Books.

Fleischman, P. (1988). *Joyful noise: Poems for two voices*. New York: HarperCollins.

Fleischman, P. (1989). *I am phoenix: Poems for two voices*. New York: HarperCollins.

Fleischman, P. & Giacobbe, B. (2000). *Big talk: Poems for four voices*. Cambridge, MA: Candlewick Press.

Fleischman, P. & Hawkes, K. (2004). *Sidewalk circus*. Cambridge, MA: Candlewick Press.

Fleming, M. (2004). *Grammar tales: The bug book*. New York: Scholastic.

Fleming, M. (2004). *Grammar tales: Chicken in the city*. New York: Scholastic.

Fleming, M. (2004). *Grammar tales: Tillie's tuba*. New York: Scholastic.

Fleming, M. (2004). *Grammar tales: A verb for Herb*. New York: Scholastic.

Fox, M. (1989). *Wilfrid Gordon McDonald Partridge*. Brooklyn, NY: Kane/Miller.

Fox, M. (1992). *Mem Fox reads*. [Cassette]. San Diego, CA: Harcourt Children's Books.

Fox, M. (1994). *Tough Boris*. San Diego, CA: Harcourt Children's Books.

Fox, M. (1997). *Whoever you are*. San Diego, CA: Harcourt Children's Books.

Fox, M. (1997). *Time for bed*. San Diego, CA: Harcourt Children's Books.

Fox, M. (2000). *Feathers and fools*. San Diego, CA: Harcourt Children's Books.

Fox, M. (2002). *The magic hat*. San Diego, CA: Harcourt Children's Books.

Fox, M. (2004). *Where is the green sheep?* San Diego, CA: Harcourt Children's Books.

Frame, J. A. (2003). *Yesterday I had the blues*. Berkeley, CA: Tricycle Press.

Freymann, S. & Elffers, J. (1999). *How are you peeling? Foods with moods*. New York: Scholastic Inc.

Gelman, R. G. (1992). *Body battles*. New York: Scholastic.

Graves, K. (2002). *Loretta: Ace pinky scout*. New York: Scholastic.

Grofe, F. (1931). *The Grand Canyon suite*. [CD]. New York: Sony.

Hartman, B. (2002). *The boy who cried wolf*. New York: Grosset & Dunlap.

Ireland, K. (2003). *DON'T take your snake for a stroll*. San Diego, CA: Harcourt Children's Books.

Jackson, E. (1994). *Cinder Edna*. New York: HarperCollins.

Jacobs, J. (Ed.). (1890). Goldilocks and the three bears. *English fairy tales*. London: David Nutt.

James, B. (2004). *My chair*. New York: Scholastic.

James, S. (1991). *Dear Mr. Blueberry*. New York: Margaret K. McElderry Books.

Johnson, D. B. (2000). *Henry hikes to Fitchburg*. Boston: Houghton Mifflin.

Johnson, S. T. (1995). *Alphabet city*. New York: Viking Press.

Kirk, D. (1994). *Miss Spider's tea party*. New York: Scholastic.

Kotzwinkle, W. & Murray, G. (2001). *Walter the farting dog*. Berkley, CA: North Atlantic Books.

Krosoczka, J. J. (2002). *Baghead*. New York: Alfred A. Knopf.

Laden, N. (1994). *The night I followed the dog*. San Francisco: Chronicle Books.

Laminack, L. L. (2004). *Saturdays and tea-cakes*. Atlanta, GA: Peachtree.

Lerman, R. S. (1997). *Charlie's checklist*. New York: Orchard Books.

Lewis, R. (2002). *In the space of the sky*. San Diego, CA: Harcourt Children's Books.

Lionni, L. (1968). *The alphabet tree*. New York: Alfred A. Knopf.

Locker, T. (2000). *Cloud dance*. San Diego, CA: Harcourt Children's Books.

Locker, T. (2001). *Mountain dance*. San Diego, CA: Harcourt Children's Books.

Locker, T. (2002). *Water dance*. San Diego, CA: Harcourt Children's Books.

London, J. (1998). *Dream weaver*. San Diego, CA: Harcourt Children's Books.

Lund, D. (2003). *Dinosailors*. San Diego, CA: Harcourt Children's Books.

MacLachlan, P. (1994). *All the places to love*. New York: HarperCollins.

MacLachlan, P. (1995). *What you know first*. New York: HarperCollins.

McPhail, D. (1997). *Edward and the pirates*. Boston: Little, Brown.

Martin, J. M. (2004). *Grammar tales: Francine Fribble, proofreading policewoman*. New York: Scholastic.

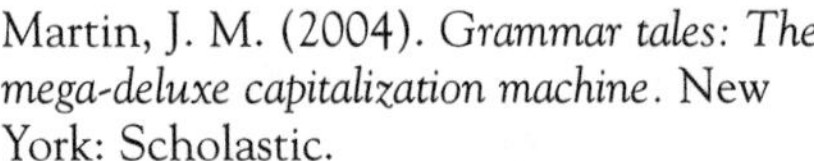

Martin, J. M. (2004). *Grammar tales: The mega-deluxe capitalization machine*. New York: Scholastic.

Martin, J. M. (2004). *Grammar tales: The mystery of the missing socks*. New York: Scholastic.

Martin, J. M. (2004). *Grammar tales: The planet without pronouns*. New York: Scholastic.

Moss, M. (2000). *Amelia's easy-as-pie drawing guide*. Middleton, WI: Pleasant Company Publications.

Pak, S. (2002). *A place to grow*. New York: Scholastic.

Palatini, M. (2001). *The web files*. New York: Hyperion.

Palatini, M. (2003). *The perfect pet*. New York: HarperCollins.

Pilkey, D. (1996). *The paperboy*. New York: Orchard Books.

Prokofiev, S. (1936). *Peter and the wolf, Op 67* [CD]. New York: RCA.

Pulver, R. (2003). *Punctuation takes a vacation*. New York: Holiday House.

Raschka, C. (1998). *Charlie Parker played be bop*. New York: Candlewick Books.

Rash, A. (2004). *Agent A to Agent Z*. New York: Scholastic Inc.

Reynolds, P. H. (2003). *The dot*. Cambridge, MA: Candlewick Press.

Ringgold, F. (2002). *Cassie's word quilt*. New York: Alfred A. Knopf.

Rowling, J. K. (1998). *Harry Potter and the sorcerer's stone*. New York: Scholastic.

Ryan, P. M. (2001). *Hello ocean*. New York: Scholastic.

Ryan, P. M. (2004). *Becoming Naomi Leon*. New York: Scholastic.

Rylant, C. (1996). *The old woman who named things*. San Diego, CA: Harcourt Children's Books.

Saints-Saens, C. (1886). *Carnival of the animals*. [CD]. New York: Decca.

Schaefer, L. M. (2002). *What's up, what's down*. New York: Greenwillow Books.

Scieszka, J. (1989). *The true story of the 3 little pigs!* New York: Viking Press.

Seinfeld, J. (2002). *Halloween*. Boston: Little, Brown.

Seuss, Dr. (1960). *Green eggs and ham*. New York: Random House.

Seuss, Dr. (1966). *The 500 hats of Bartholomew Cubbins*. New York: Vanguard.

Smith, C. R., Jr. (2003). *I am America*. New York: Scholastic.

Smith, R. K. (1984). *The war with grandpa*. New York: Random House.

Sturges, P. (1999). *The little red hen (makes a pizza)*. New York: Dutton Children's Books.

Thomas, M. (1972, 2002). *Free to be . . . you and me*. Philadelphia: Running Press Publishers.

Thomas, M. (2001). *Free to be you and me*. [DVD]. New York: Hen's Tooth Video.

Torres, L. (1993). *Subway sparrow*. New York: Farrar, Straus and Giroux.

Walton, R. (1999). *Bullfrog pops*. Layton, UT: Gibbs Smith Publishers.

Walton, R. (1998). *Why the banana split*. Layton, UT: Gibbs Smith Publishers.

Waber, B. (2002). *Courage*. Boston: Houghton Mifflin.

Webb, S. (2003). *Tanka tanka skunk!* New York: Scholastic.

White, E. B. (1952). *Charlotte's web*. New York: HarperCollins.

Winthrop, E. (2001). *Dumpy La Rue*. New York: Henry Holt.

Wood, A. (2001). *Alphabet adventure*. New York: Scholastic.

Index

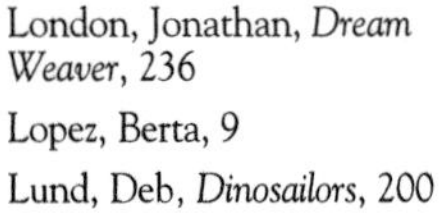